The Wages of Appeasement

The Wages of Appeasement

*Ancient Athens, Munich,
and Obama's America*

Bruce S. Thornton

ENCOUNTER BOOKS
NEW YORK · LONDON

First American edition published in 2011 by Encounter Books,
an activity of Encounter for Culture and Education, Inc.,
a nonprofit, tax exempt corporation.
Encounter Books website address: www.encounterbooks.com

Manufactured in the United States and printed on
acid-free paper. The paper used in this publication meets
the minimum requirements of ANSI/NISO Z39.48   1992
(R 1997) (*Permanence of Paper*).

FIRST AMERICAN EDITION

LIBRARY OF CONGRESS CATALOGING-IN-PUBLICATION DATA

Thornton, Bruce S.
The wages of appeasement : ancient Athens, Munich, and Obama's America /
by Bruce S. Thornton.
p. cm.
Includes bibliographical references and index.
ISBN-13: 978-1-59403-519-7 (hardcover : alk. paper)
ISBN-10: 1-59403-519-9 (hardcover : alk. paper)
1. Diplomatic negotiations in international disputes—History—Case
studies. 2. Philip II, King of Macedonia, 382–336 B.C.
3. Greece—History—Macedonian Expansion, 359–323 B.C.
4. Macedonia—History—To 168 B.C. 5. Great Britain—Foreign
relations—Germany. 6. Germany—Foreign relations—Great Britain.
7. Munich Four-Power Agreement (1938)
8. Islamic fundamentalism—Government policy—United States.
9. United States—Foreign relations—2009– I. Title.
JZ6045.T46   2011
327.1'72—dc22
2010037830

For Jakob Glen Thornton

Incipe parve puer risu cognoscere matrem

Acknowledgments

The idea for this book arose from many conversations with Victor Davis Hanson, from whose expertise and friendship I have long benefited. Roger Kimball once more has been generous with his encouragement. The bulk of this book was written with the financial support of the Hoover Institution, where I was a 2009–2010 Glenn Campbell and Rita Ricardo-Campbell National Fellow and the Susan Louise Dyer Peace Fellowship National Fellow. As always, I am grateful for the love and patience of my wife, Jacalyn.

Table of Contents

Introduction

The Temptation of Hector

"But wait—what if I put down my studded shield
And heavy helmet, prop my spear on the rampart
And go forth, just as I am, to meet Achilles,
Noble Prince Achilles . . .
Why, I could promise to give back Helen, yes,
And all her treasures with her . . .
Why debate, my friend? Why thrash things out?
I must not go and implore him. He'll show no mercy,
No respect for me, my rights—he'll cut me down
Straight off—stripped of defenses like a woman
Once I have loosed the armor off my body.
No way to parley with that man—not now—
Not from behind some oak or rock to whisper,
Like a boy and a young girl, lovers' secrets
A boy and girl might whisper to each other . . .
Better to clash now in battle, now, at once—
See which fighter Zeus awards the glory!"[1]

In May of 2008, President Bush ignited a political firestorm when in a speech to the Israeli parliament he compared some Democratic politicians to England's Neville Chamberlain and his disastrous policy of appeasing Hitler: "Some seem to believe we should negotiate with terrorists and radicals, as if some ingenious argument will persuade them they have been wrong all along. We have heard this foolish delusion before. As Nazi tanks crossed into Poland in 1939, an

American senator declared: 'Lord, if only I could have talked to Hitler, all of this might have been avoided.' We have an obligation to call this what it is—the false comfort of appeasement, which has been repeatedly discredited by history."[2]

The President's speech and the heated reaction from the Democrats and the liberal media illustrate both how toxic the charge of appeasement can be and the iconic status of English foreign policy in the Thirties.[3] This policy has become encapsulated in the word "Munich," which now describes "a conciliatory, yielding approach to the resolution of conflict ... coupled with a policy of avoiding confrontations of force by giving way to the demanding party," an approach reflecting a "foolish faith in the pacifying effect of concessions to a foe bent on aggression, or a gullible reliance on promises from a source already established as untrustworthy."[4] "Munich" thus evokes the "bad" appeasement that Winston Churchill in 1950 defined as the "futile and fatal" concessions born "from weakness and fear," in contrast to the "good" appeasement, which is "magnanimous and noble" when it comes from "strength," a legitimate tool of foreign policy and "the surest and perhaps the only path to world peace."[5] In this book, we will be concerned with defining and elaborating on "bad" appeasement, since the negative meaning now dominates our public discourse on foreign policy.[6]

Likewise, the association of appeasement with Chamberlain and his policies obscures how constant in history has been the shortsighted temptation to buy off, whether with words or treasure, an enemy intent on one's destruction. But as Hector's soliloquy reveals, such temptation is as old as conflict itself and reflects the permanent truths of human nature. Appeasement, then, did not happen just once, in the England of the Thirties. It is an eternal temptation for all peoples who for various reasons lose their nerve in the face of an enemy who wants to destroy them.

As such, appeasement can be anatomized through the study of three historical examples: Athens and the other Greek city-states threatened by the ambitions of Philip II of Macedon in the fourth century B.C.; England faced with Hitler's aggression in the 1930s; and the West, particularly the United States, confronting a renascent Islamic jihad and its most powerful state sponsor, Iran. These three states share a fundamental similarity that makes comparison illuminating: they are all constitutional democracies challenged by autocratic, illiberal regimes, and some of the reasons for appeasement can be found in the very structures of democracy, as well as in the weaknesses of democratic states, that give scope to the flaws of human nature. The processes of public deliberation and decision-making, for example, are crucial for consensual governments ruled by law and procedure rather than by force. Yet these processes mean that talk is more easily substituted for action, and transient public opinion, factional interests, and irrational passions can have a warping influence on policy. Civilian control over the military can have the same effect, as the costs of conflict and impatience with setbacks can compromise policy as well.

These similarities of political culture, however, are not as important as the permanent truths of human nature expressed through social and political mechanisms. "As long as the same passions and interests subsist among mankind," Edward Gibbon wrote, "the questions of war and peace, of justice and policy, which were debated in the councils of antiquity, will frequently present themselves as the subject of modern deliberation."[7] The anatomy of appeasement will take as its starting point the "passions and interests" rooted in human nature.

The examples of Athens and England, then, provide what the Roman historian Livy defined as history's important function: to offer from the past models of "base things, rotten through and through, to avoid."[8] Such reminders are necessary in these times, for our fight is not just against the jihadists who are using terrorist violence in pursuit of their dreams of renewed Islamic hegemony. We must also battle those in the

West who, like President Obama, see appeasement disguised as diplomatic "outreach" as the way to neutralize the enemy. And when that enemy is the theocratic regime in Iran, for 30 years a state sponsor of terrorism with American blood on its hands, and today in the pursuit of nuclear weapons that will magnify exponentially its capability for destruction, such appeasement is indeed "futile and fatal."

An anatomy of appeasement that starts with the permanent verities of the human experience, such as fear, will find no better guide to these than the Greek historian Thucydides. In his recreation of a speech delivered to the Spartans by an Athenian envoy on the brink of the Peloponnesian War, Thucydides identified the three causes of conflict: fear, honor, and interest.[9] These three motives are useful as well in identifying the causes of appeasement.

Hector's temptation to appease the Greek champion Achilles points to a one fundamental cause of appeasement. Raw fear of an enemy, whether justified or not, must be the first and most obvious factor in understanding a people's capitulation to an aggressor, their understandable horror at the carnage of war, which "he who has experienced it," the Greek poet Pindar wrote, "fears in his heart its approach."[10] The fear of death and violence inherent in human nature is a constant across time and space, as Homer shows us. Hector's fear, however, is justified, as he knows he can never defeat Achilles in battle and that his own death means the destruction of Troy. This sort of "rational" fear is not at issue in discussing appeasement. Suicidal resistance in the face of a more powerful enemy may be admirable, but most peoples are unlikely to choose that path. When in 846 the Pope promised the Muslim jihadists, who had already looted St. Peter's and St. Paul's churches, 25,000 silver coins a year to go away, his actions weren't "appeasement" born of irrational fear or weakness. He simply had no choice. Or when, starting in 1795, the fledgling United States paid a million dollars a year in tribute to the Barbary nations of Algiers, Tripoli, and Tunis to protect American shipping and ransom hostages, the absence of a Navy made this unpleasant capitulation necessary, until the construction of a fleet allowed the U.S to end those depredations in 1815.

More interesting is the fear of an enemy to whom a state is militarily superior or at least equal, an enemy intent on significantly reducing a state's power and autonomy or destroying it outright. Athens and the other Greek city-states had many opportunities to stop Philip before Chaeronea in 338 B.C., and even then the battle was a "close-run thing," as Wellington said of Waterloo. England and France, the latter possessing the largest army in Europe, could have destroyed the minuscule force with which Hitler reoccupied the Rhineland in 1936. And today, the military might of the United States dwarfs the combined power of Middle Eastern states such as Iran and Syria that support and harbor Islamist terrorists.

In addition to the fear dramatized so powerfully by Homer, we will find that "interest"— "utility," "use," "profit," "advantage," and "benefit," as the dictionary defines Thucydides's term *ôphelias*—is an important factor in appeasement. Like fear, the desire for material gain and power for one's self, one's faction, or one's nation is a constant in human nature. Sometimes old quarrels, enmities, and rivalries—the zero-sum calculus that predicates one society's power on the diminishment of another's—blind a people to a looming threat. Likewise, the prospect of short-term material gains trumps the long-term danger of appeasing an enemy, or internal political rivalries and factional interests can distract a state from an external challenge, a problem particularly acute for democracies. Conflicting state interests also compromise foreign relations and alliances. Athens's deep-rooted dislike of its rival Thebes was one reason those city-states could not form a coalition to stop Philip until it was too late. England's traditional wariness of France's power factored into its foreign policy decisions regarding a resurgent Germany. And clashing strategic, economic, and political interests and aims among the Western allies have hamstrung our collective response to jihadist terrorism.

Thucydides's last factor, honor, may seem an anachronism for analyzing our two modern examples. In fact, honor today is still an important element in the behavior of states, and the disregard of honor is a factor in appeasement, as well as obscuring the motives of one's opponent. The Greek city-states pursued their quarrels partly because they felt their enemies had dishonored them. Thebes instigated the Sacred War in 356 B.C. as a way to punish Sparta, which in 382 B.C. had occupied and garrisoned the Cadmea, Thebes's acropolis. And Athens in the fourth century B.C. struggled to reclaim the empire stripped from it after Sparta's victory in the Peloponnesian War not just for material benefits, but for the status and honor it bestowed. As Pericles put it in his famous funeral oration of 431 B.C., "For it is only the love of honor that never grows old; and honor it is, not gain, as some would have it, that rejoices the heart of age and helplessness."[11] In the 1930s as well, the bitter anger of the Germans about what they thought were the dishonorable terms of the Versailles Treaty and its "war guilt" clause was a potent element in their aggression. And today, the Islamic jihadists are driven to recover the honor besmirched by the loss of the caliphate and by the subsequent Western domination of the House of Islam on the part of infidels who for centuries trembled at Allah's armies.

For this analysis, however, "honor" is part of something larger—ideas, ideals, ideology, values, all those notions, including religion, about human nature, human behavior, human happiness, the goods a people or a state should pursue, and the proper means for acquiring those goods. All these ideals are bound up with some notion of honor: "Arguments about morality and ideology," historian Donald Kagan writes, "involve what Thucydides called honor, and nations from antiquity to our own world cannot ignore it."[12] Ancient honor was such a notion: it signified the prestige a person or state enjoyed, the public esteem in which a person or state was held. This honor determined the proper, just behavior of others, the purpose of which was to publicly acknowledge a person's own estimation of his worth and excellence. Behavior that violated a person's prestige was a powerful spur to using violence to correct the injustice, and thus for ancient states violations of honor frequently led to war. Hector's decision to await Achilles, his refusal to give in to the temptation of appeasement, and his last valiant charge at Achilles even as he knows he is doomed are all fueled by honor and its corollary, shame at dishonor.

More significant for our analysis will be the larger ideas and ideals that lie behind the actions taken by leaders faced with an aggressive enemy. One such ideal is the notion that "to jaw-jaw is always better than to war-war," as Churchill famously put it.[13] Negotiation, diplomacy, discussion—the reliance on words rather than force to defuse conflict and create peace reflects certain notions of universal human behavior and motivation that are questionable at best. Hector briefly entertains this idea, only to reject it as meaningless in the face of an enemy like Achilles. Discussion and agreement work only with the like-minded who sincerely desire to avoid conflict and who feel they belong to the same human community, as Homer's delicate simile of the whispering young lovers suggests. In the face of an implacable foe, such words and agreements are delusional. As Achilles himself responds to Hector's offer to return his corpse should Hector prevail, "Don't talk to me of pacts./There are no binding oaths between men and lions—/wolves and lambs can enjoy no meeting of the minds—/they are all bent on hating each other to the death."[14] Much modern appeasing "outreach" to a foe, whether Chamberlain's to Hitler or President Obama's to the mullahs in Iran, has illustrated the truth of Achilles's insight.

Also important for understanding appeasement will be the failure of what we can call political virtue: the shared qualities, virtues, and ideals that reinforce, sustain, and defend the political freedom that defines democracies. Courage, both physical and moral, is an important civic virtue: "happiness depends on freedom, and freedom depends on courage," as Pericles said in his funeral oration.[15] So too is patriotism, the love of one's own people and ways that drives service to the good of the state, critical for stiffening resistance to an enemy. Living with moderation and simplicity, self-sacrifice and self-restraint, renders a people more able to tolerate the hardship and suffering that conflict always entails. The weakening of these civic virtues acts as a corrosive on the people's will to defend their freedoms against the aggression of a tyrant.

Fear, interest, and ideas will all play a role in determining why a people will appease a dangerous foe. In our three historical examples, one of these three will predominate: in ancient Greece, shortsighted interests—those of one's own career, one's faction, or one's city-state—explain the failure to recognize Philip's challenge and meet it. In the years between the world wars of the twentieth century, the gruesome carnage of the First World War created an understandable horror of reprising that massive destruction, and it made possible questionable ideas, such as pacifism and internationalism. And today, various ideas about culture and human nature encourage among some Westerners a self-loathing based on a hatred of their own ways and a guilt about presumed Western crimes, such as imperialism and colonialism, that have inhibited a vigorous response to the challenge of Islamic jihad.

Of course, in all three examples fear, interest, and ideas intertwine and reinforce one another. Fear and interest can be rationalized by ideals; political virtue can be weakened by interest and competing or antithetical ideals; and ideals and interests often are advanced by the same course of action. Whether individually or together, all three short-circuit the ability of a people and their leaders to see past fear or interest or ideas and recognize an existential threat to their freedom. In our three historical examples, the stakes were (and are) high: the continuation of political freedom and autonomy, with all their attendant goods—human rights, rule by law, consensual government, equality, personal freedom, and a political system that benefits all citizens rather than the interests of a tyrant or an illiberal regime. After their defeat by Phillip II, the Greek city-states lost their "glorious sovereignty and ancient liberty," as one ancient historian put it.[16] England and France barely survived their miscalculation of Hitler's motives, at the cost of 50 million dead and incalculable destruction and suffering. And the West today, while not subject to an immediate existential threat, is nonetheless faced with a steady erosion of security and freedom at home and more wars abroad that if unchecked may leave to our children societies unrecognizable to us today, particularly if the Islamist regime in Iran acquires nuclear weapons.

This analysis obviously assumes a certain idea of human nature: the Thucydidean notion that human passions and appetites are permanent spurs of human behavior. And those actions always threaten the social and political orders and virtues that try, but sometimes fail, to restrain our destructive impulses. Thus war will be a constant in human experience, not an anomaly to be corrected. Moreover, these "imperious necessities," as Thucydides called them, contained by law and custom in times of peace, when stressed during times of crisis by disorder, want, fear, or powerful ideals concerning ultimate goods, erupt in violence and destruction that can be checked only by force and the acceptance of what Abraham Lincoln called the "awful arithmetic": the brutal calculation that killing some today means more live tomorrow.[17]

This tragic view of human life is out of fashion in our times, which endorse the progressive view: human life is perfectible, universal happiness is achievable, and ancient evils like conflict and war are primitive anomalies that can be eliminated by economic prosperity, political freedom, transnational institutions, international law and covenants, and the mechanisms of diplomacy. As this book hopes to show, the historical failure of these ideals instead confirms the wisdom of Thucydides in his famous description of the horrors wrought by revolution during the Peloponnesian War: "The sufferings which revolution entailed upon the cities were many and terrible, such as have occurred and always will occur as long as the nature of mankind remains the same; though in a severer or milder form, and varying in their symptoms, according to the variety of the particular cases."[18]

Chapter One

Athens and Philip II

————— ⚮ —————

Yet I also saw that in pursuit of power and domination,
Philip, our opponent in the struggle, had his eye knocked
out, his collarbone broken, his hand and leg maimed, in fact
that he readily sacrificed any part of his body that fortune
might take so that afterwards he might live in honor and
glory. Indeed, no one would have dared assert that a man
raised in Pella, a small, obscure place at the time, would
become so bold as to desire rule over the Greeks and to make
that his purpose, or that you—Athenians!—who every day
behold reminders of the valor of your forebears in all manner
of speeches and monuments, would be so cowardly as to
surrender your freedom to Philip voluntarily.

DEMOSTHENES[1]

Philip's Challenge

Philip II became king of Macedonia in 359, the Greek city-states for nearly a century had been fighting each other for the hegemony of Greece. The 27-year Peloponnesian War between Athens and Sparta—a "world war" wreaking havoc throughout the Greek city-states scattered around the eastern Mediterranean—had ended in 404 with the near destruction of Athens and the supremacy of Sparta. For the next three decades, Sparta expanded its power and influence in central and northern Greece, in the northern Aegean, and among the Greek city-states on the western fringe of the

I

Persian empire, now the coast of modern Turkey. Next came the turn of Thebes, whose brilliant general Epaminondas defeated the Spartans at Leuctra in 371, ending the "Spartan hegemony" and initiating a brief summer of Theban ascendancy, which itself would wane after the indecisive battle against the Spartans at Mantinea (362). Meanwhile, Athens worked relentlessly to reassert its former status as the dominant power among the Greeks, eager to recover the subject city-states stripped from her by Sparta's victory in 404, and thus to reconstitute her lost empire. Athens made a start in 379 through the Second Athenian Sea League, which at its peak comprised 75 allied city-states and islands. At Philip's ascension to the throne, then, the major powers of Greece—Sparta, Thebes, and Athens—had settled into a troubled equilibrium, ratified by a shaky treaty of common peace (362), in which each jockeyed for dominance by exploiting traditional enmities and pursuing ancient quarrels. As the historian Xenophon wrote about the aftermath of the battle of Mantinea, "The state of Greece was still more evenly balanced and disturbed after it than before it."[2]

Macedonia, a feudal world of tribal land barons evocative more of Homeric warriors than of city-state citizens, did not figure as a major player in the old polis game of power and influence. Indeed, despite decades of fitful Hellenizing, most Greeks didn't even consider the Macedonians Greek at all, occasionally describing them with the deadly epithet "barbarian," the antithesis of Greekness, despite the fact that the Macedonians spoke a dialect of Greek and had established their origins among the heroes of Homer and the gods of Olympus.[3] Historian Peter Green has summarized neatly the prevailing attitude of the Greeks, which was one of "genial and sophisticated contempt. They regarded Macedonians in general as semi-savages, uncouth of speech and dialect, retrograde in their political institutions, negligible as fighters, and habitual oath-breakers, who dressed in bear-pelts and were much given to deep and swinish potations, tempered with regular bouts of assassination and incest."[4] Incest wasn't the only sexual sin of the Macedonians: the fourth-century historian Theopompus, a harsh critic of Philip, claimed that Philip's courtiers were "man-killers by nature" but "man-whores by habit," overly fond of homosexual sodomy.[5] Macedonians were so degenerate that the Greek orator Demosthenes, Philip's inveterate enemy, in one of his attacks snorted that one couldn't even acquire a "decent slave" from Macedonia.[6]

Macedonia was more advanced and sophisticated than Greek bigotry admitted—King Archelaus (413–399) invited to his court the painter Zeuxis, the musician Timotheus, and the tragic poets Agathon and Euripides; the latter wrote his masterpiece the *Bacchae* at Archelaus's court. However, chronic infighting among claimants to the throne, interference from the more powerful southern Greek city-states, and the continual threat from Macedonia's neighbors, particularly the Illyrians to the northwest and the Paeonians to the north, kept the Macedonians weak and fragmented: "impoverished vagabonds," Philip's son Alexander the Great would say, with some exaggeration, years later, to his mutinous Macedonian troops, "most of you dressed in skins, feeding a few sheep on the hills and fighting, feebly enough, to keep them from your neighbors— Thracians and Triballians and Illyrians." The achievement of Philip was not just to transform Macedonia into a nation of cities, laws, a developed economy, and a formidable army— "he made you city-dwellers," Alexander went on, "he brought you law; he civilized you"—but also to impose its hegemony over the once powerful and more sophisticated city-states of ancient Greece.[7] As the first-century B.C. historian Diodorus Siculus wrote in his *Library of History*, Philip "ruled as king of Macedonia for twenty-four years and from the most humble of beginnings he established his kingdom as the greatest of the powers of Europe, and, inheriting a Macedonia that was a slave to the Illyrians, he made her ruler of many tribes and cities."[8]

And when Philip was assassinated in 336, he had already set in motion the conquest of the mighty Persian empire, a feat to be accomplished by his son Alexander. Yet all those achievements perhaps could not have happened if not for the failure of the free Greek city-states to recognize Philip's challenge and mount an effective response.

The Rise of Philip

In 359, however, sheer survival, not empire, was Philip's most pressing concern. First, he took care of the Paeonians, "having corrupted some with bribes and others with generous promises," Diodorus reports, thus securing the northeastern border and gaining access to the territory's silver mines.[9] Next was the turn of the Illyrians. A year earlier, these long-time rivals in the north had defeated a Macedonian army, killing 4,000 soldiers and the king Perdiccas III, Philip's brother, thus leaving Macedonia's northern territories vulnerable to further incursions. Philip avenged that defeat and shored up the northwest border in a tactically brilliant battle, killing 7,000 of the enemy. The borderland became more securely Macedonian, with Philip building cities and forts, transferring populations, and luring Macedonian settlers with tax breaks and land grants.

Philip then turned to the Greeks to his south in Thessaly. A contest for supremacy between two cities and their dominant aristocratic clans rived this powerful state, famous for its superb horsemen. In 358, one city, Larissa, invited Philip's support against its enemy Pherae. Philip entered into an alliance with the Thessalian League created by Larissa and married a Larissan woman, his third wife. With this move, Philip secured the southern passes into Macedonia, gained access to the Thessalian cavalry, which would become an important part of his reformed army, and created a mechanism by which he could interfere in Thessalian affairs. This last advantage would become one of Philip's favorite techniques for extending his influence over the Greek city-states—exploiting internecine quarrels by posing as the champion of one side over another and insinuating himself into city-state leagues as a means of controlling their policies and legitimizing his Greek credentials.

Philip's first move against the Athenians was on the city of Amphipolis. But to understand the importance of these northern Greek cities that fell to Philip, we have to sketch the geography of the north Aegean Sea, which lies between Greece and western Turkey. The northwestern corner of this sea is the Thermaic Gulf, north of which lay the coastal region of Macedonia, providing access to the trade routes of the Aegean. East of this gulf is Chalcidice, a peninsula terminating in three smaller peninsulas that jut like claws into the Aegean. East beyond Chalcidice a coastal plain ends about 150 miles away at the Hellespont (modern Dardanelles), a narrow sea passage from the Aegean into a small sea called the Propontis (Sea of Marmara), which in turn connects to the Black Sea through the Bosporus. The narrow finger of land forming the north shore of the Hellespont is the Gallipoli peninsula, which was known in antiquity as the Thracian Chersonese.

This coastal region was thickly sown with Greek cities and colonists and had immense geo-strategic importance, particularly for Athens. Apart from possessing timber and precious metals, this region bordered the sea route for the grain that Athens and other city-states imported from the Black Sea region, the largest sea-borne trade in the ancient Greek world. Imported grain was necessary—Attica, the territory of Athens, imported two thirds of its grain[10]—given the paucity of arable land in mainland Greece and the possibility of shortages because of crop failures and the burning of grain fields during war. Dependent as it was on this trade, Athens had numerous laws controlling who could import grain to Athens and the conditions of its sale. These were overseen by public officials known as "grain guardians," and the importation of grain was a regular item on the agenda of the Assembly, the Athenian democracy's main legislative body.[11] Thus Athens traditionally controlled through alliance, colonization, or outright domination the cities along the route to ensure that it remained open— an ancient orator called one city on the Hellespont, Sestos, the "corn-bin of the Piraeaus," the port of Athens.[12] Obviously, losing control of the Hellespont could be disastrous for Athens: the Spartan naval victory there at Aigospotamoi (405) cut Athens off from the Hellespont and Crimean grain. The threat of famine as grain supplies dwindled lead directly to Athens's surrender to Sparta, ending the Peloponnesian War.

Amphipolis lay in the heart of this strategically important region, just east of Chalcidice on the river Strymon, and near several lucrative gold and silver mines and timber needed for ships. It commanded as well important trade and communication routes, being the only place to cross the Strymon for those traveling by land between the Hellespont and Greece.[13] The city was founded by Athenian colonists in 437, but was captured by the Spartans in 424 during the Peloponnesian War, a loss that sent the historian Thucydides, a general at the time, into exile. In 422 an important battle was fought at Amphipolis between the Athenians and the Spartans—Socrates fought there—in which the Spartan king Brasidas and the Athenian demagogue Kleon, a favorite target of the comic poet Aristophanes, were both killed. After the war, Amphipolis became independent from Athens, but Athens never stopped scheming to recover the city, along with its mines, timber for ships, and coastal land, as an important step in recreating its empire.[14] Moreover, the loss of Amphipolis was a wound to Athenian honor, historian G. T. Griffith writes, "a little comparable to the trauma of Alsace-Lorraine on the French psyche during more than forty years."[15]

The city, however, sat on the border between Macedonia and a hostile Thrace and thus controlled Macedonia's security and expansion to the east. In other words, Amphipolis was too strategically important for Philip to let Athens regain it.

On his accession in 359, Philip faced a pretender to the throne, Argaeus, who was supported by Athens with ships and troops. Here Philip displayed his shrewdness at exploiting the short-term, shortsighted interests of his enemies. He led the Athenians to believe that the withdrawal of some Macedonian troops from Amphipolis, who a few years earlier had been invited to the city as insurance against the Athenians, was also an abandonment of Macedonian claims to it, even though the city had for some time been autonomous. The Athenian force, with the exception of a few volunteers, thus left the hapless Argaeus hanging, who on his march back from Aegae—the old Macedonian capital (it had been replaced by Pella) where Argaeus failed to rally support for his claim to the throne—was defeated by Philip's troops and killed. Philip sent the few Athenian prisoners home, and Athens made peace with the wily Macedonian, who renounced all claims to a city he had no legal claim to in the first place. Philip was then free to deal with the Illyrians and Paeonians without worrying about the Athenians and their pretender.

Once those threats had been neutralized, Philip turned again to Amphipolis. He besieged the city, which quickly fell in the summer of 357 after attacks with scaling ladders, battering rams, and unidentified "machines."[16] The Athenians, probably encouraged in this belief by Philip, expected the city to be handed to them once it fell, and so refused the pleas of help from the pro-Athenian Amphipolitans. But the Athenians were quickly disabused when Philip instead kept the city and then turned on Pydna, an ally of Athens on the west coast of the Thermaic Gulf, and took it as well, eliminating another possible base for Athens and gaining more revenues for Macedonia.

The failure of the Athenians to heed the Amphipolitans when asked for help, and their credulous acceptance of Philip's promises, was a turning point in Greek history, as the great Victorian historian of ancient Greece George Grote recognized:

"Had they [the Athenians] been clear-sighted in the appreciation of chances, and vigilant in respect to future defense, they might now have acquired this important place, and might have held it against the utmost efforts of Philip." However, what Grote calls their "fatal inaction which had become their general besetting sin" was reinforced by the promises of Philip and the anger of Athens against Amphipolis for holding on to its independence.[17] The result was the Athenians lost not just Amphipolis and Pydna, but also another important northern Greek city, their ally Potidaea. This city straddled Pallene, the westernmost "claw" of the Chalcidian peninsula, and was a home to Athenian colonists. Athenian help was again sluggish and half-hearted, and the city passed into the control of Potidaea's neighbor Olynthus, which had made a treaty with Philip. In 354, Philip seized the city of Methone, where he lost his right eye to a defender's arrow. This city, the last non-Macedonian polis on the Thermaic Gulf, sat on the northern route to the Macedonian capital, Pella, and the southern route to Thessaly, the Greek state bordering Macedonia. It thus had immense strategic importance for Philip, who followed up its destruction and the ejection of its citizens with the seizure of four other coastal towns east of Chalcidice. Once more, Athens did little to challenge Philip's seizure of this important city.

In the end, the loss of these key cities weakened Athens's hold on the northwestern Aegean and the route for Black Sea grain, although the city still maintained through its other allies and colonists a presence in the Chersonese. Philip, on the other hand, had secured his eastern borders, seized control of the lucrative gold mines near Amphipolis—a thousand talents a year's worth, according to Diodorus—and extended his influence over the strategically and economically important northern Aegean.[18]

In Philip's *annus mirabilis* of 356—when his racehorse won first prize at the Olympics, his son Alexander was born, and victories were won over Potidaea and the Illyrians—Athens became involved in the Social War, a revolt of some of its allies from the Second Athenian Sea League. Like its obsession with Amphipolis, the Athenian desire to recover the power and wealth it enjoyed during the fifth century from its naval empire—a goal the recovery of Amphipolis would advance—was another shortsighted interest that distracted it from the long-term but much more serious threat of Philip. The historian Ian Worthington speculates that Philip may have had a hand in instigating the revolt: "the timing of the revolt with respect to his own activities was too good to be a mere coincidence. It would have been easy to play on the grievances that the allies harbored towards the Athenians. . . . His motive would have been to divert Athens' attention away from his exploits in the north, especially his intended siege of Potidaea, and to weaken the city's naval power" by stripping from the fleet the allied ships.[19] In the event, by 355 Athens had to make peace after a naval defeat, and its resources and energy had been deflected for a year from confronting Philip. More important, the will to resist by relying on Athens's traditional strength, its fleet, had been compromised: "This continual aggressor," Griffith writes of Philip, "was more determined and resourceful, better equipped to deal with city walls. The naval power [of Athens] was there still, but the will that decided on its use was more hesitant, more divided in its aims in life, less concentrated on the self-preservation and self-help which sea power could serve so well."[20]

The pattern of Philip's aggressive energy and Athens's sluggish and shortsighted responses had been set. In 349, Demosthenes would chastise Athens for its continuing failure to counter Philip's aggression: "It is not surprising that Philip has the upper hand: he serves on campaign and toils hard in person, is present on the spot in every situation, and lets pass by no chance or opportunity, while you procrastinate, vote decrees and make inquiries."[21]

The Sacred War

The other Greek city-states were equally shortsighted in pursuing their parochial quarrels and enmities in a way that increased Philip's power and influence. The premier event was the conflict known to historians as the Third Sacred War, one "rending the very entrails of the Hellenic world," Grote writes, "and profitable only to the indefatigable aggressor in Macedonia."[22] The war started in 356 when Phocis, a member state of the Amphictyonic Council (a federation of city-states that managed the important shrine and oracle of Apollo at Delphi, in central Greece, and that bound its members by oath to war against violators), was ordered by the Council to pay a fine engineered by Thebes for "cultivating sacred land." The charge was a pretext: Thebes was reacting to the recent expulsion of a pro-Theban faction from Phocis as well as renewing its quarrel with its bitter enemy Sparta, which had never paid a fine levied by the Council 30 years earlier for occupying the Cadmea, the Theban acropolis and a holy site. By getting the Council to fine the Phocians, Thebes was able to bring up Sparta's outstanding debt and get the fine doubled.

The Phocians refused to pay the exorbitant fine. Instead, in 356 they seized Delphi and prepared to fight it out with the Council members, initiating a war that dragged on for nearly a decade. The Phocians, desperate for money with which to buy mercenaries, began plundering the temple treasures, eventually pilfering around 10,000 talents worth; some of the offerings ended up as gifts to wives, courtesans, and dancing-girls. This sacrilege now made the war one waged against temple robbers by the righteous on behalf of Apollo.

Philip's involvement in the Sacred War did not begin auspiciously. In 353, Philip was invited into Thessaly by his allies in Larissa to help them against their enemies in Pherae, who had made an alliance with Onomarchus, the Phocian general. The shrewd Philip was only too happy to oblige, for in addition to protecting the integrity of his southern border and his influence in Thessaly, he would also acquire Hellenic political capital by fighting the Phocian temple robbers. In the event, Worthington notes, his involvement "would prove to be a convenient stepping stone to more formal involvement in Greek politics."[23] Surprisingly, though, Onomarchus defeated Philip in two battles and sent the Macedonians back home severely disgruntled, if not mutinous. As Worthington writes, "It looked as though the whole fabric of Philip's power was starting to disintegrate, pointing to an inevitable decline in Macedonian power."[24] However, at a moment when Philip was in retreat from central Greece, the Athenian general Chares was off in the Chersonese fighting against the Thracian Cersebleptes. The Athenians attacked the important port of Sestos, Athens's "corn-bin," given its importance for the grain trade, sacking the city, killing the males, and selling the women and children into slavery. There were strategic advantages for the Athenians in this action: persuaded by the brutal fate of Sestos and by Philip's defeat by the Phocians, Cersebleptes turned from Philip and allied himself with Athens; the strategically vital Chersonese was secured. However, lost was an opportunity to counter Philip more directly, the more serious threat to Athens, at this moment of vulnerability. This failure of vision led as well to a refusal to enter into an alliance with Olynthus and the Chalcidic League, which would have created a powerful coalition on Macedonia's eastern frontier.

The Athenians were equally shortsighted in not assisting its ally Phocis more vigorously, although the bad odor of blasphemy surrounding the Phocians' appropriation of the temple treasures made it politically difficult to offer more energetic support. Perhaps the Athenians thought Onomarchus's defeat of Philip had reduced his threat. If so they were mistaken: "I didn't run away," he said of his defeat and retreat, "but, like a ram, I pulled back to butt again harder."[25] A year later, Philip returned to settle his score with the Phocians. At the Battle of the Crocus Field near the Thessalian port of Pagasae—Philip's men marched into battle wearing wreaths made from the leaves of laurel, the tree sacred to Apollo—Philip defeated the Phocians, killing 6,000. Three thousand more were captured and drowned for sacrilege against the god.[26] Athens had sent a general, Chares, and a fleet to Pagasae, but the Athenians got there too late to help the Phocians, and could only watch as the fleeing Phocians and Onomarchus tried to swim to the ships. They didn't make it. Onomarchus drowned, and his dead body was fished out and then crucified, to most Greeks a suitable fate for a temple robber and blasphemer against the gods. The Roman historian Justin described the immense prestige this victory won for Philip: "This affair brought incredibly great glory to Philip in the opinion of all people, who called him 'the avenger of the god, and the defender of religion.'"[27]

About this time Philip was elected *archon* of the Thessalian League, a lifelong office. The powers of this position probably included direct influence over the League's business and the command of some part of the army. It had the added benefit of giving Philip control of the port Pegasae and income from the harbor.[28] Philip's new prestige as the "savior of Apollo," along with his powerful position in Thessaly, which effectively became a subject of Macedonia, increased as well his power on the Amphictyonic League. Philip was now the most powerful man in central Greece.[29]

The Sack of Olynthus

Philip's next move was to march on Thermopylae, the famous "Hot Gates," where in 480, 300 Spartans and 700 soldiers from the city of Thespia died resisting the invading Persians. At Thermopylae was the narrow road between the mountains and the sea through which an army marching on Thebes or Athens had to pass, unless it marched through the easily defensible mountainous terrain to the west. Faced with the threat of Philip running loose in central and southern Greece, the city-states formed a coalition army, including 5,000 infantry and 400 cavalry from Athens, which rushed to the pass before Philip could reach it. Philip was stopped by this "unwonted act of energetic movement," as Grote put it, and he returned to operations in the north. Unfortunately, Athens did not learn the lesson of this preemptive energy.[30]

Having been turned back from Thermopylae, Philip moved north into Thrace to deal with Cersebleptes, who had made an alliance with the Athenians after their capture of Sestos. Facing a strong Athenian presence to his east, and an unreliable Thracian ally, in the fall of 352 Philip campaigned in Thrace, besieging the city of Heraion Teichos, near the Propontis and hence uncomfortably close to Athenian interests in the Chersonese. Indeed, the Athenians responded by voting to launch 40 triremes manned by citizens and imposing a war tax of 60 talents. However, on hearing rumors that Philip was ill or dead, the Athenians canceled the expedition. A few years later Demosthenes would lament this lost opportunity to confront Philip in the north: "If we had carried out our resolution in earnest and sailed to Thrace, Philip would not have survived to trouble us today."[31] That assertion may be debatable, but the alacrity with which Athens abandoned, on the strength of mere rumor, an expensive expedition and burdensome personal service points to the erosion of civic will that contributed to Philip's success. After all, Athens and her interests were as much on Philip's mind as Cersebleptes: Philip's alliances with key cities in the region, such as Cardia, Byzantium, and Perinthus, laid the groundwork for future threats to the Athenian grain trade. Meanwhile, the following year Philip continued testing the Athenians' will to respond to challenges of their interests. He harassed and plundered Athenian merchant ships, kidnapped Athenians from the islands of Imbros and Lemnos, and at Marathon made off with a sacred trireme, the ship that conveyed a state embassy to the sanctuary of Apollo on the island of Delos.[32]

After reducing Cersebleptes to a more compliant vassal, a few years later Philip turned again to Chalcidice, the region so vital to both Athenian and Macedonian interests. He set his sights on Olynthus, the powerful city that lay about a mile from the head of the Gulf of Torone between the two westernmost "claws" of Chalcidice, Pallene and Sithonia. Olynthus was the chief city of the Chalcidic Confederacy of 32 cities, and an important port for Macedonian trade, as well as possessing grain, mines, and timber. Despite its fear of Athenian ambitions in the peninsula and the material advantages of alliance with Philip, in 357 Olynthus had approached Athens to make an alliance against Philip. Athens, however, duped as we have seen by Philip's promise to return to them Amphipolis, rebuffed the Olynthians, who then made an alliance with Philip. Once again, Philip's mastery of duplicitous diplomacy obscured his real intentions from the Athenians. By 352, Philip's increasing power and his activity in Thrace were making the Olynthians uneasy—"he was too great to be trusted," as Demosthenes articulated their motives— and so they made peace with Athens and contemplated an alliance.[33] This Philip could not tolerate, and when Philip's half-brothers and potential rivals to the throne, Menelaus and Arrhidaeus, were given sanctuary in Olynthus, and the Olynthians refused to surrender them, Philip had a pretext for launching a war against Chalcidice.

By 349, Philip was ready to deal with Olynthus. The city had pro-Macedonian sympathizers within, some bribed by Philip, and the League itself was perhaps riven with factional rivalries and resentment against the predominance of Olynthus.[34] Philip proceeded to attack piecemeal the cities of the Chalcidic Confederacy in order to isolate Olynthus. He besieged and destroyed Stagira, birthplace of Aristotle, who would one day become Alexander's tutor. Ancient testimony claims the 32 cities were all destroyed, but, most likely, the example of Stagira was all it took for the others to capitulate to the Macedonians. In the midst of this campaign, Philip had to turn back an upstart in Thessaly who was rallying a Thessalian faction against Macedonian hegemony. Philip made quick work of him and returned to his reduction of the Chalcidic cities. By 348, he had taken Olynthus's port of Mecyberna, which was perhaps betrayed by a "philippising," that is, pro-Philip, faction in the city. Olynthus resisted staunchly but in two months fell, according to Diodorus because of bribery and betrayal from within.[35] "When the Macedonians took Olynthus," Worthington writes, "they went on a bloody rampage, killing indiscriminately. The Olynthians who survived the carnage were enslaved and forced to work in the Macedonian mines and field, or fled into exile, and Olynthus was razed to the ground."[36] Gangs of Chalcidic Greek slaves were seen trudging through the Peloponnese, and the Athenians taken prisoner from Olynthus were held by Philip as bargaining chips in future negotiations. The Macedonian king now had control over the strategically vital peninsula of Chalcidice, as well as its timber, grain, and nearby mines. And he had sent a brutal message to the other Greeks that resistance to his designs carried a devastating price.

The response of Athens to this calamity was typical—ill-timed or half-hearted measures that were no better than doing nothing at all. In October of 349, the Olynthian ambassadors went to Athens to seek help against Philip. After three impassioned orations on their behalf by Demosthenes,[37] the Athenians voted to make an alliance with Olynthus and sent 2,000 mercenary peltasts (light-armed troops, with javelins) and 30 ships commanded by the general Chares.[38] By the time this force got to Chalcidice, Philip was in Thessaly, and we do not know what Chares did. Most likely, he did nothing. In March 348, Athens sent out another force comprising 18 war ships, 4,000 mercenary peltasts, and 150 cavalry, commanded by Charidemus, the general stationed in the Hellespont. This force attacked the cities on Pallene, the middle "claw," already taken by Philip, but did nothing to confront the Macedonians directly. Finally, with Olynthus under siege, the Athenians sent

Chares again with 17 war ships, 2,000 citizen hoplites (heavily armed infantry), and 300 cavalry. But by the time this force was underway, the northerly summer winds known as the Etesian winds were blowing, and the force did not arrive at Olynthus until after the city had fallen.

Modern scholars generally agree that Athens, for various reasons, on its own could not have stopped Philip.[39] But one wonders what would have been the outcome if Athens, with the same alacrity with which it had earlier defended Thermopylae, had sent the third and largest force out first, in 349. Could it have taken advantage of Philip's absence in Thessaly to strengthen the defenses of the Chalcidic cities enough to deter the Macedonians, or take up a position that blocked their approach? We'll never know. And surely, the Athenians knew, when they sent out the third force, that the Etesian winds could delay its arrival. Does that mean they sent it out only as a token display? Perhaps they would have failed to stop Philip in any case, but what is significant for our discussion is the failure to provide vigorous, timely help and to formulate a clear, coherent strategic vision for the forces it did send.

The "Peace" of Philocrates and the Dangers of Diplomacy

The destruction of Olynthus, which Philip celebrated by issuing a new silver coin depicting himself as a victor, helped bring the Athenians to the bargaining table. But Philip's shrew diplomacy was as significant as the brutal fate of Olynthus. In the summer of 348, an Athenian named Phrynon had been kidnapped by Macedonian "pirates" (who operated with Philip's approval) during the Olympic truce, when travelers could not be attacked or kidnapped. Phrynon paid his own ransom, and when he returned to Athens, he demanded that an embassy be sent to Philip to recover the ransom, as it was extorted in violation of the Olympic truce. A certain Ctesiphon was chosen as ambassador, and he returned to Athens after the fall of

Olynthus. He reported to the Athenians, according to the orator Aeschines in a speech delivered in 343, "that Philip said he had not wanted to go to war with you and wanted even at that point to be rid of the war."[40] Informed nearly simultaneously about Philip's destructive power and his intention not to use it against Athens, the Athenians forgot Philip's earlier duplicity about Amphipolis and voted to make peace.

As for Philip, he was wary of Thebes and a possible alliance between that powerful city and Athens. He knew too the ancient Athenian dislike of the Thebans, and used that interest as well as fear in his courtship of the Athenians. As part of his plan, Philip needed to end the Sacred War in such a way that the Thebans would think they would benefit—the Phocians had been besting them, seizing three Boeotian cities—while in fact Philip rather than Thebes would turn out to be the dominant power in central Greece. Threatened by further Phocian success, the Thebans asked Philip for help against the Phocians. Once again, the shortsighted pursuit of parochial interests contributed to the Greek failure to unite against a common enemy.

With Macedonian help, the Thebans defeated a Phocian force near a shrine to Apollo, which provided no succor to the 500 Phocians who were burned alive in the temple. Now the Phocians turned to the Athenians and Spartans, promising them three Boeotian cities, one of which controlled the pass at Thermopylae. The Spartans sent 1,000 hoplites and their king Archidamus; the Athenians provided 50 ships. At the same time, the Athenians sent an expedition to the Chersonese, where they allied with a Thracian king named Cersebleptes, an ex-ally of Philip who was trying to regain his power. At the end of 347 or the beginning of 346, the Athenians also sent an embassy to other Greek states, inviting them to a conference to decide whether to make a collective peace with Philip or create a coalition to make war on him. Faced with these challenges, Philip needed to not only keep Thebes in check but also neutralize Athens. At the same time, he needed to bring about an end to the Sacred War, which would increase even further his power and prestige in central Greece.

Philip found an opening in the bargaining chip he had kept after the fall of Olynthus. The Athenians had long been concerned with the fate of their fellow citizens captured after the city's destruction. In early 346, they had sent an actor named Aristodemus, a friend of Philip, to Pella to find out about the Athenian prisoners. By chance, Philip at about the same time released one prisoner, Iatrocles, to communicate to the Athenians his desire for peace and an alliance with Athens. However, at the same Assembly meeting at which Aristodemus announced his news after his return, the Athenians discovered to their dismay that there had been a regime change in Phocis—Phaleacus, who had been replaced by three other leaders, was restored to power, perhaps by Philip's machinations—and the Spartans and Athenians invited to Thermopylae had been dismissed. This bad news was added to the earlier rumors that the Arcadians, from a Peloponnesian city at odds with Sparta, had asked Philip for help against the Spartans.[41] Philip's access to Thermopylae, the fate of the Athenian prisoners, and the rumors of Macedonian involvement in the Peloponnese were all factors that made peace with Philip an attractive option. The Assembly voted an embassy comprising ten Athenians, including Demosthenes, to meet with Philip and negotiate the terms of the treaty.

The history of the negotiations between Philip and the Athenian embassies is convoluted and obscured by the nature of our primary evidence—the speeches made three years later by Demosthenes and his political rival Aeschines as they battled each other in the Athenian courts over who was responsible for the failure of the peace.[42] What is clear, however, is that Philip brilliantly exploited the diplomatic process in order to obtain a settlement that advanced his interests. For one thing, he apparently was a charming man, and used this charm on the members of the embassy. Diodorus writes that Philip "enlarged his position not so much by the bravery of his deeds on the battlefield as by the diplomatic skill and affability which he brought to bear while engaged in negotiations."[43] Before he met Philip, the orator Aeschines "repeatedly labeled Philip a damned barbarian," Demosthenes reports. But after spending time with the king, Aeschines said that Philip "was, by Heracles, the purest Greek, the most skillful speaker, Athens' greatest friend."[44] Demosthenes would attribute this change to bribery, but as George Cawkwell suggests, Philip more likely simply charmed Aeschines, along with many other Greeks.[45] Demosthenes earlier in the same speech identified this same susceptibility to Philip's charms as a "terrible disease" afflicting all the Greek states: "The most prominent citizens and respected leaders in the cities are haplessly betraying their own freedom and voluntarily enslaving themselves, all the while talking euphemistically of Philip's friendship and good will and so on."[46] Indeed, Philip's "good will," if Theopompus can be believed, involved the use of lechery and debauchery as tools for achieving his political aims: "Philip, knowing that the Thessalians were licentious and wanton in their mode of life, got up parties for them and tried to amuse them in every way, dancing and rioting and submitting to every kind of licentiousness." In this way he "won most Thessalians who consorted with him by parties rather than by presents"—in other words, he didn't have to resort to outright bribery.[47]

A more important problem reflected the larger disadvantages that afflict democracies when negotiating with autocrats. As David Hunt, a classical scholar and diplomat, points out, the Athenians had no professional diplomats. As with most city-state business, a board of several citizens comprised the embassy: "There was no single ambassador," Hunt writes of Greek diplomacy in general, "or even a head of mission; the principle of collegiality was preserved and all had equal status." Regarding Athens's negotiations with Philip, Hunt adds, "It is obvious that for an autocratic ruler like Philip to negotiate with a committee of ten with equal authority but divided by internal feuds must have been a piece of cake. For since it was impossible for the Athenian assembly to delegate its authority, the political complexion of the assembly must be reflected in the mission it sent."[48] In other words, the intra-city factional strife that compromised earlier responses to Philip's designs would be duplicated in the squabbling diplomatic mission.

When the Athenians met with Philip in February of 346, the king once again mixed attractive but vague promises with conditions all to his advantage. Amphipolis was off the table—Athens would never retrieve its colony: "a bitter blow for Athens," Cawkwell writes, "which she only accepted for fear of worse if she did not."[49] Philip did recognize Athenian interests in the Chersonese; he also made vague assurances about protecting the Phocians and ending the Sacred War that in effect excluded them—Athens's ally—from the negotiations; and among other promises, including a bilateral alliance with Athens, he led the embassy to believe that the Athenian prisoners he still held would be restored once the peace was ratified.

Amid these assurances of future boons, however, Philip had one key term: each side would recognize the other's possessions at the time of ratification. This meant that Philip could continue campaigning in Thrace during the months it would take for the Athenians to return home, debate the terms, vote, and return to Philip for ratification of the peace, by which time Philip would have added more territory to Macedonia. As soon as the Athenians left, Philip returned to Thrace and defeated Cersebleptes, whom he reduced to a vassal, and took several Thracian forts east of Amphipolis, which would remain Philip's because the peace had not yet been ratified.[50] These activities shored up Philip's eastern border and compromised Athenian interests in the region.

In Athens, two Assembly meetings were held in April to debate the peace. Another item of business on one day was the proposal to create a Common Peace among all the Greek states: "As its name suggest, this would involve a general agreement of all Greek states, each one making an alliance with all the others. If one member state acted in an inappropriate manner toward another (if it attacked it, for example), the others would come to the latter's defense."[51] And any Greek state could join the Peace, including Phocis—a development, of course, that ran counter to Philip's interests. This proposal was put to the Macedonian embassy negotiating for Philip, and the ambassadors rejected what Griffith calls proposals made in "fairyland: in the hard, cold world of reality there was no chance that Philip would agree to peace on these terms."[52] That reality was sweetened by promises of boons the Athenians would enjoy after they made peace, including the reduction of Thebes's influence and "whatever arrangements we may demand of him now," as Demosthenes put it some years later.[53]

In the end, however, the options for the Athenians were either the king's terms or war, and so Athens made the Peace of Philocrates, named for the citizen who took the lead in the negotiations both in the Assembly and as one of the ambassadors. A fragment from the fourth-century historian Theopompus survives in which one Athenian, Aristophon, spoke against this act of appeasement in the face of a naked threat: "Consider how we would be behaving of all things most cowardly if we should agree to this peace and abandon Amphipolis—we who occupy the greatest of all Hellenic cities! We have a great number of allies, we own three hundred war galleys, and take income of nearly four hundred talents. This being so, who would not censure us if we, cowering before the Macedonian power, should agree to anything unjust?"[54] Perhaps Aristophon's continuing obsession with Amphipolis was unrealistic, but his evocation of Athens's glorious reputation for defending its interests and autonomy—a reputation about to be besmirched by its acceptance of Philip's conditions—was nonetheless to the point. However, war was not an attractive option for the

Athenians, particularly after another politician named Eubulus, according to Demosthenes, frightened them with the specter of increased taxes, conversion of the theoric fund into a "war chest," and personal military service.[55]

After the Athenians and their allies in the Sea League ratified the peace by exchanging oaths with the Macedonian embassy, the second embassy left to find Philip and finalize the treaty. It took well over a month, however, before the Athenians and Philip could meet. Meanwhile, ambassadors from all the major Greek powers had gathered in Pella, testifying to Philip's immense power and prestige and the consequence of these same states' inability to set aside their parochial differences and unite against a common enemy. The Thessalians and Thebans wanted the Phocians punished; the Spartans and Athenians, both enemies of the Thebans and allies of the Phocians, argued for forbearance. All the while Philip made his secret promises to both sides: "Having heard both embassies privately," Justin writes, "he promised to the one security from war, binding them by an oath to reveal his answer to nobody; to the other he engaged himself to come and bring them assistance." More significant is Justin's assessment of the spectacle of these powerful, free Greek states submitting their fates to the arbitration of an autocrat: "It was a shameful and miserable sight, to behold Greece, even then the most distinguished country in the world for power and dignity, a country that had constantly been the conqueror of kings and nations, and was still mistress of many cities, waiting at a foreign court to ask or deprecate war; that the champions of the world should place all their hopes on assistance from another, and should be reduced, by their discords and civil feuds, to such a condition as to flatter a power which had lately been a humble portion of their dependencies."[56]

The second embassy returned to Athens in July. When the members made their report to the Council (the body that recommended the business to be heard by the Assembly), the

Phocians were present to request military aid from their ally Athens, no doubt having thought harder about Philip's intentions. The question then became whether to help the Phocians and march to Thermopylae or go ahead with the peace. The Council recommended the latter, but when the Assembly met a few days later, the news came that Philip was already at Thermopylae.[57] Demosthenes railed against the peace and urged the Athenians not to abandon Phocis or allow Philip to take Thermopylae, but a letter from Philip arrived in Athens, full of protestations of affection and the desire for peace, all reinforced by "the many great advantages" for Athens enumerated by Aeschines, according to Demosthenes later.[58] The Assembly, moved more by words than by deeds and cowed by Philip's possession of Thermopylae, voted that the peace be extended to Philip's descendents and that Athens would make war against the Phocians if they did not hand back Delphi.

Before that could happen, Philip ended the war through shrewd horse-trading. His deal with the Phocian leader Phaleacus allowed the general and his 8,000 mercenaries to leave unharmed and the Phocians to surrender to Philip rather than to their enemies. However, Philip decided to let the Amphictyonic Council, filled with Phocis's bitterest enemies, decide the Phocians' fate. The Council voted to give Philip Phocis's two votes on the Council, which formalized Philip's power in central Greece: "Here then," Grote writes, "was a momentous political change doubly fatal to the Hellenic world: first in the new position of Philip both as master of the keys of Greece and as recognized Amphiktyonic leader, with means of direct access and influence even on the inmost cities of the Peloponnesus; next, in the lowered banner and uncovered frontier of Athens, disgraced by the betrayal both of her Phokian allies and of the general safety of Greece, and recompensed only in so far as she regained her captives."[59] As for the Phocians, they did not suffer what their enemies such as Thebes may have wished on them—Philip was too astute at balance-of-power politics to leave Thebes without a potential counterweight. But the punishment was still devastating. The occupiers of Delphi had their property confiscated, the city was excluded from the oracle, and its membership in the Amphictyonic Council was terminated. The Phocians had to discard all their horses and weapons until the money stolen from the temple was repaid, at the rate of 60 talents a year. All Phocian towns were destroyed, the people resettled in villages comprising no more than 50 houses. Most important for Philip, Macedonian troops were garrisoned in the Phocian towns, ostensibly to protect the Phocians from further reprisals but in reality to give Philip a military presence in central Greece and to intimidate Athens.[60] As Diodorus writes, "He had not only made a name for himself for his piety and talented generalship but had also built a sure foundation for the future increase in his power."[61]

By using mostly shrewd diplomacy—a "chess-like combination," Griffith writes, "presenting his opponents with no reasonable alternative to resigning with the pieces still intact on the board"—Philip indeed was now the most powerful man in Greece, a distinction ratified by his presiding over the renewal of the Delphic festival and games in the summer of 346.[62] As for the rest of Greece, individual city-states were now more than ever eager to use Philip's power in pursuing their quarrels at the expense of Greece's long-term interests, as did the Peloponnesian states of Argos and Messene in 344, when they courted Philip for support against their nemesis, Sparta. Elsewhere in Greece, as Grote wrote, "the movement everywhere, in or near Greece, began with him [Philip], and with those parties in the various cities, who acted on his instigation and looked to him for support. . . . Every year his power increased; while the cities of the Grecian world remained passive, uncombined, and without recognizing any one of their own number as leader."[63]

From Appeasing Peace to the War Against Freedom

Although Philip was careful not to violate the letter of the peace treaty with Athens, he continued to consolidate his power and influence in Greece in ways harmful to Athens's interests. In 344, Thessaly, Macedon's southern neighbor, had become impatient with Macedonian dominance, and unrest was brewing in both Pherae and Philip's long-time ally Larissa. Philip quickly marched into Thessaly, expelled the troublemakers, and installed Macedonian garrisons in several cities, including the most important, Pherae and Larissa. Power was given to a board of ten men, and the Thessalian "tetrarchies," the four administrative provinces of Thessaly, were subject to governors answerable only to Philip. A few years later, he replaced Arybbas, the king of the Molossians (a people living in Epirus, which lay southwest of Macedonia in what is roughly modern Albania), with his brother-in-law Alexander, who had lived with Philip for several years and was completely devoted to him—for sexually disreputable reasons, according to Justin.[64] At the same time, as we have seen, two Peloponnesian cities, Argos and Messene, were looking to Philip for help against Sparta's renewed attempts to recover its dominance over those states. It is likely they received it: Demosthenes reported in his *Second Philippic* that Philip was "actually dispatching mercenaries and forwarding supplies, and he is expected in person with a large force."[65] And evidence suggests that Philip was interfering in Euboea, the island east of Attica vital to Athenian security, as it was separated from the mainland by a narrow channel; in Elis, near Olympia, where he financed an oligarchic takeover of the city from the democratic faction; and in Megara, a city less than 50 miles west of Athens.[66]

During this same time, Philip also continued to use diplomatic overtures to provide cover for his creeping advance against southern Greece. While Philip was in Epirus in 344 deposing its Molossian king, he sent to Athens an embassy including a famous orator named Python to counter Demosthenes's increasingly vigorous attacks on Philip and the peace: "Though Philip is eager to benefit you," the orator Hegesippus would recall Python's words to the Assembly, "and prefers your friendship to that of any other state, you constantly thwart him, lending an ear to false accusers."[67] Philip also offered to amend the treaty, proposing a Common Peace among all the Greek states, something he had rejected three years earlier: "Now," Worthington writes, "he had no choice if he wanted to keep Athens as an ally and offset the people's concern over the growth in his power, especially in the Peloponnese."[68] In addition, Philip's influence on the Amphictyonic Council and the Peloponnesian cities meant that such an agreement could serve his interests.[69] Finally, Philip invited other changes to the treaty, Python alleging "that Philip was prepared to fall in with your [the Athenians'] suggestions."[70] Philip was courting Athens with these empty promises because Athens was still a power to be reckoned with and, by implication, a power that could have checked his ambitions, or served his future plans, which by this time probably included the invasion of Persia.

At this point in the debate, with the Assembly favorably disposed to Python's speech, Demosthenes delivered his famous second *Philippic*. We will examine more closely in the next section Demosthenes's efforts to rouse Athens to a more vigorous resistance of Philip. For now, Demosthenes countered Python's soothing promises with a stark assessment of Philip's ambition: "If anyone views with confidence the present power of Philip and the extent of his dominions, if anyone imagines that all this imports no danger to our city and that you are not the object of his preparations, I must express my astonishment."[71] He went on to catalogue Philip's previous betrayal of the promises he made to those states such as Thessaly and Thebes that thought they could use him for their own interests. Demosthenes also repeated what he told the Messenians when he attempted to dissuade them from trusting Philip: there is one bulwark "invaluable for democracies against tyrants," and that is "mistrust." And if the object of the state is freedom, then mistrust of Philip is necessary, "for every king, every despot is the sworn foe of freedom and of law."[72]

As a result of Demosthenes's efforts, the Assembly voted to amend the stipulation in the original treaty that "each side should keep what it possessed" to "each side should keep its own," a change that would legitimize Athens's claims to Amphipolis, Potidaea, and some Thracian fortresses. To drive this demand home, Hegesippus then proposed that Amphipolis be restored to Athens, along with the island of Halonnesus, an Athenian possession taken first by a pirate, and then by an ally of Athens, from whom Philip took it. Hegesippus lead an embassy to Philip to present these proposals, which of course Philip rejected, treating the embassy with scorn. He did not want to encourage other states to start demanding the return of cities that were now part of the Macedonian empire. Philip's rejection strengthened Demosthenes's argument that the Macedonian king was not interested in peaceful coexistence with an equal partner but was intent on becoming the master of Greece.

During these few years after the Peace of Philocrates, while Philip was vigorously increasing his intimidating power and influence closer and closer to Athens, the Athenians continued to quarrel over the peace through formal charges brought against the politicians involved, thus compromising Athens's ability to develop a coherent, consistent response to Philip's activities. Part of the problem lay in the intensely personal and partisan nature of Athenian politics, which could use the courts as venues for pursuing political quarrels and disagreements. These trials were heard in the People's Court, after the Assembly the most important political organ in ancient Athens. Trials in the People' Court were conducted in front of several hundred jurors picked by lot from a panel of 6,000 citizens. Citizens brought the charge and personally prosecuted the trial, and the jurors

were the arbiters not just of guilt or innocence but also of the
application of law. Politicians were generally subject to accusations that a decree or law was unconstitutional or that they
had worked to overthrow the democracy, betrayed the democracy to an enemy, or received a bribe to make a speech in the
Assembly that was not the best advice for the people (a charge
called *eisangelia*, "denunciation"). Any citizen could make these
accusations, the truth of which would be determined for the
most part by the jurors' reaction to speeches rather than on the
basis of reliable evidence. And the penalty frequently was death.
As M. H. Hansen writes, "Denunciation to the people gave the
People's Court enormous power over the political leaders of
Athens and the magistrates, not just because of the severity of
the penalties but still more because of the frequency off its
use"—130 prosecutions between 492 and 322.[73] Imagine our
own political system holding impeachment hearings and trials
several times a year, and you can visualize the disruption this
legal wrangling inflicted on Athens and how badly it compromised any attempt to come up with an effective, coherent foreign policy for dealing with Philip.

Two trials in particular during this period continued the
quarrel over the peace and exposed the factional divisions in
Athenian politics. First, in 343 Philocrates was charged with
acting treacherously when an ambassador by taking bribes from
Philip, and thus harming Athens's interests by making the
motion for the peace. Even though the Assembly had passed
Philocrates's proposal, responsibility for the perceived failure
of the policy it instituted was laid at the feet of the person making the proposal, with the allegation of bribery giving cover to
what was an obviously political attack. Philocrates was astute
enough to see which way the political winds were blowing and
so went into exile before the trial. He was sentenced to death
anyway, and his property was confiscated and sold.

Next came the turn of Aeschines, Demosthenes's political
rival. In 345, Aeschines had prosecuted Demosthenes's ally

Timarchus for sexual misbehavior, specifically homosexual prostitution, which invalidated his citizen rights. Now in 343 Demosthenes sought his revenge by charging Aeschines with the same offenses as those leveled against Philocrates, alleging that Aechines, bribed by Philip, had swayed the Assembly by repeating Philip's duplicitous promises of "many great advantages" for the Athenians if they made peace.[74] Again the charge was political, an attempt on Demosthenes's part "to distance himself completely from the peace," Worthington writes, "given that he had now settled firmly on a policy of resistance to Macedonia at all costs. He may also have wanted to get rid of Aeschines, who was an effective speaker and who in wanting to maintain the peace with Philip might block Demosthenes in the Assembly."[75] Aeschines narrowly escaped conviction by a margin of 30 votes out of 1,501 cast, the scant margin indicating that his exoneration was not necessarily an endorsement of the peace or the policies of the pro-Macedonian faction in Athens.

The trials of both Philocrates and Aeschines reflect the widespread Athenian view that the peace with Philip was not working out in Athens's favor. But rather than formulate a new, coordinated response, the Athenians pursued their intra-city factional rivalries at the expense of their long-term interests. The result was the same incoherent, ad hoc reactions to Philip's activities, policies that swung from ill-timed and half-baked interventions to passive inactivity camouflaged with rhetorical bluster. As Grote writes, "The activity of Athens, unfortunately was shown in nothing but words; to set off against the vigorous deeds of Philip." [76]

Philip was not done courting Athens, however; perhaps he was worried about Athenian support for the Molossian Arybbas, who was an Athenian citizen and who was actively seeking support from Athens. The trials of Philocrates and Aeschines would have likewise increased Phillip's anxiety about the stability of the peace and the extent of Athenian hostility toward him. Thus, while he was busy in Epirus dealing with Arybbas, Philip sent an embassy to Athens with a letter repeating his offer to make a Common Peace. He also proposed submitting the disputes over the Thracian fortresses and Halonnesus to third-party arbitration and forming a joint Macedonian-Athenian naval force for clearing the Aegean of pirates. During the debate in the Assembly, Demosthenes's ally Hegesippus denounced Philip's offers, particularly the one suggesting that Philip would "give" the Athenians Halonnesus as though it were his property, rather than give it *back* in recognition of Athens's claim to it.[77] Most modern historians see this point as a trivial "argument over syllables," as Aeschines put it later, and a mere pretext for the hawks in Athens to reject any agreement with Philip.[78] However, as Grote reminds us, "well-conducted diplomacy, modern as well as ancient, has been always careful to note the distinction as important. . . . No modern diplomatist will accept restitution of what has been unlawfully taken if he is called upon to recognize it as gratuitous cession from the captor."[79] Philip no doubt recognized the distinction: to acquiesce in Athens's formulation would be to open the door to other demands for the restoration of former Athenian cities, such as Amphipolis.[80] More than a quibble, Hegesippus's distinction—one ratified by the Athenians, who rejected Philip's overtures—refused to acknowledge Philip's superiority and Athens's inferiority, and rejected the bestowal of title by sheer force rather than by right. Athens was not quite ready to acknowledge that its worsened position, and Philip's increased power and influence, since the treaty of 346, were permanent.

After the Assembly's rejection of Philip's proposals, an Athenian named Antiphon, who had been stripped of his citizenship, was caught trying to set fire to the Piraeus dockyards in order to degrade Athens's most potent weapon, its fleet. Demosthenes, who prosecuted Antiphon, claimed that he was an agent of Philip, which might have been true: after the rejection of Philip's offers, as Worthington writes, "the Athenian attitude to peace and to Philip was obvious, and the king may well have wanted to try to neutralise Athens' naval power if the peace negotiations broke down completely, which would mean warfare."[81] Antiphon was convicted and executed. Not much later, in early 342, Philip also burned the territory of three cities belonging to the Cassiopaeans, a people south of Epirus. Philip gave these cities to Alexander, the new king he had installed in Epirus after deposing Arybbas. The Ambracians, likewise neighbors of Epirus, fearful that they were next, asked their mother city, Corinth (Ambracia was founded by the Corinthians), for help, and Corinth in turn sought troops from Athens, which were provided. Nearby in Euboea, Philip's general Hipponicus, with 1,000 mercenaries, drove out anti-Macedonian factions and installed "philippizing" tyrants in two cities, Oreus and Eretria.[82] Alarmed by these developments, Athens sent embassies throughout the Peloponnese, seeking allies for a coalition to resist Philip's further encroachments. Five cities, including some allies of Philip, made an alliance with Athens, which suggests that fear of Philip's growing power was not just a fabrication of the Athenian war-party's paranoia.

As relations with Athens continued to deteriorate, in June 342 Philip turned once more to the Thracians and Cersebleptes, who was attending to his own interests rather than Philip's by attacking and subjecting various cities in the Chersonese. Philip campaigned there for two years, taking cities and strongholds, founding cities, and imposing a lucrative tithe. The Greek cities of the Chersonese, according to Diodorus, "were freed from this fear [of the Thracians] and gladly joined Philip's alliance."[83] Philip installed a Macedonian general to watch over this region so vital to Athens's interests. Around the time Philip started the Thracian campaign in 341, the Athenians sent a general named Diopeithes to the Chersonese along with mercenaries and colonists to replace those who had fled earlier conflicts. In 341, Philip was drawn into a dispute between the Athenian colonists and the city of Cardia, on the western shore of the

Chersonese, near the critical entry into the Propontis. Diopeithes had attacked Cardian territory, including two cities allied
with Philip. He also held for ransom and tortured Philip's
ambassador. Finally, since Diopeithes was inadequately funded
by Athens, he robbed merchant ships on their way to Macedonia in order to pay his mercenaries. In 340, Philip sent a letter to Athens, one of 11 in this period, illustrating his tactic of
using duplicitous diplomacy to achieve his aims, mixing threats
with promises of benefits for Athens if the city played along.
This latest note demanded that Diopeithes be recalled, and
warned that Athens had broken the peace and that "I shall deal
with you about these matters," a virtual declaration of war.[84]

Athens understandably was concerned about Philip's activities in a region so vital to Athenian interests. Within a few
months of Philip's letter Demosthenes delivered three speeches
arguing that Athens was already at war with Philip, whose
actions had testified to his aggressive intent, which was to
destroy Greek freedom, especially that of Athens.[85] "He is ill-
disposed and hostile to the whole city," Demosthenes thun-
dered, "and to the very soil on which the city stands, and, I
will add, to every man in the city."[86] Thus Diopeithes was not
the point; rather, the issue was Athens's willingness to face
reality and prepare for war by creating an army and seeking
out allies, and to preempt Philip's designs on Athens rather
than waiting for him to show up in Attica: "For he who makes
and devises the means by which I may be captured," Demosthenes argued, "is at war with me, even though he has not yet
hurled a javelin or shot a bolt."[87] Demosthenes also called for
a special tax to fund the war and proposed that citizen-soldiers
rather than mercenaries do the fighting. In response, the Athenians did send out a fleet under Chares to support Diopeithes;
but the other recommendations were not followed. Worse yet,
Chares would allow Philip's fleet to sail through the Hellespont into the Propontis to support the siege of Perinthus.
Instead of directly confronting Philip, the Athenians sent a

force to liberate Oreus in Euboea from the tyrant Philip had installed and later removed another tyrant in Euboea. Embassies solicited alliances from other Greek cities, including north Aegean islands that, although they had started the Social War to free themselves from Athenian domination, now recognized Philip as a greater danger than Athens was. Demosthenes, the driving force of the anti-Philip party in Athens, in 340 was awarded a crown in recognition of his efforts, indicating that the Athenians supported, at least to a point, his views on Philip.

However, the Athenians continued to rely on half measures and mistaken policies. If they were going to violate the peace by attacking Philip's allies, as they did in attacking Cardia, then they should have realized that they were now at war and "sinned vigorously," committing fully their money and manpower to confronting Philip in the north rather than relying on poorly funded mercenaries. Meanwhile Philip defeated Cersebleptes and installed a Macedonian governor in Thrace, thereby tightening his hold on the vital Chersonese and Black Sea grain, biding his time for the climactic confrontation with Athens.

Although Athens may not have known it, Philip had declared war against the city-state with the threat that closed his letter. Thus in early 340, around the time he sent Athens the letter containing the declaration of war, he moved to besiege the city of Perinthus, which was leaning toward Athens and had refused to send Philip help for the campaign against Cersebleptes. This city sat on the north coast of the Propontis, about halfway between the Hellespont and the Bosporus. Philip's attack, then, brought him ever closer to controlling the Athenian grain route. Perinthus, however, put up a stiff fight, aided by its formidable topography—behind two walls, its houses rose in terraces up a steep slope—and by the city of Byzantium, about 45 miles to the east, which was equally apprehensive of Philip's growing power. More ominously for Philip, the King of Persia, likewise alarmed at Philip's expansionist energy, provided mercenaries to help Perinthus. In the face of these difficulties, Philip split his forces and sent half his men to besiege Byzantium, which immediately received men, money, and supplies from several Greek islands and from Persia. Clearly, the northern Aegean cities saw that Philip was a serious threat. Since dividing his forces lessened his chances of taking Perinthus, let alone Byzantium, Philip's motive may have been to provoke Athens into open war.[88] In the event, the Athenians obliged: roused by Demosthenes, they destroyed the stone on which the Peace of Philocrates had been inscribed, and sent a fleet north to help Chares. Philip immediately seized an Athenian grain fleet. He captured 230 vessels, using the timber of the 180 Athenian ships for siege-engines (he returned the 50 allied ships), and selling the grain, which earned him 700 talents, a year's income for Athens.

Faced with stiff resistance from Perinthus and Byzantium, Philip abandoned the sieges and the next year went off to campaign against the Scythians, north of the Black Sea, where the king Atheas had announced his independence from Macedonian hegemony. Lifting these sieges, however, was no defeat for Philip, nor an occasion for celebration among the Greek states. The Athenians lost an opportunity to take advantage of Philip's absence and strengthen their forces in the north or harass the Macedonians as they marched home through the Chersonese after lifting the sieges of Perinthus and Byzantium. More mysterious is the failure of the Athenian ships to pursue Philip's fleet after it escaped the Black Sea, apparently through a clever stratagem involving a false letter allowed to fall into Athenian hands.[89] Despite the failures at Perinthus and Byzantium, Philip was still an enemy to be reckoned with: he had strengthened his influence near the Bosporus to the benefit of the Macedonian economy and had damaged the Athenian fleet by destroying 180 ships. Meanwhile, he still controlled Thermopylae and counted the Thebans as his allies. In the end, Athens, not Byzantium, was the primary objective, for once Philip had dealt with Athens, the other cities would fall into line—as subsequent history would prove.

The showdown, however, would not come for nearly two years. On their way back from defeating Atheas in 339, the Macedonians had been attacked by the Triballians, Macedonia's northern neighbors, who were offended by Philip's refusal to pay for safe passage. Philip was wounded by a spear through the thigh, and the 20,000 captive Scythian women and children, along with the huge flocks and herds of livestock , were lost. However, the need to recuperate from this wound gave Philip time to take care of another problem. During this period, the Thebans would take control of Nicaea, a city commanding the pass of Thermopylae, thus blocking Philip's way into Boeotia and Attica. There was another route through the mountains west of Thermopylae, which went through Doris to Amphissa, a city in Locria, which was near Delphi and the Gulf of Corinth. The drawback of this route was a high pass usually guarded by the Phocians, but after their defeat in the Sacred War, the pass was now unguarded. That the Athenians and Thebans did not remember this route and take steps to defend it is another example of their fatal complacency.[90] Once winter was over and his wound had time to heal, all Philip needed was an excuse to march his army into southern Greece, bypassing the Thebans at Thermopylae.[91]

Philip's opportunity had begun to develop earlier while he was still besieging Byzantium. Amphissa, a member of the Amphictyonic Council, was attempting to engineer a sacred war against Athens. The pretext was some gilded shields that commemorated the defeat of the Persians at Plataea in 479. The Athenians had rededicated the shields when the rebuilding of the temple of Apollo at Delphi, which had burned down in 373, was finally finished but before it was reconsecrated. The bigger problem was the Athenians had added a caption to the memorial referring to the fact that the Thebans had "medised," that is, gone over to the Persians before the battle,

a blot on the reputation of Thebes that Alexander would use
as a pretext for destroying the city in 335. This gratuitous insult
to the Thebans, at a time when Philip was at war with Athens,
is another example of how the shortsighted pursuit of parochial
quarrels weakened the Greek states. Equally shortsighted was
the behavior of the Amphissans, no doubt encouraged by
Thebes, unless the charge was engineered by Philip to provide
a pretext for intervention in central Greece.[92] The Amphissans
wanted the Council to exclude Athenians from consulting the
oracle and fine them 50 talents, gambling that Athens would
refuse and thus justify a Sacred War—a war that would necessarily involve Philip, given his influence with the Council
through his own two votes and his control of the Thessalians.

A war was indeed started, but not the one the Amphissans
had planned. The Athenian orator Aeschines, representing
Athens at the Council meeting, ignored the charges of the
Amphissans and accused *them* of impiety because they had
cultivated the plain of Cirrha, which lay between Delphi and
the Gulf of Corinth and which had centuries earlier been con-
secrated to Apollo. The Council forgot all about Athens and
discovered that indeed the Amphissans had put up buildings
on the plain; as the Council members were making their inspec-
tion, armed Amphissans ran them off and detained a few. A
couple of months later, another Council meeting took place
near Thermopylae, where a Sacred War was declared against
Amphissa. At the spring meeting in 339, while Philip was in
Scythia and about the same time that the Thebans retook Thermopylae, Amphissa was fined and given six months to pay.
When Amphissa remained intransigent and refused to pay the
fine, at the autumn meeting, Philip was made commander of
the Amphictyonic army. His opportunity for marching south
into Greece had come.[93] Recalling these events later, Demosthenes would blame Aeschines for instigating the war and
repeat what he had said in the Assembly at the time: "You are
bringing war into Attica, Aeschines, Amphictyonic war."[94]

In the fall of 339, Philip marched south, using the undefended route that bypassed the Theban garrison at Nicaea. That Philip's purpose had little to do with punishing Amphissa became clear when he marched eastward and took Elateia. This city was strategically important, for it commanded the road between Phocis and Boeotia, the same road that linked Nicaea to Thebes and eventually Athens, which was only a three-day march away from Elateia. With this move, Philip made it clear that his objective was not Amphissa but Thebes and Athens.

When the news reached Athens that Elateia had been seized, "the city was rigid with fear," Diodorus writes. At the Assembly meeting, "a silent panic had seized the theater," for the Athenians were uncertain about which side the Thebans would take.[95] According to Plutarch, these events "drove the Athenians out of their senses: no one ventured to ascend the bema [the speaker's platform] and no one knew what ought to be said, but perplexity and silence reigned in the assembly."[96] At this moment, with the citizens "in the grip of the most extreme fear and helplessness," just when it seemed that Philip would achieve his aims by exploiting once again his enemies' parochial quarrels and their fear of a fight, Demosthenes stepped onto the bema and made the speech that would be his finest hour.[97]

Demosthenes called upon the Athenians to set aside their fear, arguing that a substantial number of Thebans had not yet thrown their lot in with Philip, no matter the number of "philippizing" Thebans. That is why Philip has seized Elateia: "He wishes both to bolster his friends and make them confident and to terrify his opponents so that they either yield out of fear or be forced to yield, which they now refuse to do." Given substantial Theban resistance to Philip, Demosthenes told the Athenians to "rid yourselves of the general fear" and forget their old hatred of the Boeotian enemy, for "if we choose to recall at this moment anything unpleasant that the Thebans ever did to us and to distrust them for being in the ranks of our enemies," then the Athenians "will bring about what Philip would pray for," strengthening the pro-Philip faction in Thebes and disheartening those who wanted to resist him. This being the case, Demosthenes further argued, the Athenians must consider the Thebans their friends—a hard sell for Athenians accustomed to considering the Thebans "Boeotian swine"— and send a citizen force of infantry and cavalry, comprising all men of military age, to nearby Eleusis, which lay on the road to Thebes, so that the Thebans "who choose to vie for freedom have you ready and willing to assist if anyone should move against them." Finally, he asked for ten ambassadors to travel to Thebes to make an alliance and coordinate the military response. Most important, Demosthenes impressed upon the Assembly that now was not the time to pursue parochial self-interest: "Ask nothing of the Thebans—it is entirely the wrong occasion. Rather, since they are in the direst straits, and we take a longer view of things than they do, announce that we will respond to a request for help."[98] The Assembly approved Demosthenes's proposals, and he was sent to Thebes as a member of the embassy.

When the Athenians arrived, Philip's ambassadors were there ahead of them. Once more, the Macedonian king was attempting to achieve his aims with diplomacy rather than force, gambling that his enemies did not have the stomach for a fight and that old hatreds would prevent these two cities from combining against him. Also, there was that considerable number of Thebans who supported Philip.[99] So the king had sent to Thebes, his formal ally, an embassy comprising representatives of the Amphictyonic states that had joined him to fight Amphissa—a reminder of his influence among the other northern Greek states. The embassy stated Philip's stark terms: join him in the fight against Athens, or at least allow free passage of his army through Boeotia, and surrender Nicaea. In return, the Thebans would join in the plundering of Athens and save their own territory from destruction. As Demosthenes recalled a few years later, the embassy explicitly tried to exploit the traditional enmity between Thebes and Athens: "They [the ambassadors] insisted that the Thebans reciprocate the favors that Philip had bestowed on them and exact retribution for the crimes inflicted by you." In short, the Thebans were called upon to pay the bill for Philip's role in ending the Sacred War to the benefit of Thebes, at the same time that Philip once again exploited the old divisive hatreds of the Greek states.[100]

Demosthenes's answer to the Macedonian ambassador has not survived, but it must have been a powerful speech. Despite the fact that Philip was a day's march away from Thebes, "the power of the orator," Plutarch wrote, quoting the fourth-century historian Theopompus, "fanned up their courage and inflamed their honorable ambition and obscured all other considerations, so that, casting away fear and calculation and feelings of obligation [Philip was their formal ally], they were rapt away by his words into the path of honor."[101] The Thebans drove a hard bargain: Athens in effect had to pay for the war while Thebes would command the infantry and share command over the fleet. That was not too great a price to pay for freedom, certainly nothing compared to what Athens in her history had sacrificed to protect her autonomy. The problem was this recognition of Philip's threat and what it would take to counter it came much too late. In the end, the Thebans expelled the opponents of war from the city and made the alliance with Athens.

Within a year, the climactic battle—"one of the most decisive battles of history," Cawkwell calls it— would take place at Chaeronea, between Philip's Macedonian army and a Greek coalition, comprising Athens, Thebes, Euboea, Megara, Corinth, Achaea, and two northwest islands, Leucas and Corcyra, a far cry from the 31 cities that 150 years earlier had fought Xerxes. The rest of Greece remained neutral, another instance of parochial shortsightedness in the pursuit of self-interest.[102] In the months leading up to the battle, a few skirmishes took place between the Macedonians and the Greek coalition troops, but we have little information about these battles. Finally, Philip once more used a ruse involving a fake letter, and surprised and killed most of the mercenaries blocking the Gravia pass on the road to Amphissa, which quickly capitulated, leaving the road open to Thebes. Philip sent embassies to Thebes and Athens, hoping to achieve his aims without bloodshed— not because he feared losing, but rather because by now his grand scheme was the invasion of Persia, for which he needed the cooperation of two of the most powerful states in Greece. But Thebes and Athens both rebuffed the king. In late summer, the Greek forces took their stand 80 miles from Athens on the plain of Chaeronea, which sat on the border between Boeotia and Phocis, the best place to block Philip's army from nearby Thebes.

In August of 338, the battle was fought that changed history. The details are sketchy and in dispute, but Philip's superior generalship and the professionalism of his army were too much for amateur citizen-soldiers who in the previous decades had not done much fighting.[103] One thousand Athenians were killed, 2,000 taken prisoner. The Thebans suffered similar casualties, and the Achaeans, according to the travel writer Pausanias, never recovered from their losses in the war. The survivors, including Demosthenes, fled south into Boeotia. The war between Greece and Macedon and the long tradition of Greek political freedom were over.

The Aftermath of Chaeronea

The reality of that loss, however, was not immediately apparent after Chaeronea. Thebes was punished with a Macedonian garrison; the soldiers taken as prisoners were sold into slavery,, and the bodies of the dead had to be paid for. This harsh treatment was Thebes's punishment for violating its alliance with Philip. The other city-states were treated with leniency. Despite a panic in Athens immediately after the battle, the Athenians were treated gently: the ashes of the dead were returned without payment demanded, the prisoners sent home gratis, and no garrison was inflicted upon the city. Philip's generosity served his long-term plans: the invasion of Persia by a Greek coalition in order to punish the desecration of Athens's temples in 480 would have a false ring to it if Philip treated Athens harshly. And in Philip's absence, a strong Athens would act as a counter force to Thebes.[104] The other states of Greece also made their peace with Macedonia, with the exception of Sparta, whose distant defiance Philip could ignore. Finally, maintaining his usual masquerade in which hegemonic ambition was cloaked in Hellenic federalism, Philip created the League of Corinth, which imposed a common peace. This League was ostensibly a federation of free Greek states, but in reality it was the instrument of Philip's power and control—he was the League's *hegemon,* "leader and master of all," as Demosthenes put it later, a position reinforced by the four Macedonian garrisons stationed at Thebes, Chalkis, Ambrakia, and Corinth, the strategic cities called the "fetters of Greece."[105] Thus the Greek states continued to work their constitutional mechanisms, but in fact were lacking the most important good that those mechanisms were supposed to serve—their civic autonomy.

If there were any doubts about the Greeks' loss of freedom, subsequent events would remove them. When Philip was assassinated in 336, Thebes made a noble attempt to regain its freedom, one that ended brutally with the literal destruction of the city and the sale of its inhabitants into slavery. Thirteen years later, on Alexander's death Athens and the Aetolian League made their own bid for freedom. After some initial successes, the coalition army was defeated near the Thessalian city of Crannon. "Their defeat," Plutarch tells us, "was not severe, nor did many of them fall," but reluctant to fight any more, the "army melted away and most shamefully abandoned the cause of freedom."[106] With the Macedonians a two-day march away, Athens surrendered unconditionally and suffered harsh punishment: some of its leaders were executed (Demosthenes committed suicide on the obscure island of Calauria), the democracy was abolished, the poorer citizens sent off as colonists, and a Macedonian garrison was installed in the port of Piraeus.

The complete civic degradation of Athens was obvious a mere thirty-one years after Chaeronea, when the Macedonian generalissimo Demetrius Poliorketes entered the city in triumph and was proclaimed a god by the descendents of those who had fought the Persians and their divine kings at Marathon and Salamis. As George Grote puts it, "The sentiment of political self-reliance and autonomy had fled."[107] The city-states of ancient Greece, which had invented the idea of political freedom and the constitutions that embodied it, would never be free again.

The Greek Response

Could Philip have been stopped? Such a question is of course difficult to answer, for it is always hard to describe the scenery on the historical road not traveled. Most modern historians believe, as George Cawkwell puts it, that "perhaps the end of Greek liberty was inevitable." Philip had more money, a professional army, and new siege technology that made fortified city-states vulnerable to capture. Moreover, Macedon was a unified nation-state ruled by an autocrat, confronting dozens of consensually governed city-states, each jealous of its own autonomy and interests. This parochial self-interest made unification difficult and the temptation to use Philip as an ally in inter-state quarrels irresistible.[108]

However, the Greeks had faced and overcome greater challenges in the past. In 480, the Persian king Xerxes invaded

Greece with a force comprising 100,000 soldiers and 1,700 ships. The Greeks met this threat with a fleet and army made up from many states, some traditional enemies: "Did not our fathers," Pericles reminded the Athenians at the outbreak of war with Sparta, "resist the Persians not only with resources far different from ours, but even when those resources had been abandoned?"[109] During the Peloponnesian War, Athens had lost 200 ships and nearly 15,000 men in its disastrous expedition to Sicily (415), yet managed to fight on for almost a decade. Even then, Persian ships and money accounted for the Spartan victory, not Athenian exhaustion. On other occasions Athens had defended itself and its interests—and set aside traditional hatreds—even when weaker than the enemy, as Demosthenes pointed out in 330: "When the Spartans ruled sea and land, Athenians, and held the territories round Attica with garrisons and military governors [395] ... when the city still possessed no ships and no walls, you marched out to Haliartus and then again not many days later to Corinth, even though the Athenians of that day could well have borne a grudge against the Corinthians and Thebans."[110] The question, then, of why the Greeks could not band together to stop Philip until it was too late cannot be answered only by noting how much poorer Athens was in the fourth century than in the fifth, or how much more formidable Philip's army was.

In fact, the issue was not money. Athens was certainly poorer in the mid-fourth century than it was when it received tribute from its subject states in its fifth-century empire. The annual income from tribute and other sources then was about 1,000 talents, compared with 400 in 340.[111] In both centuries, the money was encumbered by the cost of running a direct democracy in which citizens filled about 1,000 offices of the state. Given that most offices had one-year term limits, the number of citizens participating in running the state was enormous.[112] And by the fourth century, Athenian citizens were paid for this political service: serving as one of several hundred jurors needed for the numerous trials; attending the Assembly; serving on the Council; and serving in some of the magistracies. In Demosthenes's day there was also a fund called the *theorikon,* which started as a subsidy for poorer citizens to attend the theater but eventually included other festivals and financed other state projects as well.[113] By the second half of the fourth century, Mogens Hansen writes, "many Athenian citizens, on most days of the year, could expect a state payment of one kind or another, *misthos* [political pay] on working days and *theorikon* on festival days."[114] The total annual outlay for these payments was around 100 talents, which means that by mid-century there was still plenty of money available to Athens to spend on defending itself against Philip, even leaving aside the revenues that could be raised by a special increase in the property tax.[115] And let's not forget that Athens at this time possessed 300 triremes, making it a power still to be reckoned with in the Aegean.

Philip's military power, or Athens's alleged penury, then, are not satisfactory explanations for the failure of the Greeks to recognize and resist the threat of Macedon until it was too late. The causes will be found instead in the destructive pursuit of self-interest, whether by individual city-states or factions within a state; by the weaknesses of a direct democracy confronted by an autocrat; and by the decay of the civic virtues and political values upon which freedom rested.

Political Faction and Zero-Sum Interests

The first-century B.C. historian Pompeius Trogus, as transmitted by the later historian Justin, highlighted each Greek city's self-interest as the fatal weakness of the Greeks: "The states of Greece, while each sought to gain the sovereignty of the country for itself, lost it as a body. Striving intemperately to ruin one another, they did not perceive, till they were oppressed by another power, that what each lost was a common loss to all; for Philip, king of Macedonia, looking, as from a watch-tower, for an opportunity to attack their liberties, and fomenting their contentions by assisting the weaker, obliged victors and vanquished alike to submit to his royal yoke."[116] The second-century A.D. travel writer Pausanias identified the Peloponnesian War between Athens and Sparta as the city-state rivalry that "shook [Greece] from its foundations like an earthquake, and afterwards Philip the son of Amyntas found it already rotted and unhealthy and ruined it altogether."[117]

Demosthenes also recognized how the city-states' pursuit of their own short-term advantage was exploited by Philip: "He has hoodwinked everyone that has had any dealings with him; he has played upon the folly of each party in turn and exploited their ignorance of his own character" because "every community imagined that they were to be the recipients of his favors."[118] Traditional enmity between city-states likewise blinded the Greeks to the threat of a common enemy: Athens and Thebes, for example, were bitter enemies: "You have such a hearty dislike of them [the Thebans]," Demosthenes said in a speech, "that you would not care to hear any good of them, even if it were true."[119] He returns to this theme in the *Third Philippic* of 341, where he laments that in the face of Philip's machinations and aggression the Greeks "do not send embassies to one another"; rather, "we have so entrenched ourselves in our different cities, that to this very day we can do nothing that our interest or our duty demands; we cannot combine, we cannot take any common pledge of help or friendship; but we idly watch the growing power of this man, each bent ... on profiting by the interval afforded by another's ruin, taking not a thought, making not an effort for the salvation of Greece."[120]

Indeed, the Greeks had long recognized that inter-state rivalry was a destructive and dangerous force. "Pan-Hellenism" was an expression of this concern, an idea given its most influential expression by the Greek orator Isocrates. In 380, Isocrates's *Panegyricus* urged Athens and Sparta to set aside their differences and lead an expedition against the Persians. He called upon the Greeks to establish "more trusting relations among ourselves" by forming a coalition to fight the barbarian: "When this happens and we have removed the confusion in our lives—a confusion that dissolves friendships, causes relatives to hate one another, and drives all people to war and factionalism—then there is no way that we will not be unified and feel honest goodwill toward one another."[121] As often happens with intellectuals who lack practical political experience and who are enamored of an *idée fixe,* however, Isocrates's pursuit of this noble aim led him to turn to an autocrat for the power needed to overcome factionalism and impose unity. After considering over the years strongmen like Jason of Pherae, Dionysius I of Syracuse, and the Spartan king Archidamus, in 349 Isocrates wrote a speech to Philip calling upon the Macedonian to unite the Greeks, especially the leading states Argos, Athens, Sparta, and Thebes, in a crusade against the barbarians.[122] In his appeal, Isocrates explicitly identifies constitutional government itself as the impediment to unity and the formulation of coherent policy: "I saw all the other men of good reputation living in cities with constitutions and laws such that it was impossible for them to do anything except what those laws and constitutions prescribed." As an autocrat, on the other hand, Philip has "the power to send delegates to whomever you wish, to receive delegates from whomever you wish, and to say whatever you think best." And Philip has the "wealth and power such as no other Greek has, and these alone are naturally suited both for persuading and for compelling."[123]

Whether Isocrates was serious or merely currying favor with power, his appeal to Philip ignores the important dependence of political freedom and autonomy on precisely those "constitutions and laws" that dispersed power among the citizens and thus limited its scope. Mention here should also be made of Speusippus, Plato's nephew, and head of the Academy after Plato's death. Likewise seeking favor from the powerful, around 343 Speusippus wrote a letter to Philip that justified the king's appropriations of Greek territory with mythical fabrications purporting to show that all these territories already belonged to Philip's family and divine antecedents. Sadly, the willingness of intellectuals to flatter autocrats for personal gain or to sacrifice freedom for some utopian ideal has been a constant in history.

Within the Greek states, factional rivalries and pursuit of power also made it difficult to come up with a unified, long-term response to Philip's aggression, partly because factions could look to Philip for support. We have already mentioned the numerous political trials and indictments to which politicians could be subjected when the policies they had proposed failed. The rivalry of Demosthenes and Aeschines is merely the most famous, as several of the speeches generated by their charges and countercharges have survived. The intrusive oversight of elected generals by the Assembly was another occasion for self-destructive bickering, as Demosthenes noted in his *First Philippic:* "So scandalous is our present system that every general is tried two or three times for his life in your courts, but not one of them dares to risk death in battle against the enemy."[124] Later in the *Second Olynthiac* Demosthenes explicitly links this political quarreling to the failure to take action against Philip: "Surely you must know that all that time you have been hesitating, hoping that some other state would take action, accusing and sitting in judgment on one another, and still hoping, hoping—doing in fact pretty much what you are doing now."[125] This theme of toxic Greek factionalism is a constant in Demosthenes's career, and in fact was a commonplace. Earlier, in 354, when the Persians appeared to be the more dangerous threat to the Greeks, Demosthenes asserted that the king of Persia, just as Philip would do later, "will distribute money among them [the Greeks] and tempt them with offers of friendship, while they, anxious to bring their private quarrels to a successful issue and keeping that object in view, will overlook the common safety of all."[126]

Aid in the pursuit of factional political advantage was not the only inducement for Greek politicians to cooperate with Philip. The consensus of most ancient writers is that Philip used bribery extensively in extending his power throughout Greece. Diodorus wrote that with the plunder taken from the sack of Olynthus, Philip "distributed a large sum of money among influential men in the cities. In this way he secured the services of many men willing to betray their city."[127] Indeed, later history would accept this interpretation of how the Greeks lost their freedom through corruption. According to the Roman orator Cicero, "Philip was given to saying that every fortress could be taken which an ass laden with gold could get up to." Likewise the third-century A.D. author of "memorable deeds and sayings," Valerius Maximus, wrote that Philip was "the buyer more than the conqueror of Greece."[128]

These sources may be relying primarily on Demosthenes, who repeatedly attributed Philip's success to the bribery of treacherous politicians. In *On the Crown,* his apologia for his political record, Demosthenes asserted of the "philippizing" Greeks: "When Philip was weak and had very little power indeed, and we were continually warning, exhorting, and explaining the best policy, they were sacrificing the common good to their own base pursuit of greed, eventually reducing their own fellow citizens to slavery through deception and subversion." He then lists by name these "traitors," "foul men, bootlickers, evil demons; each of them hacked off the limbs of his own country, handed freedom on a platter first to Philip, now to Alexander, measured happiness with his stomach and basest impulses, and overturned that freedom and opposition to tyranny which for the Greeks before us was the guiding measure of what is good."[129] Demosthenes indicted his own city's politicians as well for sacrificing freedom to bribes, most famously, of course, Aeschines in 346: "Has any of you heard Aeschines raise his voice and accuse Philip?" Demosthenes asked the Athenians. "I hear nothing of the kind, and neither do you. Why? Because he was not deceived and not misled, but he hired himself out and took money to make the speech and betray us to Philip."[130] Five years later in the *Third Philippic* Demosthenes contrasts this corruption of his contemporaries with their ancestors' rectitude, the Athenians of old for whom "men who took bribes from those who wished to rule Greece or ruin her, were hated by all" and severely punished. Now, timely action, "mutual concord," and "distrust of tyrants and barbarians" are all lost, "sold in the open market." And this "corruption" vitiates the wealth of resources in ships, money, and men that "are rendered useless, powerless, worthless by these traffickers."[131]

Demosthenes's charge of bribery and treason—what he called the "terrible disease" destroying Greek freedom—has been disputed since the second century B.C. Greek historian Polybius justified the Greek city-states' deals with Philip as necessary for maintaining their own freedom.[132] Most modern historians discount Demosthenes's charges as political and rhetorical exaggerations, although no doubt a politician here and there did accept "gifts" from Philip.[133] However, the more pertinent causes of the Greek failure to resist Philip must be found elsewhere.

The Flaws of Democracy

That in a conflict autocracies have advantages over consensually ruled states is a historical truism. The king or autocrat monopolizes the authority over the army—in Philip's case, a standing professional army rather than an ad hoc citizen militia—and can plan and execute his designs without the burdensome, time-consuming machinery of constitutional deliberation: "For the swift and opportune movements of war," Demosthenes said in 349, "[Philip] has an immense advantage over us in the fact that he is the sole director of his own policy, open or secret, that he unites the functions of a general, a ruler and a treasurer, and that he

is always at the head of his army."[134] Later, in *On the Crown,*
a look back over these events in the aftermath of Chaeronea,
Demosthenes would more specifically contrast those advantages with the liabilities of democratic rule: "Consider the situation of Philip, our opponent in the struggle. First, he ruled
in his own person as full sovereign over subservient people,
which is the most important factor of all in waging war. What's
more, his people were continually under arms, he was flush
with money, and he did whatever he wished. He did not
announce his intentions in official decrees, did not deliberate
in public, was not hauled into court by *sykophants* [citizens
who prosecuted others for blackmail money], was not prosecuted for moving illegal proposals, was not accountable to anyone. In short, he was ruler, commander, in control of
everything."[135]

Demosthenes also noted that this same advantage of the
autocrat meant that a consensual government, slowed by its
political machinery, was constantly forced to react to the autocrat's facts on the ground: "For the man who always keeps a
standing army by him, and who knows beforehand what he
wants to do, is ready in an instant for anyone that he chooses
to attack, while it is only after we have heard of something
happening that we begin to bustle about and make our preparations."[136] Throughout this period, Demosthenes constantly
tried to encourage Athens not merely to react but to preempt
Philip by anticipating the longer-term goals of his aggression.
In the *First Philippic,* Demosthenes made the case for preemp-
tion with a memorable simile. "To manage a war properly," he
argued, "you must not follow the trend of events but must forestall them." Thus politicians "must guide circumstances" and
"not be forced to follow at the heels of chance." He goes on,
"But you Athenians, possessing unsurpassed resources—fleet,
infantry, cavalry, revenues—have never to this very day employed
them aright, and yet you carry on war with Philip exactly as a
barbarian boxes. The barbarian, when struck, always clutches

the place; hit him on the other side and there go his hands. He neither knows nor cares how to parry a blow or how to watch his adversary."[137]

Such advanced planning, however, was compromised by the nature of consensual governments, particularly direct democracies, that involve large numbers of citizens in the formulation of policy, a process dependent on the public deliberation and speech-making that precedes the passing of decrees. In Athens, this legislative process was further complicated by the "accounting" of those such as envoys or councilors or generals responsible for carrying out public business, and by the constant threat of denunciation in the courts if the policy approved by the Assembly turned out badly.[138] Apart from compromising timely action and making politicians risk-averse, this cumbersome process can provide cover for inaction, by substituting procedural words for military deeds. In his attempts to convince Athens to counter Philip's ambitions, Demosthenes continually criticized this penchant for substituting words for deeds, and, as he put it in the *First Philippic*, "forever debating the same question and never making any progress," passing "empty decrees," and indulging the "hopes of the [speaker's] platform."[139] In the *Second Olynthiac*, Demosthenes acknowledged that this fondness for speeches and decrees unsupported by action was a particular vice of the Athenians: "All words, apart from action, seem vain and idle, especially words from Athenian lips: for the greater our reputation for a ready tongue, the greater the distrust it inspires in all men."[140] More important, he links this oratorical indulgence to Philip's success: "If decrees could automatically compel you to do your duty, or could accomplish the objects for which they were proposed, you would not have passed such an array of them with little or no result, and Philip would not have had such a long career of insolent triumph."[141] As Demosthenes says in the *Second Philippic*, "Where either side devotes its time and energy, there it succeeds the better—Philip in action [*praxeis*], but you in argument [*logoi*]."[142]

This discrepancy between words and deeds, this habit of using deliberation as an excuse for inaction, arises as well in the failure of interstate diplomacy and negotiation throughout this period. We saw earlier Philip's masterful use of the diplomatic process to further his aims, as when in 359 he led the Athenians to believe that they could recover Amphipolis if they abandoned their support for the pretender Argaeus. Similar was his canny manipulation of all the participants in the peace negotiations of 346, convened to discuss the end of the Sacred War, when he told the embassies privately what they wanted to hear as he simultaneously pursued his own aims.[143] Philip illustrates the central problem of such diplomacy: to be successful, it depends as much on what contract law calls a "meeting of the minds" as on the terms actually agreed to in the contract. Each side has to be transparent and sincere about its intentions as publicly codified in the agreement. Otherwise, such negotiations and agreements become another weapon for the duplicitous aggressor, buying him time and obscuring his real intentions. In antiquity, Philip was remarkable precisely for his ability to manipulate the diplomatic process: "Philip is said," Diodorus reports, "to have prided himself more on the shrewdness of his leadership and on his negotiating abilities than on his prowess in battle."[144] Philip's diplomatic duplicity was noted too by Justin: "He maintained friendships more with a view to interest than good faith. It was a common practice with him to pretend kindness where he hated, and to counterfeit dislike where he loved; to sow dissension among friends, and try to gain favor from both sides."[145] This dishonesty is a potent weapon when dealing with peoples who are already disinclined to shoulder the burdens and risks of military action. Such people are vulnerable to the orators' "idle words" and fantasies based on their wishes—a liability when dealing with a hard-nosed realist like Philip, who Theopompus tells us was "formidable at stomaching facts."[146]

The Decline of Political Virtues

The most important factor, however, in the failure of the Greeks to stop Philip was the decay of civic virtues, a ubiquitous theme in Demosthenes's speeches of the period and a major cause of the Athenians' preference for speeches and procedure over action. The creation of consensual governments whose purpose was to guarantee the autonomy and freedom of its citizens depended on certain political virtues. These habits of character and behavior had to be the property of all the citizens who comprised what the Greeks called the "common thing," the state along with its offices and institutions that free citizens manage. The political issue was not necessarily the particular type of governmental "machinery" of the state, the various sorts and mixes of assemblies, offices, or procedures, but rather the qualities of character that would make a citizen know how and for what purpose to manage the machinery. To be free, citizens had to have characters worthy of freedom.

One of the most important virtues for the citizen was civic duty, the willingness to do the work and make the sacrifices necessary for running the state. This ideal of active citizen participation in the management of Athens was given memorable expression in Pericles's funeral oration, delivered at the beginning of the Peloponnesian War (431): "Unlike any other nation, we regard the citizen who takes no part in these duties not as unambitious but as useless."[147] This dedication to public service was noted also by Athens's rivals. In a speech to the Spartans by a Corinthian ambassador just before the Peloponnesian War started, the Corinthian said of the Athenians, "Their bodies they spend ungrudgingly in their country's cause; their intellect they jealously husband to be employed in her service."[148] And the most important duty of the citizen was personal military service: "Happiness depends on freedom," Pericles reminded the Athenians, "and freedom depends on courage."[149] Those who were responsible for running the state, and who enjoyed the freedom the state created, were also responsible for defending it in war, for in the end the state is the possession of the citizenry. The idea of the citizen-soldier, who risks his life for his country, and the notion of citizen control over the military were both central to the political freedom of the ancient Greek states. Indeed, this connection of citizen martial prowess to political freedom was a truism in Greek literature, perhaps best illustrated in the contrast Herodotus in his *History* drew between the Greeks running into battle at Marathon while the Persian soldiers had to be whipped by their captains.

One dimension of this civic responsibility was the office of *strategos*, or "general." Rather than a professional soldier with specialized training, as our word suggests, the ancient *strategoi* were ten elected citizen magistrates who were the commanders of the Athenian military forces, in addition to performing a few other political duties. The *strategos* was as much a political office, then, as the *rhetor*, or speaker in the Assembly, courts, or Council, and the two were often paired to create the equivalent of our word "politician."[150] One manifestation of the weakening of the ideal of personal military service was the growing division in the fourth century between the *rhetor* and the *strategos*. In the fifth century, as Mogens Hansen points out, the "normal thing" was for the same citizen to perform both functions: "Men such as Themistiokles, Aristeides, Kimon, Perikles, Kleon, Nikias, and Alkibiades were elected and re-elected to the generalship and simultaneously engaged in politics as speakers and proposers in the Assembly. The close relationship between being a *rhetor* and being a general shows that at that period, like Clausewitz, the Athenians regarded war as 'politics continued by other means.'" In the fourth century, however, "The Assembly was increasingly dominated by speakers trained in rhetoric, and the citizen militia increasingly gave way to mercenaries under the command of professional generals, sometimes even *condottieri*, who often came from other states."[151]

One ill effect of this professionalization of these civic functions was the increased opportunities for personal profit in the form of "gifts" or bribes, since many generals and speakers were now professionals for hire pursuing their own interests rather than citizens performing their civic duty. More important, this professionalization weakened the citizen's sense of being an active manager of the state's business, responsible for its well-being, and hence his own freedom, rather than a mere beneficiary of its largess and privileges.

This division between the general and the speaker also contributed to a breakdown in the coordination of political policy with the military execution of policy, along with a weakening of citizen oversight of generals in the field, at the same time that the generals were still subjected to trials and audits after the fact. In his speech *On the Peace*, delivered in 355 at the end of the Social War between Athens and its allies, Isocrates lamented this development: "We also differ greatly from our ancestors in that they chose the same men as leaders of the city as generals, for they realized that the one best able to advise them from the speaker's platform would also be the one who could make the best plans when by himself. We, however, do the exact opposite. The men we take as advisors about the most important matters we do not think are intelligent enough to be voted generals, but those whom no one would consult on matters of private or public concern we send out with full powers, thinking that somehow they will be wiser out there and will more easily decide about the affairs of Greece than they do about issues proposed here in the Assembly."[152] And when mercenaries were sent out with a professional general more often than were citizen-soldiers, then the breakdown in accountability and political oversight of policy execution was worsened, as is evident in the history of Athens's response to Philip during the two decades before Chaeronea.

The decay of this ideal of personal military service and the reliance on mercenaries and professional generals are both repeatedly lamented by Demosthenes in his speeches.[153] Early in his career (354), Demosthenes proposed a reorganization of the methods for financing the navy in order to spread the fiscal burden more fairly. Apart from fairness, Demosthenes saw this reform as a way of engaging citizens more directly in, and hence taking more responsibility for, the business of the state: "Whenever you have collectively formed some project, and thereafter each individual has realized that it was his personal duty to carry it out, nothing has ever escaped your grasp; but whenever you have formed your project and thereafter have looked to one another to carry it out, each expecting to do nothing while his neighbor worked, then nothing has succeeded with you."[154] Three years later, in the *First Philippic*, Demosthenes again exhorted the Athenians "to throw aside all this pretence of incapacity, and to act where his duty bids him, and where his services can be of use to his country," and to leave off from "slothful apathy."[155] In most of the speeches of the next few years, Demosthenes calls on the Athenians to throw aside their "disinclination to do our duty" and instead to act, rather than indulging their "indolence," "indifference and carelessness," and "outrageous and incurable slothfulness." He exhorts them to stop taking thought first for private "pleasure" and allowing self-serving politicians to weaken their civic courage by exploiting their apathy: "The politicians hold the purse-strings and manage everything, while you, the people, robbed of nerve and sinew, stripped of wealth and allies, have sunk to the level of lackeys and hangers-on, content if the politicians gratify you with a dole from the Theoric Fund or a [religious] procession."[156]

The most important duty that Demosthenes is calling for in these speeches is personal military service. In the 20 years during which Athens confronted Philip, it wasn't until Chaeronea that a significant number of citizen-soldiers were put into the field. Instead, mercenaries, often underfunded, were usually sent out, sometimes with a small force of citizens accompanying them. As early as the *First Philippic* of 351, Demosthenes recognized the dangers of this reliance on mercenaries and argued for citizen-soldiers to take the field: "Do not speak to me of ten thousand or twenty thousand mercenaries. I will have none of your paper-armies. Give me an army which will be the army of Athens, and will obey and follow the general whom you elect, be there one general or more, be he one particular individual, or be he who he may."[157] The problem with mercenaries led by a professional general was accountability and oversight of actions in the field, as those who fight for hire quite often pursue their own interests and needs rather than the policies and interests of the state: "Ever since your mercenary forces have gone to war alone," Demosthenes continued, "it is your friend and allies that they conquer, while your enemies have grown more powerful than they should be." Without oversight, and shorted of funds, the mercenary army plunders even Athens's allies. So, Demosthenes proposes, "I bid you take away their excuses both from the general and the soldiers, by supplying pay and placing citizen-soldiers at their sides as spectators of these mysteries of generalship."[158] Citizen-soldiers are necessary in the field because they are fighting for their own interests, undergoing hardship and risk on behalf of the "common thing" they own and whose benefits they enjoy. In addition, their presence at the front acts as a monitor of the army, ensuring that it pursues the interests and policy aims of the city.

In his speech of 341, *On the Chersonese,* Demosthenes summarized all the various problems that resulted from citizens relying on badly funded mercenaries rather than serving themselves, all the while carping and second-guessing and preferring words to deeds: "We refuse to pay war-taxes or to serve in person; we cannot keep our hands off the public funds, we will not pay Diopeithes [the general sent with mercenaries to check Philip's activities in the Chersonese] the allowances agreed upon, nor sanction the sums that he raises for himself; but we grumble and criticize his methods, and ask what he intends to do, and all that sort of thing; and yet, while maintaining that attitude, we refuse to perform our own tasks; with our lips we praise those whose speeches are worthy of our city, but our actions serve only to encourage their opponents."[159] In addition to personal service, Demosthenes here touches on another failure of the Athenians to perform their civic duty—providing the funds necessary for financing a credible resistance to Philip.

Indeed, the issue of money surfaces repeatedly in Demosthenes's speeches of this period. The calls for personal service are invariably accompanied by the demand to provide money for the military, as in the *Third Philippic* of 341: "We must make provision for defense, I mean with war-galleys, funds, and men; for even if all other states succumb to slavery, we surely must fight the battle of liberty."[160] Of particular concern was the *theorikon*, the dole given to citizens for attending the theater and religious festivals. In the mid-fourth century, a law was passed that transferred the state's surplus revenue into the theoric fund rather than into the *stratiotikon*, the military fund. In February 348 an Athenian named Apollodorus proposed that the Assembly vote on whether the surplus should go to the military fund. His proposal passed, but he was subsequently indicted and fined 15 talents, suggesting that Athenians were more interested in their dole than in their defense. Shortly after, a law was passed that made any such transference a capital crime.[161] More important than the actual amount of the distribution was the "habit of mind," as Demosthenes put it, which this state money fostered, as evidenced by the political sanctions against tampering with the fund.[162] The willingness to forgo a stipend for attending festivals would indicate that the citizens were collectively taking seriously their obligation personally to pay for defending the states' interests rather than assume that somebody else would take the responsibility.

Demosthenes addresses these issues in the speeches he made in 349 arguing for vigorous assistance to Olynthus. In the *First Olynthiac,* he dismissed the argument that there was not enough money to fund help for the Olynthians: "With regard to the supply of money, you *have* money, men of Athens; you have more than any other nation has for military purposes. But you appropriate it yourselves, to suit yourselves." At this point, Demosthenes was careful not to suggest anything technically illegal regarding the theoric fund, but he made it clear that without shifting money from financing festivals to paying for a war, only a special war tax could fund the expedition.[163] A little later, in his next speech on the Olynthian crisis, Demosthenes called for changing the law on the administration of the theoric fund, so that money went to soldiers in the field rather than to festival-goers at home.[164]

Demosthenes repeatedly emphasizes throughout this period that the Athenians are more concerned with their domestic entitlements and pleasures than with protecting their interests and freedom through the provision of funds for defense and through personal service. In his first speech addressing the threat of Philip, the *First Philippic* of 351, he scolded the Athenians for efficiently organizing and funding their festivals, with enthusiastic participation of all the citizens, while their military expeditions are mismanaged and starved of resources.[165] These misplaced priorities reflect the decay of political virtue that hamstrung Athens in its confrontation with an aggressive autocrat. A law was passed on the eve of Chaeronea that transferred theoric money to the war fund, but by then it was too late.

That citizen entitlements corrupted political virtue was certainly the estimation of the historian contemporary with these events, Theopompus. He blamed Eubulus, the politician who was instrumental in the management of the theoric fund and the laws regulating its use, for making the Athenians "less courageous and more lax" because of the money he distributed to them for attending the festivals, upon which, Theopompus alleges, "the Athenian people thoroughly squandered their state revenues." Later, Theopompus makes an explicit connection between what he describes as the hedonistic Athenian lifestyle and the neglect of military duty: "The young men dallied over prostitutes in the little flute-girl establishments, men slightly older than they over drinking [and] dice and similar debauchery, and the entire citizenry spent more on public festivals and sacrifices than on the management of the war."[166] Theopompus is a severe moralist and perhaps exaggerates, but his connection between Athens's failure to resist Philip adequately and its loss of civic virtue is consonant with Demosthenes's opinion and has the ring of truth.

Based on the arguments of Demosthenes, the decay of political virtue—as evidenced in the reluctance of citizens to serve in the army, their unwillingness to forgo the public dole, and the corruption of some politicians by bribery—stands out as the premier cause of the Greeks' failure to resist Philip and defend their freedom. Modern historians cast a more jaundiced eye on Demosthenes's policies and prescriptions, noting the rhetorical exaggerations, distortions of fact, and failures of Demosthenes's character, such as his vanity and ambition. But in the estimation of those closest to the events, his fellow Athenians, Demosthenes was prescient in his recognition of the threat Philip represented, and what was at stake, and in his analysis of what needed to be done to counter Macedonian aggression. Although Demosthenes's policies had led to defeat at Chaeronea, the Athenians chose him to deliver the funeral oration for those who died in that battle, an honor typically bestowed on the leading citizen: "By the honor and respect which they paid to their counselor," Plutarch writes, "they made it manifest that they did not repent of the counsel he had given them."[167] Aeschines's later failure to convict Ctesiphon for proposing a crown for Demosthenes in recognition of his service to Athens—having failed to get one fifth of the jurymen's votes, Aeschines by law had to pay a fine and subsequently went into exile—likewise testifies to the Athenians' regard for Demosthenes. Some 40 years after Demosthenes's suicide, the Athenians erected a bronze statue of the orator and decreed that the oldest male in his household would enjoy public meals at the prytaneium (the public building where the prytany, the steering committee for the Council, met), an honor reserved for public benefactors and distinguished visitors.[168] Indeed, before the present age and its revisionist mania, the West's estimation of Demosthenes, from Cicero to French statesman Georges Clemenceau, was consistent with that of the orator's fellow citizens—as the model of resistance to tyranny and the defense of freedom.

Indeed, whatever criticisms we can make of Demosthenes's character or policies, in one factor he was absolutely correct: what was at stake in the struggle with Philip was the very survival of political freedom. In 341, Demosthenes put the case to his fellow citizens in precisely these terms: since the Athenians were famous for being "quick to confound the plots of the ambitious and to vindicate the freedom of all mankind," Philip "does not want to have the Athenian tradition of liberty watching to seize every chance against himself." Thus in this struggle "the first thing needful [is] to recognize in Philip the inveterate enemy of constitutional government and democracy, for unless you are heartily persuaded of this, you will not consent to take your politics seriously."[169] That, finally, is both the value of Demosthenes's speeches for any analysis of why free states succumb to an autocratic enemy and the basis of his enduring reputation. As British historian A. W. Pickard-Cambridge, writing in 1914, on the brink of the near-suicide of the West in the Great War, put it, "The claim of Demosthenes to be ranked among the heroic men of the past rests above all on the constancy and sincerity with which he defended the noblest cause known to the Greeks—that of Hellenic liberty; and only those who have failed to recognize that most of what was best in the Greek, and, above all, in the Athenian character sprang from and was bound up with political liberty, can seriously censure his choice."[170]

The Greek city-states did not lose their political freedom because of the "fear and weakness" that Churchill saw as the causes of appeasement in his own times. To be sure, Philip's ruthless destruction of Olynthus "alarmed the other cities that were at war with him," Diodorus reports, and such fear may have been a factor in Athens's willingness to begin peace negotiations.[171] However, during this whole period fear of Philip was not the primary cause of Greek appeasement. Indeed, *more* fear of Philip's ultimate aim might have induced the Greek states to band together sooner to thwart his designs. Instead, the interests of cities and the political factions within each city found in Philip a ready ally, and a generous purse, for pursuing their own ambitions.

This concern with short-term interests over long-term security partially reflects the weakness of Greek political freedom, which for most Greeks remained a particular good for the citizens of that particular state rather than a universal good for all Greeks, let alone all mankind. Despite the efforts of Demosthenes, it was impossible to overcome that xenophobic parochialism and create a federation of Greek states held together by the belief that political freedom is superior to autocracy and tyranny, and hence more important than ethnic, historical, or regional differences. The limitations of the Greek idea of freedom, then, have a role in the Greek failure to defend that very freedom. The weaknesses of constitutional government likewise compromised the response to Philip. The machinery of discussion, voting, and accountability that undergirds political freedom paradoxically weakened an effective response to Philip's aggression against the free states. This process can favor words over deeds and give cover to those unwilling or unable to act.

Finally, the decay of political virtue is the most important factor in the loss of Greek freedom. That is, the *failure* of an important ideal—rather than the attempt to implement some utopian program, such as pacifism in the 1930s—destroyed the

foundations of virtue and character upon which political freedom rests and left the Greeks vulnerable to the aggressor. Citizens who see the state as a source of largess rather than as
their own "common thing" in whose defense they must sacrifice their lives and treasure, will be loath to take up the duties
and make the sacrifices required to protect freedom against
those who would destroy it. In the anatomy of appeasement,
then, the experience of the Greeks shows us that the causes
will not be material but will arise from the limitations of human
nature and from the failure of political ideals.

Chapter Two

England and Germany

———— ᴥ ————

It is my purpose, as one who lived and acted in these days, to show how easily the tragedy of the Second World War could have been prevented; how the malice of the wicked was reinforced by the weakness of the virtuous; how the structure and habits of democratic States, unless they are welded into larger organisms, lack those elements of persistence and conviction which can alone give security to humble masses; how, even in matters of self-preservation, no policy is pursued for even ten or fifteen years at a time. We shall see how the counsels of prudence and restraint may become the prime agents of mortal danger; how the middle course adopted from desires for safety and a quiet life may be found to lead direct to the bull's-eye of disaster.

WINSTON CHURCHILL[1]

Hitler's Challenge

Sir Neville Chamberlain is one of those historical figures whose misfortune is to live on as the father of a failure the parents of which were legion. If Hitler is the embodiment of pure evil, Chamberlain is the epitome of weakness and fear in the face of such evil, "a timorous, bumbling, and naïve old gentleman, waving an umbrella as a signal of cringing subservience to a bully," as historian Telford Taylor describes the caricature.[2] Yet, however much Chamberlain's idealism, vanity, and weakness were the driving force behind the disaster of Munich, it was in fact the consequence of a certain sensibility and a complex of ideals, pacifism, and "moralizing internationalism," which were fueled after World War I by a toxic mix of fear and short-sighted national interests.[3] We forget that for a few months "Munich" was not the emblem of craven capitulation to tyranny, as it is for us now and it was for a few prescient dissenters, such as Winston Churchill then, but rather the proof that the horrors of war they had been expecting could be averted by diplomacy and negotiation. When on September 28, 1938, Chamberlain announced to the House of Commons his intention to meet Hitler in Munich, he was greeted with thunderous cheering and a five-minute standing ovation. And when Chamberlain returned to England two days later, he was greeted as a hero by thousands of people at Heston airport, invited to Buckingham Palace by George VI, praised by the Archbishop of Canterbury, and acclaimed by crowds at No. 10 Downing Street, where from the balcony of the Prime Minister's residence he proclaimed the soon to be infamous phrases "peace with honor" and "peace for our time."[4]

Munich, then, was the culmination of a process that began the moment the Treaty of Versailles was signed on June 28, 1919. The conflicting national interests of the victorious allies, the widespread idealism articulated by Woodrow Wilson's Fourteen Points, and the lingering horror at the industrial carnage of the Great War all created serial opportunities for a Germany eager to reclaim the great power status it had spent a century acquiring, and the loss of which was a bitter humiliation and affront to German honor. This judgment is not meant to endorse the historical revisionism that attributes the subsequent disasters of Nazism and World War II to an unjust Versailles Treaty poisoned by the victors' greed, revenge, and, in the case of the United States, isolationism. As Margaret MacMillan in her history of the treaty puts it, "That is to ignore the actions of everyone—political leaders, diplomats, soldiers, ordinary voters—for twenty years between 1919 and 1939."[5] In fact, the treaty was not the "Carthaginian Peace" described by John Meynard Keynes in his influential 1919 book, *The Economic Consequences of the Peace.* On the contrary, after Versailles Germany was not, Zara Steiner writes, "reduced to a power of the second rank or permanently prevented from returning to great power status": Germany's productive and industrial potential were intact; the most populous state in Europe, its population was a third greater, its birthrate far larger, and its steel production nearly twice that of its Continental counterweight, France. In addition, the war had left Germany with weak, ethnically fragmented states on its eastern borders and its powerful traditional rival, Czarist Russia, extinct.[6] "Though weakened by the war," Gerhard Weinberg points out, "Germany had been weakened less than her European enemies, and she had thus emerged relatively stronger potentially in 1919 than she had been in 1913."[7] Finally, the seemingly astronomical reparation payments that disgusted Keynes—the money Germany was supposed to pay to compensate the Allies, particularly France, for the costs and damages of the war—were reduced several times, averaging for the period 1919–1931 only 2 percent of Germany's annual national income.[8]

The problem with the Versailles Treaty, then, was not its harshness, but rather its fundamental incoherence. At the most obvious level, as historian Donald Kagan writes, the Treaty "was neither conciliatory enough to remove the desire for change, even at the cost of war, nor harsh enough to make another war impossible."[9] More particularly, the lofty idealism of President Woodrow Wilson's Fourteen Points, the last of which called for what would become the League of Nations and was incorporated into the Versailles Treaty as its first 26 articles, never addressed specifically the issue of the enforcement of such utopian provisions. This problem worsened when the United States Senate refused to ratify the Treaty, thus leaving its enforcement in the weaker hands of France and England, and the U.S.

reasserted an isolationism expressed by Theodore Roosevelt in an article posthumously published in March, 1919: "I do not believe in keeping our men on the other side to patrol the Rhine, or police Russia, or interfere in Central Europe or the Balkan peninsula."[10]

Other contradictions vitiated the Treaty's provisions. The desire to transcend the nationalist *amour propre* that many believed had led to the war, evident in the creation of the League of Nations, was compromised by the principle of national sovereignty and ethnic self-determination: "National aspirations," Wilson told Congress in 1918, "must be respected; peoples may now be dominated and governed only by their own consent."[11] National self-determination, however, was a principle poorly defined or understood; as American Secretary of State Robert Lansing mused at the time about Wilson's demand for "self-determination," "What unit has he in mind? Does he mean a race, a territorial idea, or a community?"[12] In addition, minorities were not concentrated in neat, homogenous enclaves that could be turned into nations simply by providing borders and a flag—30 million people in Europe lived as ethnic minorities. They were intermingled and scattered, so that population transfers would have been necessary to provide them with a coherent state.[13] This contradiction between internationalism and ethnic self-determination as the basis of a state's identity would later come back to haunt the Allies when Germany under Hitler schemed to incorporate the German minorities in Austria, Czechoslovakia, and throughout Eastern Europe back into the Fatherland, cloaking territorial aggrandizement with the banner of ethnic self-determination. "The causes of the Second World War in Europe," historian Niall Ferguson writes, "were not economic . . . at least, not in the sense Keynes had in mind. They were territorial—or, to be more precise, they arose from the conflict between territorial arrangements based on the principle of 'self-determination' and the realities of ethnically mixed patterns of settlement."[14]

Finally, Germany quite simply did not accept the legitimacy of the "peace of shame"—as a yet obscure, twice-decorated, wounded war veteran named Adolph Hitler would soon be calling it—the perceived injustices of which led German Chancellor Phillip Scheidemann in 1919 to thunder, "What hand would not wither which placed this chain upon itself and upon us?"[15] German honor particularly bristled at Article 231, the so-called "war guilt" clause that made Germany completely responsible for the war and justified the reparations Germany would have to pay the Allies.[16] In fact, Article 231 says nothing about guilt, assigning instead "responsibility," but in Germany it became politically useful to speak of an unjust "war guilt" in order to discredit the whole Versailles settlement. And why should Germany, many Germans wondered, take sole responsibility and pay for a war started as a justified preemptive strike against the Slavic hordes threatening from the east and in response to provocations from England and France? Equally galling to Germans were the demands that it alone should be disarmed, its military neutered. After all, Germany did not surrender like a defeated power—it signed an armistice with its troops on foreign soil, its soldiers keeping their guns, and it did so partly because German leaders assumed that Wilson's more conciliatory Fourteen Points, which called for a "peace without victors," as Wilson put it to the U.S. Senate in 1917, would provide the basis of the final peace treaty.[17] Forcing Germany to give up its army, which in fact at the time of the Armistice was on the brink of dissolution due to disease and desertion, seemed to Germans an underhanded way to finish by treaty what the Allies could not finish on the battlefield, with the help of socialist traitors at home who had inflicted the infamous "stab in the back."

Germans could indulge this fantasy of being cheated rather than defeated, and then unjustly treated by the victors, partly because their country had not suffered the wartime devastation France and Belgium had. Nor had Allied soldiers occupied

German territory to provide a concrete, daily reminder of the wages of aggression and national arrogance. Absent these mind-concentrating experiences, Germany more easily refused to accept its defeat as the fruits of its own actions for which it bore the lion's share of the responsibility. This delusion was enabled by many in England who sympathized with Germany and felt the Versailles Treaty was an unjust instrument of French national vindictiveness. Thus long before Hitler and the Nazis came to power, many Germans were anxious to undo what they saw as a dishonor inflicted on their national power and prestige.

The Dismantling of Versailles

During the 1920s the German assault on the Versailles Treaty focused on four provisions, an assault met by serial appeasement on the part of England. The first, largely symbolic but no less galling for all that, was the elimination of the "war guilt" clause, which was seen as an unjust humiliation of a proud civilization that its culturally and racially inferior enemies were attempting to reduce to "slaves and helots," in the words of the German Chancellor.[18] Germany attacked the clause through the sponsorship and promotion of research into the war's origins that exculpated German responsibility. A periodical called *The War Guilt Question* was launched in 1923, its editor an employee of the German Foreign Office. "This periodical," Martin Gilbert writes, "gave prominence to all evidence pointing to Russian, French, British, and even Serbian 'responsibility' for the war. The documents to which it gave prominence quickly found their way into the historical works of British historians who, from 1919, tended to be more critical of the British case."[19]

The slew of such books and memoirs in the following years fostered "war guilt" among many in England in the 1920s and 1930s. Rather than a great victory against a brutal aggressor, the Great War increasingly became characterized as "a great carving of human flesh which was of our boyhood, while the old men directed their sacrifice, and the profiteers grew rich, and the fires of hate were stoked up at patriotic banquets and in editorial chairs," as war correspondent Philip Gibbs described it in 1920.[20] This angst and doubt helped to build sympathy for Germany and made it easier for its violations of the Versailles Treaty to be rationalized or ignored, a sensibility typified in 1937 by *Times* editor Geoffrey Dawson's admission to his correspondent in Geneva that "I do my best, night after night, to keep out of the paper anything that might hurt their [German] susceptibilities.... I have always been convinced that the peace of the world depends more than anything else upon our getting into reasonable relations with Germany."[21] Many politicians, particularly in the Labour Party, likewise believed, as one Labour M.P. put it after Munich, "It is perfectly true that we did not act, not merely wisely and generously, but even justly to Germany after the war.... I repeat that we bear a very heavy responsibility for the tensions and menaces of the present international situation."[22] This "war guilt" helped to legitimize a policy of appeasement as a necessary and just correction of the Treaty's harsh and vindictive terms.[23]

The next three Versailles provisions anathema to Germany were more practically linked to its recovery of the military, political, and economic preeminence to which its citizens believed it worthy: the reparations owed to the Allies for the costs and damages of the war (Articles 231–247), which included cession of the Saar basin coal mines to France as "part payment" of the total reparations bill (Articles 45–50); the disarmament and reduction of the German military (Articles 159–213); and the demilitarization and Allied occupation of the Rhineland (Articles 42–44). All these attacks on the Versailles settlement, however, served a much larger and more dangerous foreign policy aim—the undoing of the territorial losses suffered by Germany after the Great War. Germany had lost 5 percent of its population and 15 percent of its agricultural land, especially by means of the so-called "eastern settlement," which gave the coal-rich region of Upper Silesia to Poland and sundered East Prussia from Germany by the "Polish corridor" that linked the "free city" of Danzig to Poland.[24] Further goals included reintegration into Germany of the 10 million ethnic Germans marooned in Czechoslovakia and Austria, and the eventual strategic and economic domination of Eastern Europe.[25]

The Myth of Punitive Reparations

From the beginning, German reparations were as much a political as an economic issue. English and French leaders had to please domestic constituencies eager to punish Germany: as British Prime Minister Lloyd George said, "Somebody had to pay. . . . Those who ought to pay were those who caused the loss."[26] The French were even more vehement, since among the Allies they had suffered the greatest loss of people, resources, and territory. Setting a precise figure, however, was difficult. If it were too small, voters in England and France would howl, yet a figure high enough to placate voters would be impossible for Germany to pay and further alienate already angry Germans and weaken the fragile Weimar government. Consequently, the treaty did not set a figure, which allowed Germans to claim they were signing a "blank check" that condemned them, in the words of the German delegation, "to perpetual slave labor."[27]

Pressing national economic interests likewise complicated the issue of just how much, and for what specific damages and costs, Germany owed to the victorious Allies. France had suffered the most: in addition to 1.3 million dead and 700,000 wounded, its ten northern departments, the main battlefields of the war, had been hammered by millions of tons of high explosives, and its industrial heartland had been severely damaged.[28] In addition, France owed the United States $4 billion and England $3 billion.[29] The triumph over Germany, earned with the expenditure of so much blood and treasure, created for the French the opportunity to ensure their future power and security by rebuilding their economy with money justly exacted from the German aggressor. The French, then, were eager to make Germany pay as high a bill as possible.

Britain, on the other hand, had its own $4.7 billion debt to the United States. An economically prostrate Germany would not be able to pay its reparation debt, nor would it be a trading partner for England. As for the United States, a return to "normalcy" meant a return to its traditional fear of "entangling alliances": "This meant," Donald Kagan writes, "support of the rapid return of Germany to full prosperity as a rich market for American industry and commerce [and] an opportunity for profitable investment."[30] And America wanted the money that France and England had "rented," in Calvin Coolidge's famous quip, to be repaid. These economic aims of both America and England would more likely be met if Germany recovered economically, something that would not happen if astronomical reparation payments hamstrung the German economy.

Missing in the shortsighted calculations of England and the United States, however, was the historical reality that a powerful Germany for the last half-century had been the font of continental disorder that, in a "globalized" economy, would not be limited to Europe. Moreover, nothing in Germany's behavior or demeanor after the war indicated that defeat had extinguished its prewar drive for dominance, predicated on a powerful belief in German cultural and racial superiority expressed as early as 1806–7 in Johann Gottlieb Fichte's *Addresses to the German Nation* and furthered by decades of what G. K. Chesterton in 1915 called "Teutonism," "rubbishy fairy-tales about the Teutonic Race being the natural conqueror of all others."[31] Indeed, British Prime Minister Lloyd George recognized that wounded German *amour propre* was fomenting "a German war of revenge—a revenge which it requires small knowledge of the German character to be sure that the country will systematically and relentlessly pursue so long as she has a chance of success."[32] So too Marshall Foch, the French Supreme Commander of the Allied armies, who, when he heard that the peace treaty had been signed, commented prophetically, "This is not Peace. It is an Armistice for twenty years."[33] Yet despite these forebodings, the English continued to see France as, in the words of Foreign Secretary Lord Curzon in 1919, "the great power from whom we have most to fear in future," at the same time it underestimated Germany's capacity for recovery of its economic and military power.[34] This miscalculation on England's part led to a division among the Allies that hampered enforcement of the Versailles Treaty and provided Germany with opportunities for ignoring or weakening those provisions.[35]

In the event, the actual figure set by the Reparations Commission in 1921 was 132 billion gold marks ($33 billion), to be paid in cash and in commodities like timber and coal.[36] This amount was one-sixteenth of the figure bruited during the treaty negotiations, and the intricate method of payment called the London Schedule of Payment in effect reduced that figure even further, to 50 billion gold marks ($12.5 billion), less than what Germany itself had earlier offered to pay), to be paid in cash and kind over 36 years, an obligation most historians now believe was within Germany's power to meet.[37] Nevertheless, Germany resisted payment, making the still widely accepted argument that payments were fueling the rampant inflation in the immediate postwar years, often blamed by historians then and now for helping to grease Germany's skid into Nazism. As historian Sally Marks points out, however, the inflation predated reparations, and "the inflation mushroomed in the period from the summer of 1921 to the end of 1922 when Germany was actually paying very little in reparations." Moreover, inflation was a deliberate policy pursued by German leaders, for it "enabled the German government to pay off its domestic debts, including war debt, and those of the state enterprises in worthless marks. Certain industrialists close to the German cabinet profited greatly as well."[38]

Germany's resentment of Versailles—coupled with American and English pursuit of their own economic interests that favored an economically recovered Germany as a market for exports and an opportunity for investment—led both to German default and to Allied disagreement over what to do about it. In January 1923 the Reparations Committee found the Germans to be in default on coal deliveries—the 34th time in 36 months. In response, the French and Belgians occupied the Ruhr, the important German industrial region. This attempt to enforce the Treaty, however, was met by resistance from the U.S. and from England, whose ambassador to the Weimar Republic, Lord D'Abernon, thought that the French occupation of the Ruhr "has shown that the real danger of military violence at the present moment is infinitely greater from France than from Germany."[39] Left hanging by the British, and faced with strikes by German workers in the Ruhr, eventually France had to yield to an international commission that produced the Dawes Plan in 1924, which allowed Germany to avoid making payments for two years and "which reorganized Germany's finances, supported by a large international loan[,] and effectively reduced its reparations debt and payment schedule." The Germans agreed to the Dawes Plan, since they saw it as a way to get the French out of the Ruhr and lower reparations payments, with an eye to further reductions later on. Later that same year at the London Conference, France was indeed required to end the occupation, and the Reparations Commission was revised so that it became impossible to keep Germany from defaulting.[40]

Historian Correlli Barnett summarizes the malign consequences of England's undermining of France and the Versailles Treaty: "The course of the Ruhr crisis marked a major shift of power from the victors towards Germany ... It demonstrated

to Europe, and particularly to Germany, that England was no
longer at France's side. . . . France had failed to destroy Germany's capacity to revive in the future as a super-power."[41] Thus
began the demoralization of France that eventually led to the
passive, defensive posture embodied in the Maginot Line, the
supposedly impenetrable border fortifications that France mistakenly believed would check German aggression, but that in
fact fatally damaged French military strategy; rather than a
"strong offensive component that was mobile and swift and
always ready to attack" in order to deter German aggression
with a credible threat from the west, "[French] military planners designed only a mass army that could fight only after a
long delay, one entirely unsuited for the most important task."[42]

The Dawes Plan was not the end of German efforts to
reduce the reparations payments. In 1929, on the brink of the
bigger payments due from Germany called for in the Dawes
Plan, the Young Committee began work on a final resolution
of the reparations problem. The Young Plan, true to reparations settlements from the beginning, did not back up the
expectations with provisions for enforcement.[43] On paper, the
total was 114 billion marks, but only a third of that was owed
without conditions, and the remainder could be postponed or
renegotiated depending on Germany's economic circumstances.
Worse, Germany linked its acceptance of the Young Plan to
the Allied evacuation of the Rhineland, which under the Versailles Treaty the Allies were scheduled leave in 1935. Once
again indulging its immediate interests at the expense of long-
term ones, England supported Germany in both reducing the
payments, increasing England's share threefold along the way,
and moving up the evacuation to June 1930, thus saving the
expense of the British occupation troops. These moves, however, left France isolated as the only Ally left that wanted to
enforce Versailles and check a reviving German power.

That a significant number of Germans were, despite these
concessions, still resentful and eager to reassert Germany's

preeminence should have been obvious in the reaction to the Young Plan. Despite the reductions in Germany's obligations, now a fraction of the original debt codified in the London Schedule of Payments, almost six million Germans voted in a popular referendum for a so-called "Freedom Law" that "demanded repudiation of the war-guilt clause and immediate evacuation of all occupied German territory. It declared the signing of the Young Plan as high treason and insisted that the Chancellor and his ministers be imprisoned for their role in its negotiation."[44] The proposal was defeated in the Reichstag, but the referendum indicated that a large number of Germans were angry at the continuing dishonor of their nation and unlikely to be mollified by new agreements or more concessions. This portent became political reality when in 1930 the previously marginal Nazi Party increased its number of voters eight-fold in just two years and won 107 seats in the Reichstag, becoming the second largest party in Germany.

The end of reparations came at the Lausanne Convention in 1932, where another complex agreement was signed that on paper committed Germany to a final payment of 3 billion gold marks but that in reality was "a paper fiction, a sop to French opinion."[45] In the end, between 1919 and 1932 the Germans actually paid 19.1 billion gold marks ($4.8 billion), a far cry from the London Schedule's 132 billion—and a figure likely less than that exacted from France by Germany after the Franco-Prussian War in 1870–71.[46] Even more damning for the thesis that the punitive reparations sanctioned by the Versailles Treaty mortally damaged Germany's economy, during that same period, Germany "received 27 billion gold marks in net capital inflows, mostly from private investors, mainly American, who subsequently lost considerable sums following the German defaults in 1923 and 1932."[47] The disparity between the amounts publicized and the amounts actually paid, in addition to the complexity of the payment schedules and the general public's ignorance about private foreign investment, led both the German sense of dishonor at being extorted by their rapacious conquerors, and English sympathy for a people supposedly being ground down by the greed and vengeance of France.

Stealth Rearmament

The next affront of Versailles the Germans resented and diligently worked to undo was Articles 159–213, detailing the dismantling of Germany's military power. The German Army was reduced to seven infantry and three cavalry divisions, with no more than 100,000 men and 4,000 officers. Universal conscription was forbidden, the German general staff was eliminated, and munitions and weapons limited, the excess beyond the limits to be destroyed or handed over to the Allies. Germany could not manufacture or import poison gas, armored vehicles, or military aircraft. The Navy was reduced to a fraction of its prewar size, and submarines were forbidden. Finally, an Inter-Allied Commission of Control (IACC) was established to monitor Germany's compliance. This minute, detailed intrusion into Germany's affairs—even the numbers of students in military academies were strictly limited, and no organizations or clubs could "occupy themselves with any military matters"— galled bitterly a nation with a proud military tradition and record of victory, not to mention millions of sullen, discharged veterans still in possession of their weapons. It is no surprise, then, that sabotaging and subverting these terms became a constant obsession with Germany throughout the 1920s.

Germany's method of subverting the disarmament provisions ranged from petty harassment of the IACC to serious preparations for the swift reconstitution of German military power when future events made this possible.[48] IACC officers were housed in shabby quarters, stood up by German officers with whom they were scheduled to meet, attacked with clods and stones by soldiers they were supposed to inspect, and even threatened with bayonets. Germany dragged its feet on destroying munitions and demobilizing its army to meet the 100,000–man limit set in the Treaty. In March 1920 an "uprising" of Bolsheviks in the Ruhr— most likely orchestrated by the German government—provided a pretext for Germany to send 18,000 troops into the Ruhr. In response, France occupied five towns in the Rhineland. This incident also gave Germany an argument for keeping the army larger and undoing other disarmament provisions. This attempt failed, yet ominously, England chastised France—partly for using "savage" black Moroccan troops—and the Allies positively responded to the German request for increasing troop numbers, which opened the door to revisions of Treaty articles regarding the issue of "the internal order and economic well-being of Germany." A concrete result of this appeasing attitude was that the Germans were given an extra year to meet the military manpower limitations. As Kagan and Kagan note, this crisis made it clear that "the allies would not insist on 'too literal' an interpretation of the treaty. The Germans were free to continue to undermine the treaty and obstruct the Allied inspections with redoubled efforts."[49]

Germany, however, pursued rearmament in ways much more aggressive than merely obstructing the work of the IACC. During the Twenties, military theorists like General Groener and Georg Thomas developed plans for conducting a total war that mobilized the state's economic as well as military resources, integrating the former into the latter: "In 1924 the army established an economics staff (*Wirtschaftsstab*), whose job it was to plan for the time when Germany could embark on rearmament in earnest. A network of ex-officers working in business was set up to establish close links between industry and the military." In 1925 a "statistical society" was founded by the Army Armaments Office and several industrialists, the goal of which was "to underpin and promote the work of the defence ministry' and to establish contact with key firms not yet involved in military production."[50]

During this same period, under the leadership of head of army General von Seeckt, the foundations of the future German

Army and General Staff were being laid in order to provide the continuity of experience, training, and theoretical developments necessary for a world-class military—all contrary to the terms of the Versailles Treaty. Officers were camouflaged in Departments of Reconstruction, Research, and Culture; secret training manuals, focused on military innovation and theory, were written and studied and short-service training of soldiers conducted; paramilitary organizations were "dissolved and its members reformed with dazzling ingenuity as labor gangs, bicycle agencies, traveling circuses and detective bureaus"; the limits on officers were evaded by creating astronomical numbers of noncommissioned officers, which were not limited by the Versailles Treaty;[51] and even military exercises were conducted for officers commanding not the treaty-proscribed seven divisions but a planned minimum of 63 divisions.[52]

At the same time, weapons and munitions were steadily and secretly stockpiled. New weapons were designed and manufactured abroad: "The massive arms firm of Krupp acquired control of the Swedish firm of Bofors and the Dutch firm of Blessing. Its most skilled and important personnel went to Sweden and Holland, where they continued to design and build artillery, antiaircraft guns, and light tanks."[53] And in Germany, factories funded by American and English investment money were designed to be quickly converted into munitions plants, manufacturing tanks and other weapons, an evasion of disarmament strictures that was common knowledge to most Germans. "In the Berlin cabarets," MacMillan writes, "they told jokes about the worker who smuggled parts out of a baby carriage factory for his new child only to find when he tried to put them all together he kept getting a machine gun."[54] Apparently, many English and French were not in on the joke. In an even more ominous development, Germany secretly worked with the Soviet Union to evade the Versailles military restrictions. Under General von Seeckt's "Special Branch R," Germany provided military training and technical assistance in

exchange for raw materials and space for developing, manufacturing, and testing weapons far from the IACC. Aircraft
prototypes built in Holland were tested in Russia, as were German tanks and poison gas.[55]

"Locarny-Blarney"

This rebuilding of Germany's war machine accelerated after
the Locarno Treaty in 1925. This multinational pact aimed to
ensure European peace and end Germany's exile from the international order, as confirmed by Germany's joining the League
of Nations with a permanent seat on the League Council. The
agreement comprised the Rhineland Pact, a nonaggression
pact by Germany, France, and Belgium, along with mutual
guarantees among those countries and Italy and England to
keep the Rhineland demilitarized and to defend those nations'
borders. Any of the nations included in the treaty that suffered
violations of its provisions would receive military assistance
from the others.[56] Locarno also included arbitration agreements among Germany and France, Belgium, Poland, and
Czechoslovakia.

Ignoring issues of Germany's good faith and England's willingness and ability to meet its obligations codified in the treaty,
both politicians and voters greeted Locarno with enthusiastic
approval based on the illusion that the treaty had finally closed
the books on the Great War and the Versailles Treaty and was
ushering in a new age of peace and international friendship,
in which increasing trade and prosperity would make possible
the reductions of armaments and armies whose proliferation
was thought to have sparked the Great War. When the German delegation was received into the League in 1926 on the
twelfth anniversary of the Battle of the Marne, French Prime
Minister Aristide Briand, who later won the Nobel Peace Prize
for his role in creating the treaty, orated, "Away with rifles,
machine guns, cannon. Clear the way for conciliation,

arbitration and peace." England's Foreign Secretary, Austen Chamberlain, who also won the Peace Prize for Locarno, believed the treaty would "close the war chapter and start Europe afresh."[57] A *New York Times* headline concluded, "France and Germany Bar War Forever."[58] Given these expectations, Locarno gained, Marks writes, "an instant sanctity normally accorded only to motherhood," thus putting its provisions beyond criticism.[59] The poet A. P. Herbert called this sentimental faith in the treaty "Locarny-Blarney."

In reality, the treaty was, Barnett summarizes, "so far as England and her guarantee were concerned, no more than a hollow gesture to soothe the French; a bogus commitment, a fraudulent IOU that was given only because the English government never thought for a moment that they would ever have to make it good."[60] For Germany, on the other hand, the treaty was a "great victory," with "the certainty that its position would improve still further," specifically by dismantling the Eastern settlement.[61] France was left with few military options for checking German aggression east or west, or even punishing violations of the Versailles Treaty. Finally, Germany, despite its growing economic power and industrial growth, was not placated or appeased by these concessions, but continued to work toward the complete dismantling of Versailles.[62]

The weakening of the Versailles disarmament articles quickly became evident after Locarno, despite an IACC report five months before the treaty was signed in which the violations of the Germans were documented and the conclusion reached that "the Reichswehr, instead of being organized for internal purposes as laid down in the [Versailles] treaty, is being built up under the direction of the High Command to prepare the nation for war."[63] After Locarno the work of the IACC stopped in July 1926. German industrial power, financed mainly by American loans, was expanding much faster than that in its one-time foes England and France, with government involvement ensuring that all this industrial capacity could be quickly harnessed to create a war machine.[64] "When Hitler came to power," Kagan and Kagan summarize, "he inherited a state that had little military power, but enormous military potential. It had a large base of semi-trained military manpower, an industrial base configured to move rapidly to war production, and a highly sophisticated research and development system that had already designed the equipment that military industry would produce."[65] The delusion that Germany was disarmed reinforced England's wishful thinking that Germany was not an immediate threat, and in turn further eroded the Versailles Treaty's provisions to ensure that Germany did not again become a threat.

England's misreading of its own interests and Germany's intentions, coupled with a delusional faith in the efficacy of treaties like Locarno, accounts for the willingness to wink at the resurrection of German power. Failing to recognize its responsibilities and obligations to the new geopolitical order created by the Great War and the Versailles settlement, England continued to believe that its main foreign policy interest lay in defending the Empire and ensuring that no one power would dominate the Continent. To achieve this latter aim, England needed to function as a "mediating" power, whose support of one side could deter the other from achieving a preponderance of power. To do that meant avoiding binding treaties that would hinder England from playing this role. As a Foreign Office memorandum in 1926 put it, "We keep our hands free in order to throw our weight into the scale on behalf of peace."[66]

The prostration of Germany, which left France as the dominant Continental power, aroused concern in England that the next war would be against its one-time ally—with whom England over the centuries had gone to war several times.[67] Moreover, the clash of British and French interests in the Middle East soured relations further after 1919, leaving England disinclined to guarantee France's borders against future German expansion. France was also seeking alliances in Central and Eastern Europe as a buffer against Germany, which raised suspicions in England that France was aiming at Continental hegemony.[68] Thus "no British statesman would allow France to increase its power at the expense of Germany and alter the Versailles balance in its favour. However distrustful of Germany, most British politicians (the military thought differently) argued that the security and prosperity of Europe depended on the recovery of Germany." Because of this confluence of economic interests and shortsighted foreign policy strategy, England "exaggerated French power and underestimated the German capacity for recovery."[69] The recovery of Germany, abetted by British appeasement and codified in the Locarno Treaty, would restore the balance of power on the Continent and ensure that England would not have to intervene again in a European war.

The Temptations of Unilateral Disarmament

Another factor in England's willingness to ignore Germany's violations of the Versailles Treaty was England's own precipitous disarmament that as the decade went on left it with few options for using force to punish Germany and deter further infractions, and to support its foreign policy aims or treaty obligations. Between the armistice in November 1918 and 1920, English forces were reduced by nearly three million men. As early as October 1919, Secretary of State for War Winston Churchill commented that "the Army had melted away."[70] In that same period, again failing to anticipate its responsibilities in enforcing Versailles and protecting its international interests, England formulated the "Ten Year Rule," which assumed that "'the British Empire will not be engaged in any great war during the next ten years, and that no Expeditionary Force is required for that purpose.'" Subsequently, the defense budget was reduced by four fifths between 1919 and 1921, and it continued to decline, though not as steeply, until 1933.[71] These cuts left England incapable of playing any meaningful Continental role, either in maintaining the balance of power or punishing German aggression against the Versailles settlement. Nor could England fulfill its guarantee to protect France's border with Germany. These reductions also meant that the English arms industry languished, falling behind in investment and technological development. Thus, "as the Germans carefully nurtured a deceitful program to maintain their arms industries . . . the British carelessly destroyed their own."[72]

England continued to weaken its military preparedness at the Washington Conference of 1921–22, where it accepted a 5:5:3 ratio of naval ships with America and a newly assertive Japan and a ten-year moratorium on the building of new capital ships limited to 35,000 tons displacement, despite the fact that England had not built a new warship since 1919 and thus was already behind in maintaining its naval strength. In addition, to mollify Japan for accepting a lower number, England promised not to build any new bases north of Singapore. This "disastrous mistake," as Barnett terms it, resulted from a failure once again to recognize England's unique global responsibilities and obligations.[73] This mistake was repeated in 1931 at the London Naval Conference, where the ten-year "naval holiday" was extended until 1936 and England accepted parity in cruiser tonnage with the United States. The net result, as detailed in 1931 by Admiral of the Fleet Sir Frederick Field, was that British naval strength had been "so diminished as to render the fleet incapable, in the event of war, of efficiently affording protection to our trade."[74] Nor had the Army or the Air Force done much better during the Twenties. The target established in 1923 for "a force of 52 squadrons, 394 bombers, and 204 fighters," to be met in 1928, was eventually postponed until 1938.[75]

By 1934 the shortfall in funding was so severe that "it would have cost more than England spent on defense for a year just to make good the deficiencies in one service [the army], to say nothing of actually preparing for the war that was to come."[76] These reductions and neglect left England incapable of fulfilling its various international obligations and interests, let alone defend itself against a possible aggressor, a contingency dismissed by the extension of the "ten-year rule" in 1928, although it was abandoned four years later.[77] By the critical period of 1938–39, when Hitler's aggression became manifest, Germany was spending five times as much on its military than was England, and it was manufacturing at least twice the munitions of England and France put together.[78] Even so, after his return from Munich, Chamberlain told the Cabinet that making good Britain's "deficiencies" was "not the same thing as to say that as a thank offering for the present détente we should at once embark on a great increase in our armament programme."[79]

Once again, throughout this period economic self-interest and political constraints were an important factor in England's behavior. At the time of the Washington Naval Conference in 1921 and 1922, England's economy was ailing, suffering from foreign competition and high unemployment.[80] In addition, interest payment on the national debt, which by 1927 was 172 percent of gross domestic product, reached 40 percent of government spending by the late Twenties.[81] At the same time, demands for increasing spending on social welfare programs were increasing. Many politicians agreed with Prime Minister Lloyd George, who "defended spending on social programs both as part of his program to make England 'a land fit for heroes,' and as part of a more urgent plan to placate a restless and increasingly unhappy populace. He was, therefore, much less likely to accept cuts in government programs in housing, for instance, than to cut the military."[82] Economic expediency, moreover, was reinforced by the principle of disarmament as the way to prevent war and maintain international order. The Great War was popularly blamed on an "arms race" fomented by the "merchants of death," greedy weapons manufacturers.

Universal disarmament would thus "remove the nations' fears of each other and make aggression or resistance to the League's authority impossible."[83]

This utopian ideal, abetted by a growing pacifism and faith in collective security that we will explore further in the next section, was enshrined in Article 8 of the Versailles Treaty, regarding the functions of the League of Nations: "The Members of the League recognize that the maintenance of peace requires the reduction of national armaments to the lowest point consistent with national safety and the enforcement by common action of international obligations. . . . The Members of the League agree that the manufacture by private enterprise of munitions and implements of war is open to grave objections. The Council shall advise how the evil effects attendant upon such manufacture can be prevented. . . . " Apart from the problems of determining, "consistent with national safety," the limits to the numerous military services of 40 nations, "weapons systems were different, equivalents hard to find, and ratios difficult to establish. Methods of control and inspections raised fundamental questions about sovereignty and independence."[84] And, of course, as we today continue to experience in international attempts to disarm a nuclear North Korea or prevent Iran from obtaining nuclear weapons, international agreements or monitors, absent the threat of force, will not deter states eager to possess weapons. Like Germany during the Twenties, these states will simply cheat, using such agreements to buy time, misdirect scrutiny, or camouflage clandestine activity.

The political popularity of disarmament, fueled by still-fresh memories of the carnage of the Great War, continued to be strong at the beginning of the 1930s. And the Great Depression intensified the need for economy in government spending. This sentiment ultimately led to an ill-fated World Disarmament Conference in early 1932, which took place despite ominous harbingers of threats to world peace: "battleships abuilding in Germany, sabers rattling in Italy, bombs bursting in Manchuria, and rearmament in progress in Russia and also in France."[85] Germany remained truculent and attempted to use the pressure for disarmament to effectively gut the Versailles limitations by demanding "equality of status," which meant compelling other nations to disarm to Germany's level—all the while, of course, that Germany continued the clandestine preparations for the reconstitution of its military.[86]

This demand for armaments equality, moreover, despite the danger it represented to England's national security, was met in England with widespread approval, the *Times* speaking of "the timely redress of inequality" between German and Allied armaments.[87] With this domestic political support, further negotiation finally led to the "MacDonald plan," which proposed to reduce France's Army from 500,000 to 200,000 and allow Germany's to match that number. Other restrictions on artillery and military aircraft were also proposed to placate Germany. Speaking in Parliament, Winston Churchill identified the grave danger in appeasing a militant, vengeful Germany: "Nothing in life is eternal, but as surely as Germany acquires full military equality with her neighbours while her own grievances are still unredressed and while she is in the temper which we have unhappily seen, so surely shall we see ourselves within a measurable distance of the renewal of general European war." However, despite these "scarcely comprehensible" concessions, as Churchill put it, the talks collapsed after Hitler came to power and Germany walked out of the conference in October 1933.[88] Hitler correctly calculated that he could now blatantly rearm and so no longer needed negotiation and multinational treaties to achieve his goals and camouflage his activities. The failure of the Disarmament Conference illustrates once again that a reliance on diplomatic talk is vitiated by the simple fact that any sovereign nation can just stop talking when talk no longer serves its interests.[89]

Remilitarizing the Rhineland

The Versailles provisions concerning the occupation and demilitarization of the Rhineland were perhaps the most galling
Allied affront to German honor, for it involved the stationing
of foreign occupation troops on the Fatherland's sacred soil.
Yet the Rhineland—the German territory west of the Rhine
river—was crucial both for French security and the deterrence
of German aggression: "Five times in a hundred years,"
Churchill wrote, "in 1814, 1815, 1870, 1914, and 1918, had the
towers of Nôtre Dame seen the flash of Prussian guns and
heard the thunder of their cannonade."[90] Keeping the Germans east of the Rhine would prevent yet another attack on
France and deter aggression against the weak, new states on
Germany's eastern border by maintaining a credible threat of
an attack on Germany from the west. For England as well, the
advent of aerial bombardment meant that the Channel was no
longer England's defensive frontier. As early as 1923, the British
Foreign Office had called the Rhine England's frontier, a trope
made famous by Prime Minister Stanley Baldwin in 1934: "The
old frontiers are gone. When you think of the defence of England you no longer think of the chalk cliffs of Dover; you think
of the Rhine. That is where our frontier lies."[91] France's solution in 1919 was to establish a separate buffer state in the
Rhineland, but this was vetoed by England and America as a
violation of the principle of ethnic self-determination. Instead,
the Rhineland and the east bank for 50 kilometers were "permanently" demilitarized, and Allied troops would occupy the
west bank for 15 years.

As we have already seen, the Young Plan moved up the evacuation of the occupying troops to June 30, 1930. England pressured France into accepting this erosion of its security by
threatening to pull out its troops unilaterally. The end of the
occupation was a great victory for Germany, met with jubilant
celebrations by the *Stahlhelm*, the "Steel Helmet" paramilitary

veterans group, on the French and Belgian borders. While England looked to its short-term economic and misunderstood strategic interests that an appeased and revived Germany supposedly would serve, Germany had taken another huge step in the dismantling of Versailles and the recovery of its national prestige, both necessary for achieving the ultimate goal of once more dominating the Continent: "The evacuation of the Rhineland," Barnett concludes, "led therefore to a calamitous weakening of France's defensive position. But this was not all. Perhaps more serious, it removed the last positive French hold over Germany. . . . The European balance of power, heavily tilted at Locarno, had taken a great lurch away from France and England toward Germany." Nor had this appeasement mollified Germany, which demanded further weakening of the Versailles settlement. Meanwhile, voters increased the legislative power of the Nazi Party, whose explicit foreign policy objective was the total destruction of the Versailles Treaty as the key step in the restoration of Germany's Continental dominance.[92]

The Failure of the League of Nations

When Hitler came to power in January 1933, then, the ground for German expansion had already been prepared by over a decade of appeasement fueled by fear, shortsighted national interests, and delusional idealism. Moreover, the great hope for international peace through collective security, the League of Nations, had long been exposed as a toothless sham, lacking a military force capable of punishing aggressors and compromised by the contradiction between an international organization, created to provide collective security, made up of sovereign states with their own peculiar interests and aims that necessarily must conflict with those of other states.

The first test of the League came in 1923, when Mussolini used the murder of some Italian diplomats in Epirus to begin engineering the takeover of the Greek island of Corfu as part

of advancing Italian designs on Albania. After an Italian fleet
sailed into the island's main harbor and bombarded a fortress
housing Greek and Armenian refugees from Turkey, killing 15
people, Greece appealed to the League of Nations. As Harold
Nicolson, then with the British Foreign Office, recognized at
the time, this incident was exactly the sort of crisis that the
League had been created to resolve. More important, Nicolson saw that "should the [League] Assembly fail, in such fla-
grant circumstances, to enforce obedience to the Covenant,
it was realized that the authority of the League would be forever impaired."[93] In the end, national self-interest—the French
wanted Mussolini's support over the Ruhr occupation and the
British refused to use its fleet unilaterally—bypassed the League
for the Council of Ambassadors* where such national interests and *realpolitik* horse-trading took precedence over the
idea of collective security based on the lofty principles of the
League Covenant. Despite being blameless, Greece was made
to pay Italy reparations as the price of Italian withdrawal. In
the end, England's prestige was tarnished, and Mussolini's violations were rewarded rather than punished, a harbinger of
further aggression to come. Worse, as the Secretary-General
of the League wrote, "[T]his challenge has brought into question the fundamental principles which lie at the root of the
public law of the new world order established by the League."

Despite some minor successes in defusing conflict in the
Balkans and Iraq during the Twenties, the League's weakness
in deterring the aggression of a determined great power, evident in the Corfu crisis, was confirmed by Japan's attack on
Manchuria in September 1931.[94] The League could not punish Japan even symbolically with a condemnation or expulsion,
as Japan could veto any such action since it was a permanent
member of the League Council. As for military force, there

*The Council of Ambassadors, comprising representatives from England, France,
Italy, and Japan, was created in 1919 to implement the Versailles Treaty.

was no League member able or willing to fight Japan over Manchuria, which would be politically unpopular even in England, where support for the League was strongest. And even if England or France, the two greatest League powers, could summon up the will to use force, Sally Marks writes, "[a]fter years of budget slashing, shrinking armies and naval disarmament, neither had the military power to embark on a course which, in any event, would probably bring down their depression-burdened Cabinets and invite Japanese retaliation against their trade and their Asian colonies."[95]

Given the priority of national interests for the nations upon which the viability of the League depended, in the end nothing was done about the brutal invasion of Manchuria: "The League, unable to evade the issue altogether, assiduously avoided action and limited itself to hollow phraseology."[96] A resolution was passed urging Japanese withdrawal in three weeks, but it was non-binding because Japan voted against it. Another resolution called for withdrawal without a time frame, but a loophole allowed Japan to pursue "bandits," an elastic category guaranteeing the continued killing of Chinese. And in another attempt to substitute words for action, a "commission of inquiry" was sent to China, which nearly a year after the invasion did nothing but again request Japan's withdrawal and assert the "nonrecognition" of Manchukuo, the puppet state created by the Japanese as camouflage for their conquest. Japan was not branded an aggressor, which would have led to sanctions according to the League Covenant. Despite this flabby response, Japan resigned from the League in protest. Any shrewd aggressor could see that the League was nothing but a mechanism for dressing inaction in the rhetorical robes of utopian internationalism, as became even more obvious during the Spanish Civil War (1936–39), when Italy and Germany blatantly provided men and arms to the Nationalists while the League remained neutral.

Thus in 1933 England was militarily weak and suffering from a national failure of nerve, France was equally dispirited and huddling behind the Maginot Line, America was still mired in isolationism, and the League of Nations had been exposed as a "cockpit in the Tower of Babel," as Churchill would describe it after the Second World War.[97] With the victors in the Great War unwilling or unable to check German aggression, nothing stood in Hitler's way of realizing both what had been Germany's goal since 1919, to dominate the Continent once again, and his own grandiose ambitions for a German world empire, clearly outlined nearly a decade earlier in *Mein Kampf* and later in many public speeches.

The Fool's Gold of Pacifism and Diplomatic "Engagement"

The final dismantling of the Versailles Treaty would be the prelude to the neutralization of England and France and the conquest of Eastern Europe in the pursuit of racial purification and *lebensraum*. Hitler began this process incrementally, each step encouraging the next by the flaccid response of an England duped by his conciliatory and moderate tone during the first few months of his regime; with this strategy Hitler "was making his assessment of the attitude that the various Powers would be likely to adopt when he began to move toward his real objectives. This was a process that involved a series of graduated probes intended to test their ability to collaborate effectively to preserve the *status quo* and their willingness to resort to force in order to frustrate his designs."[98]

The first test came when Hitler pulled Germany out of the disarmament conference and the League of Nations in October 1933. England's response indicated that neither the government in power nor critical sectors of the citizenry had any interest in accelerating the pace of rearmament despite the Nazi Party's well-known brutality and Hitler's well-publicized aggressive ambitions. In July 1934, in response to government proposals to increase the Royal Air Force by 820 planes in five years, the Labour Party, with support from the Liberals, moved a vote of censure, which asserted that the "policy of rearmament [was] neither necessitated by any new commitment nor calculated to add to the security of the nation, but certain to jeopardize the prospects of international disarmament and to encourage a revival of dangerous and wasteful competition in preparation for war."[99] In the face of all evidence demonstrating Germany's hostile intentions, disarmament continued to be pursued as the philosopher's stone that could transmute the dross of interstate conflict into the gold of international peace and friendship: "[L]ong after Germany had walked out of the Disarmament Conference ... the English Cabinet clung desperately to the hope of reaching some general agreement on disarmament or arms limitation. As late as November 1935 the Government was talking arms limitation in its public speeches, and pursuing such an agreement until well into 1936."[100]

The politicians, however, were in part responding to the mood of the people, which was ambivalent at best and downright pacifist at worst. In February 1933, the Oxford Union debated the motion "That this House will in no circumstances fight for its King and Country." The motion passed 275–153 and caught the attention of Mussolini, who was already formulating his expansionist designs.[101] Similar resolutions were passed in more than 20 other universities. The next portent was a by-election in a London district in 1934, in which the Labor candidate accused his Conservative opponent of being a warmonger, and the Labor Party leader, George Lansbury, told the Labor candidate that he would "close every recruiting station, disband the Army and disarm the Air Force. I would abolish the whole dreadful equipment of war and say to the world 'do your worst.'"[102] The Labor candidate won, the first of a string of byelection victories, "all fought on the issue of 'peace,' in which the swing against the Government varied between 24.88 per cent and 19.9 percent," a trend that continued throughout the rest of 1934 and into 1935.[103]

In the spring of 1935, a survey sanctioned by the League of Nations Union, the so-called "Peace Ballot," polled 11.5 million people about their support for the League of Nations and disarmament and whether aggressor nations should be stopped by economic and other nonmilitary means or by force if necessary. About 10 million people answered "yes" to all the questions. "This nation-wide knocking on doors," Ronald Blythe writes of the survey, "and beating of breasts quite drowned out the sounds from German dockyards, where the [battleships] *Scharnhorst, Gneisenau, Bismarck* and *Tirpitz* were being laid down."[104] Some historians argue, as did Churchill, that the endorsement of force evidenced in the affirmative reply to the question about using military power to resist aggression argued for a more vigorous sentiment among the British people, one that could have led to a more muscular foreign policy if the politicians had been able clearly to formulate and present such a policy.[105]

Be that as it may, the overwhelming endorsement of the League and disarmament ratified the government's policy of seeking arms limitations rather than rearmament as the response to Germany's growing assertiveness. Even those "those service chiefs, cabinet ministers, and backbenchers who were more concerned about Britain's defences than disarmament had to put their case carefully in public. Few would openly risk the danger of being called 'warmongers.'"[106] Lord Cecil, the long-time champion of the League of Nations, interpreted the ballot's results on disarmament as confirming that the elimination of weapons and armies was "the way of true security for the world against the greatest of man-made perils." In this assessment, Lord Cecil was in tune with the Labor and Liberal Parties' consistent, public opposition to rearmament, such as that of Labor MP George Hall, who said in the House of Commons, "[I]t is madness to assume that more and bigger armaments are required to preserve peace, to give security, and to deter aggression."[107] What Churchill later wrote about the

Oxford debate no doubt applies to these other displays of England's appeasing mood: "[I]n Germany, in Russia, in Italy, in Japan, the idea of a decadent, degenerate Britain took deep root and swayed many calculations."[108]

Further behavior by England confirmed this estimation. Despite Germany's withdrawal from the disarmament conference, in February 1935 England and France came up with a new disarmament plan that would give Germany equality in armaments in exchange for an agreement to accept conventions limiting air war and some weapons, along with new treaties to provide security to Germany's eastern neighbors and its return to the League of Nations. This massive concession was met in March with Hitler's revelation that Germany now possessed an air force and that he no longer would honor the military articles of the Versailles Treaty. Worse, he intended to expand the German army to over half a million men comprising 36 divisions. If left unchecked, Hitler's actions would "change fundamentally the European balance of power," for France could not match Germany's new army, given the political mood in France.[109] A meeting in Stresa in April with officials from England, France, and Italy, the latter troubled by Germany's designs on Austria, led to nothing but empty rhetoric and promises to resist further violations of the Versailles Treaty—with sanctions ruled out in advance by England—that Hitler had effectively gutted. Hitler responded with more rhetorical misdirection, resorting "to his old technique of defusing potentially dangerous situations by saying all of the things that peaceful people want to hear."[110] In May he offered to enter into bilateral agreements in which he would promise to recognize Austria's independence and respect the Locarno Treaty and its prohibition against militarizing the Rhineland. Many in England were delighted with these promises, the *Economist* praising the speech's "overwhelming impression of sincerity," and the Archbishop of York opining that "Hitler had made in the most deliberate manner offers which are a great contribution to the secure establishment of peace."[111]

For those in England who still believed that pleasing words could be transmuted into the reality of peace and friendship, Hitler's cynical and mendacious offer was met with enthusiasm. Liberals and socialists in England called for an international conference to take advantage of an opportunity "to call a halt in the armaments race," as Clement Attlee, leader of the opposition in Parliament, put it. And the Cabinet said that Hitler's speech "should be welcomed and promised careful and sympathetic consideration."[301] Given the strength of pacifist sentiment among English voters, Hitler's unilateral repudiation of the Versailles settlement and his dangerous disruption of the European balance of power was nonetheless rewarded in June 1935 with the Anglo-German naval treaty, which gave Germany the right to a fleet up to 35 percent of the British, along with a 45 percent ratio for submarines that Germany could raise to parity, although Hitler did promise never to use submarines against merchant shipping. The treaty was a blow to British security, given the role its Navy had to play in defending its far-flung global empire, particularly in the East, where an expansionist Japan threatened Hong Kong and Singapore. In addition, Germany was not subject to any limits, as was England, by the Washington Naval Agreement, on the size of ships or armaments.[113] For Germany, the treaty was a huge victory. England had weakened Versailles, further alienated the French, and, according to Admiral Erich Raeder, head of the German Navy, "sanctioned Germany's right thereafter to rearm."[114] It had now "become morally certain," Barnett summarizes, "that France and England would not make use of their existing joint strategic superiority, whatever the provocation; and this was perfectly apparent to Hitler."[115]

And it was apparent to Mussolini as well. An important lesson taught by England's appeasement of Hitler is that giving in to one aggressor encourages another who has witnessed the weakness of the appeasers. Moreover, given that his alliances are based on expediency rather than shared principle, an aggressor may calculate that a fellow aggressor is more useful to his own interests than is a weak democratic state whose leaders are electorally answerable to citizens and hostage to public opinion. Between Hitler's ascension to power in 1933 and the Munich conference in 1938, Hitler and Mussolini were spurred to new attacks by the weak response of England and France to previous aggression. This was the view of British historian T. P. Conwell-Evans, who in 1932 had written a book arguing for England's responsibility for World War I: "He [Hitler] scorns the attitude of England," Conwell-Evans wrote after Mussolini's invasion of Ethiopia, "whose fine phrases contributed nothing to the Negus [king of Ethiopia]. If England hesitated to tackle the Italians. . . . how much more would the English hesitate to grapple with the Germans—a much tougher proposition, he thinks."[116] Here is an important danger of failing to resist hostile actions: any act of appeasement empowers not just one, but any number of other aggressors who may be watching from the sidelines and calculating chances.

Having witnessed England's appeasement of Germany, then, Mussolini decided that the time was right to pursue his dream of reconstituting the old Roman Empire by expansion into Africa with an invasion of Abyssinia (Ethiopia). This goal was not a secret and should have been obvious at the Stresa Conference. There the agreement to oppose "any unilateral repudiation of treaties which may endanger the peace" was altered by Mussolini with the important phrase "in Europe," with no objections from England despite the phrase's obvious relevance for Italy's well-known plans to invade Ethiopia, and the dangers to peace the invasion would create.[117] "Mussolini," Churchill wrote, "like Hitler, regarded Britannia as a frightened, flabby old woman, who at the worst would only bluster, and was anyhow incapable of making war."[118] Encouraged by England's weakness and France's courtship of him to counterbalance England's appeasement of Germany, Mussolini invaded Ethiopia in October 1935, spurred on by England's back-channel assurances that it would not respond militarily or close the Suez Canal.

Hitler in his turn surely was encouraged in his designs by the ineffectual response of both England and the League of Nations to Mussolini's aggression against a fellow League member. The League condemned Italy and imposed economic sanctions, but oil was excepted, the one commodity that Italy was short of and that was crucial to the success of an overseas invasion. England was internally divided by "the contradiction and confusion that underlay the government's policies and public opinion."[119] The military, overestimating both Italy's naval strength and England's naval weakness, advised against any action that could stop Italy. The politicians agreed but were still committed to the League and the notion of collective security, and they were pressed during an election year by a public opinion strongly opposed to Italy's actions—when England and France later concocted a deal that rewarded Mussolini's aggression with 60,000 square miles of Ethiopian territory, the angry reaction of the people torpedoed it. The people wanted something to be done but did not want to support the one thing that could stop Mussolini, military action, as the incoherent results of the "Peace Ballot" had suggested that spring. This contradiction was resolved by the magical thinking that made the League of Nations the instrument for stopping aggression without the costs and risks of using force, a fantasy particularly exploited by the Labor Party, which won the election in October 1935.

This confused policy of resistance with words rather than deeds angered Mussolini without stopping his aggression: "In the end, Britain's attempt at a double policy was a disaster that brought about results worse than following either one consistently. Mussolini had achieved his goals, the League and collective security were finished, Britain's prestige was badly damaged, and Italy was alienated, shortly to join forces with Hitler. The democracies seemed weak, indecisive, and cowardly, and their failure and inaction gave courage to their enemies."[120] Churchill confirms the impact of England's failure on German public opinion, quoting an English diplomat living in Bavaria: "I am impressed by the note of contempt in references to Great Britain in many quarters . . . It is to be feared that Germany's attitude in the negotiations for a settlement in Western Europe and for a more general settlement of European and extra-European questions will be found to have stiffened."[121] By May 1936 Italy had completed its conquest of Ethiopia, the ineffectual sanctions were lifted, and Hitler's remilitarization of the Rhineland was two months old.

Like Mussolini's designs on Ethiopia, Hitler's aim of remilitarizing the Rhineland was well known to both the British and French governments. Maurice Gamelin, Commander-in-Chief of the French Army, warned three months before Hitler moved in his troops that militarization of the Rhineland was necessary for Hitler's ambitions to undo the Eastern settlement by first neutralizing the French. Even earlier, in November 1935, the French ambassador to Germany had warned that Hitler would use France's signing of a pact with the Soviet Union as a pretext for remilitarization.[122] Despite this foreknowledge, on March 7 Hitler was allowed to send 22,000 unseasoned troops and 14,000 local police into the Rhineland in gross violation of Articles 42, 43, and 44 of the Versailles Treaty, not to mention the Locarno Treaty, which Germany had signed without coercion. Facing them were 76 French and 21 Belgian divisions, with promises of support from Poland, Czechoslovakia, and Rumania. Hitler was bluffing, as he confessed: "If the French had then marched into the Rhineland we would have had to withdraw with our tails between our legs, for the military resources at our disposal would have been wholly inadequate for even a moderate resistance."[123] Instead of resistance, France complained to a League of Nations which Mussolini was in the process of emasculating.

By that time the "cult of the defensive" had paralyzed the French military, and French public opinion on both the left and the right was opposed to action. The left was particularly pusillanimous, one newspaper writing, "Hitler has torn up a treaty, he has broken all his promises, but at the same time he speaks of peace and Geneva [i.e., disarmament]. We must take him at his word."[124] The same faith in negotiation and disarmament, held by both the politicians and the people, vitiated any response from the British as well, many of whom had long been sympathetic to Germany, despite the thuggish nature of the Nazi regime, and felt that Hitler had been provoked.[125] Rather than seeing the crisis as a serious threat to England's security, the Labor Party thought the Rhineland crisis "pregnant with new and great possibilities for the future of the world."[126] Historian Arnold Toynbee, after visiting with Hitler, came away convinced "of the Führer's sincerity in desiring peace in Europe and close friendship with England."[127] As for the general public, its attitude was summed up in a statement attributed to a taxi driver: "I suppose Jerry can do what he likes with his own back garden, can't he?" Such thinking, Kagan writes, "reflected the understandable ignorance of most people about the strategic importance of what had happened and the character of the regime that had carried out the coup, as well as eighteen years in which educated opinion had minimized the threat from Germany, sympathized with its grievances, and complained of the aggressive unreasonableness and selfishness of France."[128]

Political and economic interests, mixed with idealistic dreams of collective security and pacifism nurtured by fear of war, had driven most of England's leaders during this period, making it easier to ignore the hard strategic truths and looming dangers that it was their responsibility to communicate to their fellow citizens. However, as Churchill later wrote, "Virtuous motives, trammeled by inertia and timidity, are no match for armed and resolute wickedness. A sincere love of peace is no excuse for muddling hundreds of millions of humble folk into total war."[129]

The failure to contest the remilitarization of the Rhineland is the key act of appeasement in Europe's descent into the maelstrom of World War II. With his spectacular bluff, Hitler had put his army 100 miles closer to France and recovered the traditional jumping-off point for German armies invading France.[130] Work would soon begin on the Siegfried Line (what Germans called the West Wall), a wall of fortifications that would further neutralize France as a threat to Germany's western border, leaving Hitler free to pursue his destruction of the Eastern settlement with attacks on Austria, Czechoslovakia, and Poland. And the nascent Luftwaffe's bombers now had bases closer to their future targets in England. The Rhineland militarization was the final act of a decade-long tragedy of shortsighted national interests, wish-fulfilling idealism, and paralyzing fear; it was also the first step in the sequence of further appeasement that would culminate in Munich and sign the death warrants of 50 million people.

Austria and the Prelude to Munich

With this critical step accomplished, Hitler had completed the destruction of most of the Versailles settlement: disarmament, reparations, and the demilitarized Rhineland were all dead letters; or as some influential English appeasers approvingly telegraphed to Prime Minister Baldwin, "Versailles is now a corpse and should be buried."[131] And Hitler had achieved all this restoration of Germany's prestige and power not through military force but, like Philip II, through political and diplomatic skill and daring. As 40,000 Hitler Youth sang a few years later at the Nuremberg Party rally, "Germany suffers no longer,/The Führer came as the orderly of God and made it free./Blood is stronger than enemy power/And what is German must belong to Germany!"[132] The last two verses pointed to the next phase of Germany's expansion—the dismantling of the Eastern settlement and the fulfillment of Hitler's dream,

as he told his war cabinet in 1937, "to make secure and to preserve the racial community and to enlarge it," which required
reintegration of the German people whom the iniquitous Versailles Treaty had sundered from what Hitler in *Mein Kampf*
called the "great German motherland"; and the acquisition of
lebensraum, "living space" for the German *volk,* which could
be achieved "only by means of force."[133] The first step was to
bring back the Germans marooned in Austria—who, according to Hitler, "were subjected to continuous suffering because
of their sympathy and solidarity with the whole German race
and its ideology"—by exploiting the principle of ethnic self-
determination that the post-war settlement put at the center
of international relations.[134]

In manipulating this pretext, Hitler was abetted by the fear
of war and the illusory idealism of Neville Chamberlain, who
had become Prime Minister in May 1937. Chamberlain, who
had lost a beloved cousin in the Great War, had a visceral horror of war, which he believed "wins nothing, cures nothing,
ends nothing." He was not a complete pacifist, but he did see
war as the last resort, subject to a "vital cause," one that "tran-
scends all the human values." In another context, he specified
that war could be fought against "a claim by one state to dominate others by force," or "for the preservation of democracy,"
although he allowed Germany to "dominate" Czechoslovakia
and destroy its democracy. Moreover, Chamberlain was naïve
about the potential goodness of human nature, and he was
determined to find "decency even in dictators."[135] In the view
of Foreign Secretary Anthony Eden, who resigned in February
1938 over Chamberlain's naïve outreach to Mussolini, the Prime
Minister "believes that he is a man with a mission to come to
terms with the dictators."[136] Thus Chamberlain believed that
diplomatic discussion could arrive at agreements and treaties,
and that conciliation and appeasement of grievances could diffuse conflict and create peace. Like many in Europe, including many today, Chamberlain failed to take seriously the power

of ideology and an irrational commitment to it, in trumping economic and other material considerations, such as the African colonies the English mistakenly thought would satisfy Hitler's ambitions, or "economic appeasement," financial help for a German economy that in fact was doing much better than England's.[137]

Fatally misjudging Hitler and Nazi ideology, Chamberlain believed that concessions on the remaining Versailles provisions—particularly the Eastern settlement, still angering the Germans—would placate Hitler and avoid war rather than encourage his aggression. Thus the soon-to-be Foreign Minister, Lord Halifax, on a visit to Germany for a hunting exhibition, told Hitler, "On all these matters [Danzig, Austria, Czechoslovakia] we were not necessarily concerned to stand up for the *status quo* as to-day, but we were concerned to avoid such treatment of them as would be likely to cause trouble. If reasonable settlements could be reached with the free assent and goodwill of those primarily concerned, we certainly had no desire to block." Halifax was confirming the opinion of another influential and frequent visitor to Hitler, Lord Philip Lothian, who in May 1937 had told him, "Britain had no primary interests in Eastern Europe."[138] So too the British ambassador to Germany, the pro-German Nevile Henderson, who had told a gathering of high-ranking Nazi officials that many in England had "an entirely erroneous conception" of the Nazi regime, focusing too much on "Nazi dictatorship" instead of "the great social experiment which was being tried out in Germany."[139] Given these sentiments, it is no surprise that according to the American ambassador, William Dodd, Henderson had "informed the German Government that England would make no objections if Hitler seized Austria and Czechoslovakia."[140] As Kagan says, Halifax gave Hitler the green light to dismantle the Eastern settlement, which in any case England had opposed in 1919 and still disfavored, "if only he behaved with some small degree of decorum."[141]

Hitler thus employed two tracks in his assault on Austria—covert subversion and diplomatic pretense to placate and distract world opinion; in May 1935, Hitler in a speech to the Reichstag had said, "Germany neither intends nor wishes to interfere in the internal affairs of Austria, to annex Austria or to conclude an *Anschluss*."[142] Even before this bald-faced lie, Germany had subverted Austria's independence through the machinations of the Austrian Nazi Party, which had assassinated the Austrian Chancellor Engelbert Dollfuss during an attempted *coup d'état* in July 1934. Since that failure, which had alarmed Mussolini and moved him to join England and France in the short-lived Stresa Front, Hitler had relied on terrorist activities such as bombings and violent demonstrations by Austrian Nazis to undermine the Austrian government, all the while German public diplomacy pursued better relations with Austria and the legitimization of the Austrian Nazi Party. As part of this strategy, in February 1938 Hitler summoned the Austrian Chancellor Kurt von Schuschnigg to Berchtesgaden and bullied him with threats of invasion into signing a "protocol" that made Austrian Nazis Ministers of the Interior, Finance, and the Armed Forces; gave a general amnesty to all Austrian Nazis in detention; and legitimized the Austrian Nazi Party. Hitler's speech in the Reichstag a few days later illustrates how the pleasing rhetoric of a spurious diplomatic settlement can mask the brute application of terror, threats, and force: "I should like to express . . . my sincere thanks to the Austrian Chancellor for his great understanding and the warm-hearted willingness with which he accepted my invitation and worked with me, so that we might discover a way of serving the best interests of the two countries. . . . I believe that we have thereby made a contribution to European peace."[143] As Churchill would write later, "Once can hardly find a more perfect specimen of humbug and hypocrisy for British and American benefit. . . . What is astounding is that it should have been regarded with anything but scorn by men and women of intelligence in any free country."[144]

However, maintaining such verbal pretexts was in the end unnecessary, given that it was clear to all that England, let alone France, was not going to use force to protect Austria's territorial integrity. Hitler certainly was confident that both countries would not fight for Austria: during his threats to von Schuschnigg at Berchtesgaden, he answered the Austrian's feeble claim that "We are not alone in the world" with this accurate assessment: "Don't believe that anyone in the world will hinder me in my decisions! . . . England? England will not lift a finger for Austria . . . And France? Well, two years ago when we marched into the Rhineland with a handful of battalions—at that moment I risked a great deal. If France had marched then we should have been forced to withdraw . . . but for France it is now too late!"[145] This estimation was consistent with the sentiments of many in the English government, such as Sir Alexander Cadogan, permanent undersecretary at the Foreign Office, who criticized those worrying about Austria "when we can't do anything about it," and who wrote after the *Anschluss,* "Thank goodness Austria's out of the way. . . . After all, it wasn't our business: We had no particular feeling for the Austrians: We only forbade the *Anschluss* to spite Germany."[146] Hitler was correct: years of unilateral disarmament, appeasement of aggression, and sheer wishful thinking had done their work and sapped the will of England and France.

So too had the delusional faith in diplomacy and negotiated settlements. Hitler's plan of phased subversion through diplomacy and intrigue had to be abandoned when in March von Schuschnigg scheduled a referendum to decide the issue of the Austrian German minority. Faced with this possible wreck of his phased approach, on March 12 Hitler sent the German Army into Austria, which the next day was annexed to the German Reich, giving Germany control over southeastern Europe and threatening Czechoslovakia from the south. However, despite this ruin of his hopes for a negotiated agreement, or at least for a pleasing pretext of respect for international law and nonviolent adjudication of grievances, Chamberlain kept his faith that continued engagement with a ruthless dictator could create peace. He blamed the crisis on "Schuschnigg's blunder" in holding the plebiscite and told the Cabinet that he "did not think anything that had happened should cause the Government to alter their present policy; on the contrary, recent events had confirmed him in his opinion that that policy was the right one and he only regretted that it had not been adopted earlier."[147]

Nor was the obvious brutality of Nazism, one immediately inflicted on Jews in Austria, a deterrent to those who blamed Versailles for Germany's aggression and believed coexistence was possible, provided any remaining grievances were satisfied. Seven months before the occupation of Austria, the influential liberal historian G. M. Trevelyan had written in the *Times*, "Dictatorship and democracy must live side by side in peace, or civilization is doomed," and he attributed Nazism to "Allied and British injustice at Versailles." Chamberlain had used similar words, when a month after the *Anschluss* he told the House of Commons: "You may say we may not approve of dictatorships .... We have to live with them .... We should take any and every opportunity to try to remove any genuine and legitimate grievance that may exist."[148] In this vein, he contemplated telling Hitler, "'It is no use crying over spilt milk [Austria] .... The best thing you can do is to tell us exactly what you want for your Sudeten *Deutsch*. If it is reasonable we will urge the Czechs to accept it and if they do you must give us assurances that you will let them alone in future.'"[149]

Thus a misplaced idealism and faith in human nature sealed the fate of Czechoslovakia at Munich. What makes this faith even more astonishing is that the nature of Nazism was obvious upon Hitler's accession to power, when within a week the Reichstag gave him dictatorial powers and within months Jews were being boycotted and beaten in the streets, trade unions were outlawed, political enemies were arrested and imprisoned without trial, and concentration camps constructed. In addition, British ambassadors sent back to England reports of the nature of Nazism and the Führer. British ambassador Sir Horace Rumbold, who had read *Mein Kampf* and quoted from it to support his analysis of Hitler and Nazism, reported accurately the nature of the new regime until he left Berlin in June 1933.[150] Rumbold described German audiences listening enthusiastically "to his [Hitler's] derogatory remarks about 'such nonsensical ideas' as international understanding, peace pacts, and spirit of Locarno, the policy of conciliation and the like."[151] When Rumbold left his post in Berlin, he sketched further the irrational bellicosity and racialist views of Germany's new leader: "Pacifism is the deadliest sin. . . . Will and determination are of the higher worth. Only brute force can ensure the survival of the race," which required that "the new Reich must gather within its fold all the scattered German elements in Europe" and acquire more territory. To achieve this goal, the young must be "educated to the maximum of aggressiveness. . . . It is the duty of the government to implant in the people feelings of manly courage and passionate hatred." A year later, Rumbold's successor, Sir Eric Phipps, wrote back to London, "If his [Hitler's] neighbours allow him, he will become strong by the simplest and most direct methods. . . . If he finds that he arouses no real opposition, the *tempo* of his advance will increase." Moreover, Phipps made it clear that this malign ideology could be checked only "by the knowledge that the Powers who desire peace are also strong enough to enforce it."[152]

In 1935, Winston Churchill on a BBC broadcast confirmed for the average Englishman the diplomats' estimation of the nature of Nazism and its imminent dangers:

> Only a few hours away by air there dwells a nation of nearly seventy millions of the most educated, industrious, scientific, disciplined people in the world, who are being taught from childhood to think of war and conquest as a glorious exercise, and death in battle as the noblest fate of man. There is a nation

which has abandoned all its liberties in order to augment its collective might. There is a nation which, with all its strength and virtues, is in the grip of a group of ruthless men preaching a gospel of intolerance and racial pride, unrestrained by law, by Parliament or by public opinion. ... Now they are rearming with the utmost speed, and ready to their hands is this new lamentable weapon of the air, against which our Navy is no defence, before which women and children, the weak and the frail, the pacifist and the jingo, the warrior and the civilian, the front line trenches and the cottage home, lie in equal and impartial peril.[153]

Nevertheless, knowledge of Hitler's aims, methods, and nature could not penetrate the delusional idealism of a whole generation of British leaders.

The "Little Worms" of Munich

Hitler's destruction of Czechoslovakia was, as historian Gordon Craig describes it, a "virtuoso performance, diminished only by the fact that his antagonists made things easier for him than he deserved."[154] The same methods that had destroyed Austria's independence were employed: manufactured ethnic grievances that exploited the ideal of ethnic self-determination and covert subversion employing violence and propaganda, all camouflaged by phony "negotiations" meant to distract England and France, the latter bound by treaty to defend Czechoslovakia, as was the Soviet Union. But the Soviets were obligated to act only if France did, and France had no intention of acting without British support. The British Chiefs of Staff, overestimating German military power and minimizing that of the Allies, concluded that "we are not yet ready for war." This "failure of intelligence," as we might describe it, gave ammunition to Chamberlain's argument that a negotiated settlement predicated on appeasement of German grievances could avert a war that England was presumably not prepared to fight and could also serve his foreign policy goal of a rapprochement with Germany.[155]

The "pretext," as Thucydides would put it, for the German assault on Czechoslovakia was the alleged sufferings of the Sudeten Germans—the "brutal treatment of mothers and children of German blood," as Reichsminister of Propaganda Joseph Goebbels put it.[156] This pretext gave Czechoslovakia's allies a public excuse for inaction by holding out the promise that if only a settlement that alleviated these sufferings could be negotiated, then war would be averted. As part of this charade, Hitler in March 1938 instructed Konrad Henlein, leader of the Sudeten German Party, that "demands should be made by the Sudeten German Party which are unacceptable to the Czech Government," which Henlein paraphrased, with Hitler's approval, as "we must always demand so much that we cannot be satisfied."[157] Once the demands became so egregious that the Czechs broke off negotiations, Hitler would then have a pretext for invading and taking over the whole country, his aim from the start. Duped by this diplomatic misdirection, the French and particularly the English pressured Czechoslovakia to appease the Sudeten Germans and satisfy their supposed grievances: Chamberlain's Foreign Minister Lord Halifax informed the Czechs "that in the interests of international peace every possible step should be taken to remove the causes of friction or even of conflict arising out of the present minority problem in Czechoslovakia."[158] The flawed assumption, of course, was that Hitler was sincerely concerned with settling the Sudeten issue through negotiation and that the Sudetenland was "the last territorial claim I have to make in Europe," as Hitler said later on September 24.[159] In fact, his aim all along, clear to anyone who paid attention to the dictator's speeches and writings, was the destruction of the whole Eastern settlement as the prelude to Germany's march to the domination of Europe and the acquisition of *lebensraum*.

For the next several months, increasing demands from Hitler, provocations in the Sudetenland, and the "pathetic, pointless charade," as Taylor describes it, of negotiation proceeded apace.[160] In April, during negotiations in Karlsbad between the Henleinists and the Czech government, Henlein, obedient to his master in Berlin, announced eight demands, the last of which called for the Sudetens to have "full liberty to profess the German nationality, and the German political philosophy."[161] This last demand was impossible for the Czechs to accept, since the result would be a virtually separate Sudeten state that would endanger other minority groups. The Czechs were outraged, and in May rumors of German troop movements led the Czech government to call up their reservists and occupy the frontier forts and the Sudetenland. The British and French, fearful of war, blamed the Czechs for the crisis: the French Foreign Minister warned that if the Czechs were "unreasonable," France "considered herself released from her bond."[162]

As for the British, they thought the solution was "for Prague to get a real twist of the screw" so that the Czechs gave in to the demands of the German minority, which is to say, of Hitler.[163] "The general feeling," First Lord of the Admiralty Duff Cooper observed, "seemed to be that great, brutal Czecho-Slovakia was bullying poor, peaceful little Germany."[164] While the British and French increased diplomatic pressure on the intended victim of German aggression, Hitler wrote in his attack plan, "It is my unalterable decision to destroy Czechoslovakia by military action in the foreseeable future."[165] However, a rare display of English fortitude, in the form of a warning to Hitler on May 22 "not to count on this country being able to stand aside if from any precipitate action" war broke out, made the Führer reconsider for the moment a reliance on brute force to achieve his aims.[166]

Meanwhile, Hitler was angered by the perception abroad that the Czech mobilization and Britain's diplomatic warning had deterred him from invading. Thus he used diplomatic feints to confuse the Allies until he could be sure they would not come to Czechoslovakia's aid. In July he sent his personal aide to London to gull the English into thinking he was eager for a settlement. Once more displaying the unfortunate penchant of democracies to substitute talk for action, in late July Chamberlain sent to Prague a commission headed by Lord Runciman as "independent mediator," whose task was to negotiate a settlement between the Czechs and the Henleinists. This investigation achieved nothing other than the application of more pressure on the Czechs and was seen by many Sudeten Germans as an effort on their behalf: "What do we need Father Christmas for/We have our Runciman evermore!" a popular song went.[167] Amid increasing tensions, in early September Czech President Edvard Benes agreed to all the Sudeten Germans' eight demands given to him at the Karlsbad conference. This decision to accept the *de facto* dismemberment of his country was forced on Benes by the English through their Minister in Prague, Basil Newton, who accused Benes of "spinning out the negotiations without any sincere intention of acting on the immediate and vital issue," and advised him to "go forthwith to the very limit of concession, which limit ought not to stop short of the eight Karlsbad points if a settlement could not be obtained otherwise."[168] This offer, suicidal as it was for the Czechs, could have created a problem for Hitler, since he was preparing to attack on October 1 with the aim of conquering all of Czechoslovakia. But rioting between Czechs and Sudeten Germans instigated by SA forces and Henlein, false reports of Czech attacks on German villages, and an incident on September 7, most likely staged, in which a Sudeten Party official was struck by a Czech policeman, created a pretext for breaking off negotiations.

At the Nuremberg rally on September 12, Hitler dropped the mask of seeking a negotiated settlement and declared, in the presence of British ambassador Sir Nevile Henderson that the Germans and Czechs were "irreconcilable" enemies amenable to no amount of "forbearance"[169] Given this imprimatur at Nuremberg—delivered in a violent rant to the "roars of *'Seig Heil!'* from the frenzied audience, bawled out like the battle-cry of a horde of savages," as Harold Macmillan described it—Henlein now demanded explicitly the *de jure* secession of the Sudetenland.[170] This mountainous region was the site of the fortifications that provided Czechoslovakia its most important defense against attack and the loss of which would leave Czechoslovakia helpless before an invader.

Faced with a blatant assault against a sovereign nation that the British were morally, and the French by treaty, obligated to defend, Chamberlain once more turned to the fool's gold of diplomacy to resolve a crisis that could be settled only by force or at least a credible threat of force. And so began the three-act tragedy of Munich, in which Hitler played on the French and British fear of war and their failure of nerve in order to achieve cheaply his aim of devouring Czechoslovakia. Still under the delusion that Hitler would not attack if the issue of the Sudeten Germans were resolved, on September 15 Chamberlain flew to Berchtesgaden and assured Hitler that in effect he would first persuade the French to abandon the Czechs, and then France and England would, without consulting them, compel the Czechs to agree to let Germany swallow the Sudetenland. As Churchill wrote, "The British and French Cabinets at this time presented a front of two over-ripe melons crushed together; whereas what was needed was a gleam of steel." Instead, early in the morning of September 20, Czech President Benes was urged by the British and French Ministers to accept partition "before producing a situation for which France and Britain could take no responsibility."[171]

Armed with what he thought was a diplomatic coup, Chamberlain the next day flew to Bad Godesberg to give Hitler the news. What he heard instead of agreement were new demands: "I am very sorry," Hitler responded, "but all that is no longer

any use" because of recent "developments," that is, more rioting instigated by the Sudeten Germans.[172] Now Hitler
demanded that German troops occupy strategic areas of
Czechoslovakia after Czech police, civil, and military author-
ities had evacuated them. Then plebiscites would determine
the fate of those regions. Sudeten prisoners held by the Czechs
would be released, and nonaggression treaties would not be
signed with Czechoslovakia until Polish and Hungarian claims
to Czech territory were satisfied, Hitler once more exploiting
the ideal of ethnic self-determination to mask his aggression.
This ratcheting up of demands was predictable, given the weakness Chamberlain had already displayed by flying hat in hand
to Berchtesgaden in order to surrender Czechoslovakia under
the cover of diplomatic camouflage. Hitler's aim in making this
new demand was most likely to force the Czechs to refuse,
whereupon the British and French would abandon them and
Hitler's army could take over the whole country. Faced with
this new development, Chamberlain obtained from Hitler a
pledge not to move his forces before October 1—the date, of
course, on which Hitler had already planned to launch the
attack. Once again, Chamberlain served as Hitler's messenger
announcing to Prague Czechoslovakia's annihilation.

However, Chamberlain first had to persuade an English
public growing ever angrier over the sacrifice of a democratic
state to a dictator. One poll found 44 percent "indignant" at
Chamberlain's policy, and the evening of September 22, 10,000
people gathered at Whitehall and shouted, "Stand by the
Czechs!" and "Chamberlain must go!"[173] France too objected
to what the Minister of War Édouard Daladier called "the stran-
gulation of a people" and voiced a resolve to honor the treaty
with Czechoslovakia, which would compel England to back
France.[174] Chamberlain was horrified by the possibility of war,
however, and still deluded about the ability of diplomatic negotiation to defuse a crisis, as well as nursing a vain faith in the
power of his personality and negotiating skills. "How horrible,

fantastic, incredible," he broadcast to the British people on September 27, "it is that we should be digging trenches and trying on gas masks here because of a quarrel in a far-away country between people of whom we know nothing. It still seems impossible that a quarrel which has already been settled in principle should be the subject of war."[175] In his reports to the Cabinet, he raised the specter of aerial bombardment of London, dangled the possibility of an Anglo-German alliance, and attested to Hitler's sincerity in aiming at a solution to the "racial problem" rather than at the domination of Europe. The Prime Minister was "satisfied Hitler was speaking the truth," and asserted that "he had established some degree of personal influence over Herr Hitler." At the next Cabinet meeting, he averred that Hitler "would not deliberately deceive a man whom he respected and with whom he had been in negotiation, and he was sure that Herr Hitler now felt some respect for him. When Herr Hitler announced that he meant to do something it was certain that he would do it."[176] These deliberations ended with the Cabinet's decision to send a letter to Hitler suggesting a four-power conference, the purpose of which, as Barnett writes, was "avert a war at all costs" and to "hand over the swag to the criminal in return for a due receipt, in order to save him the trouble of having to rob his victim."[177]

Chamberlain's delusional assumption that Hitler was a man like himself, interested in peace and amenable to reasoned negotiation, coupled to his personal vanity and the culture-wide fear of war, all found in diplomatic discussion a convenient excuse for avoiding hard facts and making hard decisions. As for Hitler, faced with seemingly renewed martial spirit in the French, the British mobilization of their fleet, the apparent reluctance for war among the German people, the doubts of his general staff, and the Czech mobilization of its forces, which complicated his plans for a surprise attack, he "decided," as Craig puts it, "that it would be best to take the cherry in two bites."[178] Hitler sent a conciliatory letter to

Chamberlain in which he said, "I regret the idea of any attack on Czechoslovak territory," and professed himself "ready to give a formal guarantee of the remainder of Czechoslovakia."[179] Thus gulled once again, Chamberlain on September 29 for the third time flew to Germany. As a joke in the British Foreign Office had it, "If at first you don't concede, fly, fly, fly again"[180]

The result, of course, of the negotiations in Munich was the infamous settlement that rewarded subversive violence and aggression and provided for both the patina of international diplomatic legitimacy. Hitler's only concession was to spread the occupation over ten days. Yet Chamberlain wanted a bigger prize—an agreement that would lift the threat of war for good. So he presented Hitler with the following agreement: "We regard the agreement signed last night and the Anglo-German Naval Agreement as symbolic of the desire of our two peoples never to go to war with one another again. We are resolved that the method of consultation shall be the method adopted to deal with any other question that may concern our two countries."[181] Hitler signed this diplomatic persiflage, dismissing Ribbentrop's alarm by saying, "Oh, don't take it so seriously. That piece of paper is of no further significance whatsoever."[182] Chamberlain, that "silly old man," as Hitler described him, on his return to England waved the agreement to the delirious crowd at Heston airport.[183] Before then, General Syrovy had announced to the Czech people their forced acceptance of "terms which are without parallel in history for their ruthlessness. We were deserted. We stood alone."[184]

There is perhaps no greater symbol than the Munich agreement of the deluded faith in negotiated settlements and diplomatic "consultation" to stop an aggressor who will say anything and sign anything in the pursuit of aims he is ready to accomplish by force. Amid all the acclaim for Chamberlain's achievement, there were those in England who saw what a disaster the Munich agreement was. Duff Cooper, who resigned in protest from the Cabinet, clearly identified in his farewell speech the central problem of Chamberlain's approach: "The Prime Minister has believed in addressing Herr Hitler through the language of sweet reasonableness. I have believed that he was more open to the language of the mailed fist."[185] And Churchill prophesized in the House of Commons the consequences of Chamberlain's delusions and the "total, unmitigated defeat" they had wrought: "And do not suppose that this is the end. This is only the beginning of the reckoning. This is only the first sip, the first foretaste of a bitter cup which will be proffered to us year by year unless, by a supreme recovery of moral health and martial vigour, we rise again and take our stand for freedom as in the olden time."[186]

Hitler soon proved the truth of Churchill's prophecy. The Führer made it clear that the Munich agreement meant nothing in the face of a newly assertive Germany bent on recovering its children stranded outside its borders: "It would be a good thing," he said in a speech on October 9, "if in Great Britain people would gradually drop certain airs which they have inherited from the Versailles epoch. We cannot tolerate any longer *the tutelage of governesses.* Inquiries of British politicians concerning the fate of Germans within the frontiers of the Reich, or of others belonging to the Reich, are not in place."[187] This reference to Germans "belonging to the Reich," as Niall Ferguson points out, "implied a German empire stretching from the Rhine to the Volga," something far beyond what British statesmen thought to be Hitler's demands.[188] Consistent with this ominous warning, in March 1939 the German Army marched into Prague without resistance, and Czechoslovakia was no more, its 40 divisions gone, its armament industry in Hitler's hands, and its borders with Poland now filled with German troops. Even then, Chamberlain voiced his intention to substitute "the method of discussion for the method of force in the settlement of differences."[189] The Versailles settlement was now a dead letter, and the next phase of Germany's resurrection from the humiliation of defeat—the conquest of Poland— would soon begin.

And why not? Against the fears of his general staff, who knew Germany was not yet ready for a war with France and England, Hitler had three times put all his chips on the table—in the Rhineland, in Austria, and in Czechoslovakia—and all three times he had bluffed the Allies into folding their better hands. Thus Chamberlain's warning, after the destruction of Czechoslovakia, that "any attempt to dominate the world by force was one which the Democracies must resist," while popular at home, was met with contempt by Hitler, who saw England's guarantee of Poland's independence as a weak bluff, since it was backed up by half-hearted measures unlikely to deter Hitler, and had been made only because England thought that Poland was in no danger from Germany.[190] "Even after Prague," Kagan writes, "and the shift to a policy of deterrence in the political and military spheres Chamberlain continued to employ appeasement by offering economic and colonial concessions. Small wonder that Hitler never seems to have taken his opponents' warnings seriously. As he laid plans for the attack on Poland he discounted the danger from the leaders of Britain and France. 'I saw them at Munich,' he said. 'They are little worms.'"[191]

As always, Churchill has drawn the proper moral of the disaster of Munich and its naïve reliance on an idealism divorced from the tragic reality of human nature:

> The Sermon on the Mount is the last word in Christian ethics. Everyone respects the Quakers. Still, it is not on these terms that Ministers assume their responsibilities of guiding States. Their duty is first so to deal with other nations as to avoid strife and war and to eschew aggression in all its forms, whether for nationalistic or ideological objects. But the safety of the State, the lives and freedom of their own fellow-countrymen, to whom they owe their position, make it right and imperative in the last resort, or when a final and definite conviction has been reached, that the use of force should not be excluded.[192]

Fear, misguided idealism, and shortsighted national interests had paved the way for the most destructive war in history, one whose victory ultimately rested as much with luck and Hitler's mistakes as with the heroic efforts and sacrifices of the Allies. Hard upon this struggle, moreover, came the Cold War and the confrontation with an expansionary, nuclear-armed Soviet Union that the war had turned into a superpower, a conflict that risked human civilization itself. Political freedom was indeed saved from fascism, but at the cost of horrors the effects of which still shape our world today

England's Response

In his famous "Sinews of Peace" speech delivered in Fulton, Missouri, in 1946, Churchill said, "There never was a war in all history easier to prevent by timely action than the one which has just desolated such great areas of the globe. It could have been prevented in my belief without the firing of a single shot." Churchill was speaking of the period before 1935, when Germany's serial violations of the Versailles Treaty were met with appeasement rather than resistance. But after 1935, too, the war could have been prevented, though not "without firing a single shot." Just starting with the militarization of the Rhineland in 1936, when 36,000 German troops confronted 76 French and 21 Belgian divisions, we know that Hitler was bluffing, and by his own admission the Germans would have had to "withdraw with our tails between our legs" had France resisted.[193] A more powerful German Army enforced the *Anschluss,* yet the invasion of Austria was beset with difficulties: some army units weren't assembled on schedule, and the Second Panzer Division arrived 12 hours late, out of gas and dependent on tourist guides for maps, while abandoned vehicles and Panzer tanks, as many as 70 percent of the latter in some places, lined the roads.[194] "The German war machine," Churchill wrote later, "had lumbered falteringly over the frontier and come to a standstill."[195] These miscues suggest that Hitler's military still needed some fine-tuning if it was going to confront two major powers simultaneously.

As for Czechoslovakia, if England and France had supported the Czechs the Germans would have had a hard fight, particularly if the Poles intervened, let alone the Soviets.[196] The Czechs, Churchill pointed out, had "a million and a half men armed behind the strongest fortress line in Europe, and equipped by a highly organized and powerful industrial machine," including the Skoda works, "the second most important arsenal in Central Europe." The productive capacity of the Skoda works after they fell into German hands was nearly equal to the production of all British arms factories combined.[197] In the west, 56 French and Belgium divisions faced eight German divisions and would have easily broken through the Siegfried line, which in the summer of 1938 was not even a third finished. According to historian Williamson Murray, if the Allies had resisted the invasion of Czechoslovakia, "Germany would have faced overwhelming Allied superiority . . . [T]he results would have been inevitable and would have led to the eventual collapse of the Nazi regime at considerably less cost" than that of World War II.[198]

Yet such "what if" questions miss the point. Wars are won not just by material superiority, but by determination and confidence in the rightness of one's cause and beliefs, and in England these had for the previous two decades been sapped by fear, shortsighted interest, and delusional ideals.

The role of national self-interest in the failure to resist Germany's two-decades-long undoing of the Versailles settlement is obvious from the preceding historical narrative. England's traditional wariness of Continental entanglements, along with its distrust of a powerful France, undermined France's attempts to enforce the Versailles Treaty and check a revanchist Germany. Even after Hitler came to power and the brutality of the Nazi regime was obvious, England continued to see advantages for its imperial interests rather than danger in a Germany restored to power, and thus sought an Anglo-German alliance even at the expense of Czechoslovakia's independence. These foreign policy interests were reinforced by economic ones, which needed a prosperous Germany as a trading partner and investment opportunity, and by the Liberal and Labor parties' demands for social welfare expenditures that partially drove the reductions in armaments budgets. Like the city-states of ancient Greece, England and France let parochial self-interest and traditional interstate enmities keep them from recognizing the greater threat posed by Germany.

The Long Shadow of the Great War

The second member of the Thucydidean triad, fear, played an overwhelming role in legitimizing the policy of appeasement and fostering the pacifism that compromised military preparedness. The impact of the Great War on the imagination of Europeans in the Twenties and Thirties can be seen throughout the literature, culture, art, and even the strategic thinking of military planners. This profound effect on the European mind reflected the unprecedented misery and horror of trench warfare, an inferno of mud, rain, rats, vermin, snipers, endless artillery bombardments with shells weighing as much as a ton, the no-man's land infested with rotting corpses, the seemingly pointless charges through coils of barbed wire and storms of machine-gun fire, the shredded and mutilated bodies, and the astronomical numbers of dead and wounded (a million casualties just in the first battle of the Marne in September 1914)—as Churchill would write in his history of the conflict, "When all was over, Torture and Cannibalism were the only two expedients that the civilized, scientific, Christian States had been able to deny themselves: and these were of doubtful utility."[199]

These horrors were documented and publicized in numerous novels, plays, poems, and memoirs throughout the postwar period. In 1927 15 books about the war were published in England, in 1928 21, and in 1929 29. One of the most influential novels was Erich Maria Remarque's *All Quiet on the Western Front,* published in 1929, the same year that saw Robert Graves's *Goodbye to All That* and Ernest Hemingway's *A Farewell to Arms.* Though written by a German, *All Quiet on the Western Front* became an international bestseller, selling a million copies in Germany and in translation another million in France, England, and the United States, where it was turned into a film in 1930, winning the Oscar for best picture.[200] Even more war novels and memoirs, testifying to the fascination with the Great War and its horrors, followed the novel's success. These "trench reminiscences," Barnett writes, "told much the same story: of idealism turning into sour disillusion, of the futility of the fighting, of the obscenity of death and mutilation on a modern battlefield, of the terrors of battle."[201] The effect of these works and the terrifying experiences they documented was to discredit not just the Great War but *all* war. In the critical period after 1928, when another war was becoming a real possibility, these books "had an immediate relevance to the present and the future. What began as an epitaph ended as a warning. As a warning, the war books seemed to say that war was so terrible and futile that the British ought to keep out of another one at any cost."[202] As Prime Minister Stanley Baldwin said of the British in 1935, "We live under the shadow of the last War and its memories still sicken us."[203] Given this pervasive fear of war, "Never again" became both the epitaph for the war dead and the policy for the future.[204]

The impact of the Great War on the psyches of the victors was manifested not just in a pacifism nourished by fear of modern warfare. British military and defense strategy had been powerfully affected by the bombing of England by German air attacks during the Great War. From 1914 to 1916, Zeppelin attacks across England killed 500 and wounded nearly 1,300. In May 1917, German Gotha planes bombed a shopping arcade in Folkestone, killing 95 people, and a week later destroyed London's Liverpool Station, leaving 162 dead. In December of that year, Gotha bombers dropped ten tons of incendiary bombs on London.[205] Long after the war, many in England still remembered huddling in cellars or stifling London Underground stations, or the evacuation of towns like Hull and Hythe. These attacks had brutally revealed the novel reality of modern total war, in which civilians now were objects of sudden attack from the skies. For the English in particular, the traditional security that came from being an island protected by its powerful navy evaporated. Given this new devastating threat, military planners became obsessed with a "knock-out blow" enemy bombers could inflict on England by destroying its industrial capacity and so demoralizing its citizens "that they would insist upon an armistice," as the Committee of Imperial Defence reported as early as 1922.[206] The war would be over before land forces could even come to grips with the enemy army.

This fear of sudden death and destruction from the air reflected not just the memories of Gotha bomber and Zeppelin attacks during the Great War but also the theories of military strategists, such as Sweden's K. A. Bratt, whose *That Next War* (English ed. 1930) predicted the "knock-out blow" achieved by bombing population centers; Italy's Giulio Douhet, whose *The Command of the Air* (1931) argued for the military supremacy of air power and aerial bombardment of the enemy's homeland; and England's Lionel Charlton, whose *War from the Air* (1935) likewise discussed the strategic bombing of cities and factories. These professional views on the superiority of strategic bombing were popularized in the months before Munich by Charles Lindbergh, an international celebrity and aviation guru since his famous trans-Atlantic flight in 1927. His visits to Germany's aircraft factories in 1936 had convinced him "that German air strength is greater than that of all other European countries combined." In the days before Chamberlain's outreach to Germany, Lindbergh met with various British

Air Force officials, whom he counseled "to avoid war at almost any cost" since "the German Air Force could 'flatten out cities like London, Paris, and Prague.'" In this view, Lindbergh was confirming the exaggerated estimates of German air strength already made by the British Air Ministry.[207] Such speculations reflected and reinforced the received wisdom that there was no defense against aerial bombardment since "the bomber will always get through," the famous formulation of Prime Minister Stanley Baldwin in 1932: "I think it is well also for the man in the street to realize that there is no power on earth that can protect him from being bombed. Whatever people may tell him, the bomber will always get through."[208] Speculation seemingly became reality five years later during the Spanish Civil War, when the Germans bombed Guernica, a town of no military significance, killing 1,654 civilians and destroying the city center.

In 1938, Irish poet W. B. Yeats in "Lapis Lazuli" memorably captured this widespread mood of impending destruction: "For everybody knows or else should know/That if nothing drastic is done/Aeroplane and Zeppelin will come out,/Pitch like King Billy bomb-balls in/Until the town lie beaten flat."[209] Yeats's lines reflect how thoroughly these nightmare scenarios imagined by politicians and military leaders circulated throughout the public's consciousness. In the mid-Thirties Major-General J.F.C. Fuller described the imagined effects of one air raid on London: "London for several days will be one vast raving Bedlam, the hospitals will be stormed, traffic will cease, the homeless will shriek for help, the city will be a pandemonium. What of the Government at Westminster? It will be swept away by an avalanche of terror. Then will the enemy dictate its terms."[210] Various projections of civilian casualties added to the imagined horror. Churchill, trying to goad his country into spending money on armaments, in 1934 estimated in a speech in the House of Commons that 30,000 to 40,000 people would be killed or injured in 7 to 10 days of bombing, and 3 to 4 million would evacuate the city.[211] A few years later, military experts predicted that in a war with Germany, the Germans "would launch an attack that would last for sixty days, producing casualties of 600,000 dead and a million injured. Other estimates added millions suffering from psychological disorders."[212]

Popular culture fed on this fear, providing graphic details in films like *Things to Come* (1936), based on a novel by H. G. Wells, in which the destruction of London is the prelude to the end of civilization. At least 80 "next-war" novels were published in Britain between the world wars, many imagining apocalyptic destruction wrought by aerial bomb and gas attacks.[213] And pacifists found in these ghoulish predictions fodder for their arguments for disarmament. During the 1933 Oxford Union debate on the motion "that this House will in no circumstances fight for its King and Country," the philosopher C.E.M. Joad, author of the pacifist manifesto *Why War?* (1936), in his speech supporting the motion "described a future war in which bombers would attack Britain within twenty minutes of the outbreak; aerial defenses would be useless since 'a single bomb can poison every living thing in an area three quarters of a square mile.'"[214] One of the most influential pacifist tracts of the period, philosopher Bertrand Russell's *Which Way to Peace* (1936), likewise made liberal use of such predictions, painting lurid scenes of destruction caused by thermite bombs, which "will cause rivers of molten steel, and water will be powerless to extinguish the fires produced by it"; or by gas like Lewisite, which "poisons the burns by means of the arsenic which is one of its constituents," and is "so poisonous that fifty bombers, given perfect conditions, could carry enough of it to poison all London and its suburbs."[215]

Years later, Harold Macmillan would write during the Cold War, "We thought of air warfare in 1938 rather as people think of nuclear warfare today."[216] Indeed, it was the seeming liberation from this fear of apocalyptic destruction from the air that contributed to the joyous relief greeting Neville Chamberlain on his return from Munich—"I find an immense sense of *physical* relief," Harold Nicolson wrote in his diary, "in that I shall not be afraid tonight of the German bombs"—and that had figured into the discussions preceding Chamberlain's overtures to Hitler.[217] Before the trip to Berchtesgaden, General Edmund Ironside counseled Chamberlain that England could not "stand up against German air bombing," an assessment with which the Air Staff concurred.[218] In his own report to the Cabinet after his meeting with Hitler at Godesberg, Chamberlain had touched on this general fear: "That morning he had flown up the river over London. He had imagined a German bomber flying the same course. He had asked himself what degree of protection we could afford to the thousands of homes he had seen stretched out below him, and he had felt that we were in no position to justify waging a war today in order to prevent a war hereafter."[219] He also exploited the same fear in his talks with the French Minister of War, Édouard Daladier, predicting a "rain of bombs" that would fall on Paris if war broke out.[220] It is understandable that ordinary people in England would be joyfully relieved that such horrors had been avoided, and that they would not need the trenches, gas masks, air-raid drills, evacuation plans, antiaircraft batteries, and sandbags they had been feverishly preparing during these critical times. But statesmen have a larger responsibility to see beyond present fears and take measures to defend against the threats that have created the fear rather than let emotion dictate policy.

The belief that a country could not defend itself against bombers and that aerial bombing could traumatize a people and degrade their industrial capacity, thus delivering a swift "knock-out blow," had deleterious affects on England's military planning. For some politicians and strategists, a powerful air force, whether as an offensive or defensive weapon, in conjunction with the navy's command of the seas, was seen as enough of a deterrent that an expeditionary army was unnecessary: in 1937 during rearmament discussions, the Cabinet "had in mind the proposition that air forces would be the most powerful factors in the future and therefore it might not be wise to spend too much on our land forces at the expense of air forces."[221] Such assumptions rationalized cutbacks in money for the army, at the same time supporting the traditional British abhorrence of committing troops on the Continent, a reluctance seemingly confirmed by the enormous casualties suffered in the Great War. "To the British," Barnett writes, "re-armament came to seem almost a question of air power alone. Cabinet discussion tacitly assumed that the next war, if it came, would take the form of a direct, almost private duel between the British and German air forces; the implications of another decisive land battle in the west, of which the French would bear the brunt, were largely ignored."[222] The malign consequences of this thinking were apparent in 1940 when France and the Low Countries quickly fell to German land forces, the paltry British Expeditionary Force was barely saved from complete destruction at Dunkirk, and the Luftwaffe was now based closer to England and thus was able to inflict the bombardment that many in England had long feared.[223]

This fear, which for over a decade permeated British society, partly explains the exaggerations of and misunderstandings about German air power that justified these policies. In reality, the Luftwaffe was developed not primarily for strategic bombing but as a tactical force in support of ground forces; thus, "such bombers as they had and were building lacked the range to be effective against Britain from German bases and were vulnerable to attacks from fighters. The fighter escorts that might have protected them had even shorter ranges."[224] The problems the RAF identified for its own bombers' ability to inflict significant damage on Germany—distance, weather, target-finding, and aiming—were often ignored when estimating Germany's capabilities for bombing England. As late as July 1938, the Air Staff was projecting a daily average of 600 tons of bombs Germany could drop on England, a bombing rate and amount actually achieved only briefly in 1941 despite the use of closer bases in France and the Low Countries.[225] In actuality, the German bombing of England during the war, including attacks from V-1 and V-2 rockets, however devastating for the victims, came nowhere close to inflicting the apocalyptic damage imagined for years by novelists and politicians alike, let alone a quick "knock-out blow." And what damage that was inflicted came at a high cost to the attackers in pilots and planes.

The Pacifist Delusion

This general culture-wide fear of modern total war reinforced two influential ideas about international relations and human flourishing that had been developing for centuries in the West: pacifism and internationalism. These ideas were interconnected: to achieve peace and abolish war, national interests and aims had to be subordinated to transnational institutions and international laws that could monitor and deter belligerent states.

Before World War I, pacifism was found predominantly among evangelical Protestant sects, such as Baptists and Mennonites. A more significant influence for the secular pacifist movement was Leo Tolstoy's anarchic and eccentrically Christian pacifism set out in his tract "What I Believe" (1885), for it legitimized pacifism outside the Orthodox Christian tradition and linked pacifism to the restructuring of social institutions necessary before war could disappear.[226] Also important were organizations such as the London Peace Society, which, like Tolstoy, whom it called "the foremost and most uncompromising Peace advocate in the world," believed in societal transformation to abolish not just war but social ills such as alcoholism, slavery, prostitution, and brutal imprisonment.[227] Significantly for the interwar period we are examining, these organizations focused on establishing international organizations and laws that used arbitration codified in treaties to diffuse conflict, at the same time that they agitated for disarmament. Finally, equally important for the social and political mood that facilitated policies of appeasement in the Thirties were the socialist and labor movements. While not absolute pacifists—capitalistic imperialism was unlikely to be overthrown without force—these movements saw war between states as a violation of their universalistic ideal of human brotherhood and an expression of capitalism's inherent corruption. "Only when countries adopt a Socialist form of government," said British Labour Party leader George Lansbury in 1937, "will the world be finally secure for peace."[228]

After the Great War, the gruesome scale of its destructiveness, graphically documented in the many novels and memoirs mentioned earlier, gave impetus to pacifism by seemingly confirming the pressing need to eliminate war and thus prevent a repeat of the horrors that had been instigated by arms manufacturers and jingoistic nationalists. George Orwell commented on the pacifism and antimilitarism pervasive in the postwar period, particularly among those who were too young to have fought: "Ours was the one-eyed pacifism that is peculiar to sheltered countries with strong navies. For years after the war, to have any knowledge of or interest in military matters, even to know which end of a gun the bullet comes out of, was suspect in 'enlightened' circles. 1914–1918 was written off as a meaningless slaughter, and even the men who had been slaughtered were held to be in some way to blame."[229] Various organizations sprang up to channel this sentiment, such as the British No More War Movement, for which Bertrand Russell wrote an essay in 1922 entitled "The Prevention of War." In it Russell counseled people to be a "leavening" influence by signing pledges to "to take no part" in any war.[230] The War Resistors International was another such group. Its membership included internationally famed physicist Albert Einstein, who in 1928 advised people "not to participate in any war, for any reason."[231] Another significant organization was the Peace Pledge Union, founded by Anglican clergyman Dick Sheppard, which numbered around 100,000 members shortly after its creation in 1936: "The PPU had a formidable array of sponsors including a retired general . . . a number of persons prominent in the literary and artistic worlds, an array of dignitaries from both the established church and the nonconformist bodies, and leading representatives of the World War I generation of war resisters alongside veterans of that conflict." There were 800 local chapters of the PPU and a weekly newspaper, *Peace News*.[232] All together, there were 19 major pacifist organizations active in England during the Thirties.[233]

Though embodying a variety of views on the legitimacy of force and the circumstances in which war might be necessary, these pacifist movements shared some general ideas that affected public opinion and government policy in the interwar period: they distrusted free-market capitalism and its ethos of competition; an imperialism seen as an extension of capitalism's need for new markets and resources to exploit; and a patriotism that fostered jingoism and militarism, which in turn empowered and profited the arms industry, all of which fomented war. And most pacifists believed in transnational organizations and international law as the way to correct these evils by enforcing disarmament in order to create global peace and prosperity. This was the general philosophy of the influential League of Nations Union, created three days before the Armistice in 1918. By its peak in 1931, the Union had over 400,000 paid-up members and an annual income of 40,000 pounds, making it "the most substantial peace association in history."[234]

The notion that disarmament was the key to peace was widespread between the world wars, reflecting the notion that an arms race created by "merchants of death" had caused the Great War. In 1914, H. G. Wells had linked the manufacture of armaments to the lust for profits on the part of the weapons industry, decrying the "incalculable folly in permitting private men to make a profit out of the dreadful preparations for war."[235] In 1926, a group of international writers and intellectuals, including Wells and Bertrand Russell, signed a petition demanding "some definite step toward complete disarmament and the demilitarization of the mind of civilized nations."[236] This notion that peace would follow disarmament was a major principle of the Labor Party, whose leader Clement Attlee said in 1935, "Our policy is not one of seeking security through rearmament, but through disarmament."[237]

Here we see concentrated all the false knowledge and received wisdom of the previous decades, also evident in the ideas of Neville Chamberlain and the other appeasers: the demonizing of the Versailles Treaty as an act of irrational revenge against Germany; the faith in unilateral disarmament as the way to create peace; and the delusional view of human nature—even for dictators clear about their aggressive aims—as essentially rational, peace-loving, and fair-minded, and thus amenable to the negotiated settlement of conflict and appeasement of grievances.

In short, these pacifist movements contributed to the culture-wide failure of nerve and disaffection with the British political, economic, and social order after the Great War, while fostering a doomed faith in international institutions, multilateral diplomacy, and negotiated settlements as the way to create peace. Winston Churchill made the connection between pacifism and this malaise in 1936: "We view with the strongest reprehension activities like those of [Labor Party leader] Mr. Lansbury and Canon [Dick] Sheppard, who are ceaselessly trying to dissuade the youth of this country from joining its defensive forces, and seek to impede and discourage the military preparations which the state of the world forces upon us."[240] Churchill could have added to his list C.E.M. Joad, who in 1933 counseled "the inauguration of an intensive campaign to induce the maximum number of young people to announce

their refusal to fight in any war between nations."[241] This alienation of many British citizens from their own country in turn
helped to bring about the disastrous policy of appeasement.

The Internationalist Utopia

The disaffection of the British public also reflected a widespread notion that nationalism and patriotism, along with the
old balance-of-power foreign policies, had led to the First World
War. Thus the Enlightenment dream of a transnational organization that created and enforced international laws to which
states were subjected was reinvigorated as the way to prevent
a new war and create global peace. Such a belief in turn
reflected the notion that human nature and civilization were
progressing away from the violence and disorder fostered by
irrational superstitions, such as ethnic or nationalist loyalties,
to a world in which the essential rationality of human nature
would be liberated and thus able to create a more stable and
just universal social and political order. Immanuel Kant articulated this ideal in his influential 1795 essay "Perpetual Peace,"
which laid out a series of "articles" that could achieve this goal,
such as a "federation of free states" that would form a "pacific
alliance . . . different from a treaty of peace . . . inasmuch as it
would for ever terminate all wars, whereas the latter only fin-
ishes one."[242]

Although Kant acknowledged the difficulties of such a project, not the least being that such a federation would still have
to depend on nation-states with sovereign power,[243] at the end
of his essay he expressed the optimism that would character-
ize the subsequent two centuries of this idealism founded on
the belief in human progress fostered by reason:

> If it is a duty, if the hope can even be conceived, of realizing,
> though by an endless progress, the reign of public right—per-
> petual peace, which will succeed to the suspension of hostil-
> ities, hitherto named treaties of peace, is not then a chimera,

but a problem, of which time, probably abridged by the uni-
formity of the progress of the human mind, promises us the
solution.[244]

This vision became increasingly attractive in the interwar period,
when the rise of fascism's brand of militaristic nationalism
threatened another world war, which perhaps explains the
appearance of an English translation of Kant's essay in 1932.
As American Nicholas Murray Butler, president of the Carnegie
Endowment for International Peace, wrote in his introduction
to that translation, "The most pressing single problem before
the world of today is that of establishing and securing international peace by placing it upon a foundation of international
understanding, international appreciation, and international
cooperation."[245]

This revival of internationalism had decades of earlier efforts
to build on. In the nineteenth century various multinational
treaties had been signed that institutionalized the notion of
international cooperation as the means for creating peace and
order or for regulating war once it broke out. The First Geneva
Convention (1864) sought to establish laws for the humane
treatment of sick and wounded during conflict on land; the
Second (1906) did the same for naval engagements. In 1929,
the Third covered the treatment of prisoners of war. More significant were The Hague Conventions, the aims of which were
more ambitious: "the maintenance of the general peace" and
"the friendly settlement of international disputes," aims that
followed the recognition of a supposed "solidarity which unites
the members of the society of civilized nations" and their alleged
shared desire for "extending the empire of law, and of strengthening the appreciation of international justice," as the Preamble to the First Hague Convention (1899) put it. To achieve
this goal, the Convention called for the establishment of an
international Court of Arbitration. In addition, restrictions
were placed on aerial bombardment, the use of poison gas,

and exploding bullets. The Second Hague Convention (1907) expanded these restrictions to include practices and armaments specific to naval warfare. The restrictions on armaments were an important goal of these agreements, for as Tsar Nicholas II, who convened the convention, put it, "the accelerating arms race" was "transforming the armed peace into a crushing burden that weighs on all nations and, if prolonged, will lead to the very cataclysm it seeks to avert."[246]

This process of ever more ambitious multinational agreements designed to limit war intersected with widespread pacifist sentiment to create in 1928 the Kellogg-Briand Pact, eventually signed by 49 nations, including the future Axis powers, Germany, Japan, and Italy. By the terms of this agreement, the contracting parties "condemn recourse to war for the solution of international controversies, and renounce it, as an instrument of national policy in their relations with one another," and "agree that the settlement or solution of all disputes or conflicts ... shall never be sought except by pacific means."[247] This treaty—which in three years Japan would violate with impunity when it attacked Manchuria—seemingly validated the existence of the League of Nations, at whose conclaves in Geneva world leaders uplifted "the multitude with sermons praising the reconciliation of ancient enemies and the growing unity of mankind." Meanwhile, the League of Nations Union "busied itself in the schools, assuring the children that there could never be another war, because the League would 'stop it.'"[248]

All these agreements were attempts, through rationally devised and codified restrictions, to mitigate the effects of war, if not eliminate it altogether. They assumed that people universally were reasonable and capable rationally of determining their true interests, these being a peace and prosperity generated by global free trade. Norman Angell, in his influential *The Great Illusion* (1910), argued that in a world united by trade, finance, and industry, nationalism and the pursuit of national interests through war were irrational because they were unprofitable. This argument took for granted, however, that all people were indeed rational and through tutelage or experience were able to cultivate their reason and recognize their true interests, which turned out to be those of liberal-democratic Europeans. From this perspective, war was, in Angell's terms, a "failure of understanding" to be corrected by improving people's thinking: "The world of the Crusades," Angell wrote, "and of heretic burning . . . was not a badly-meaning, but a badly-thinking world. . . . We emerged from it by correcting a defect in understanding; we shall emerge from the world of political warfare or armed peace in the same way."[249]

This way of thinking took it for granted that avoiding conflict and achieving peace and prosperity through commerce were the primary interests and desired aims of all states and their peoples: "International law and order," historian Arnold Toynbee wrote in 1935, "were in the true interests of the whole of mankind," while "the region of violence in international affairs was an anti-social desire which was not even in the ultimate interests of the citizens of the handful of states that officially professed this benighted and anachronistic creed."[250] Yet the whole history of mankind demonstrated that war was not a distortion of a pacific, rational human nature, an anomaly reflecting the temporary ascendancy of the irrational or a cabal of evil rulers, but rather an instrument by which states pursued their various perceived interests, whether these be rational or irrational, interests moreover shared by a critical mass of the people who did the fighting and dying.

In short, history demonstrates that, as Plato's Cleinias put it in the *Laws*, peace is "only a name; in reality every city is in a natural state of war with every other."[251] However, the Great War, rather than proving that truth, seemed to many in the postwar period to prove that war was indeed a correctable anomaly, contrary to humanity's true interests; and also to confirm urgently the need for even more expansive international institutions, agreements, and laws that could rein in irrational nationalist passions and the "merchants of death," the arms manufacturers who had, in the words of American philosopher John Dewey, "waxed fat and bloated."[252]

The creation of the League of Nations was directed toward this goal, but as Kagan writes, it "represented a flight from reality. A product of the idealistic Kantian tradition of internationalism, it was introduced into a world of nationalistic states, unwilling to abandon any sovereignty." Moreover, "it provided no certain mechanism for peacefully adjudicating quarrels between states nor for bringing force to bear to maintain peace or prevent aggression."[253] Article 16 of the League Covenant did direct the League Council to recommend "what effective military, naval, or air force the Members of the League shall severally contribute to the armed forces to be used to protect the covenants of the League." This provision, however, was interpreted by many nations, particularly those with small militaries, as a nonbinding option rather than a contractual obligation.[254] Enforcement of League decisions thus rested on the military forces of a great power, as Churchill told the House of Commons in 1935: if the League "is now a reality and is now gripping all men's minds" rather than remaining "an academic apparition," it is because "there has been behind it . . . the Royal Navy."[255]

But if a great power was unwilling—increasingly likely in an era of disarmament, economic straits, and widespread pacifism—to provide the force necessary to back up a League decision, then any League sanction remained diplomatic bluster, as the Japanese invasion of Manchuria in 1931 demonstrated. This dependence on a great power to enforce militarily a League sanction was even more obvious in 1935, when England refused to use its Mediterranean fleet to blockade the Suez and thwart Mussolini's designs on Ethiopia. As we have seen, ineffective sanctions were imposed instead, and as Churchill later snorted, "The League of Nations therefore proceeded to the rescue of

Abyssinia [Ethiopia] on the basis that nothing must be done to hamper the invading Italian armies."[256] The Spanish Civil War, in which Germany and Italy blatantly armed and fought for the Nationalists, and British shipping was attacked in international waters, further confirmed the impotence of the League.

The reliance on a multinational organization like the League of Nations to keep and restore order through diplomatic discussion and negotiation suffers from other weaknesses. Diplomacy and negotiation are vulnerable to the potential bad faith of those doing the negotiating. As we saw earlier, diplomacy can be used by an aggressor to mislead an enemy or to camouflage his true intent in order to buy time. Or an aggressor can simply stop talking, or he can leave an international organization once it no longer serves his interests, just as Hitler pulled Germany out of the disarmament conference and the League of Nations in 1933.[257]

Also, despite the internationalist rhetoric about transcending state power and nationalist interests in order serve the global community, the League was dominated by the great powers, which directed the League's business in accordance with their national interests: as an Italian delegate to the League wrote in 1935, he "never saw a dispute of any importance settled otherwise than by an agreement between the Great Powers," the League's procedures being "a system of detours, all of which lead to one or other of these two issues: agreement or disagreement between Great Britain, Italy, France and Germany."[258] International idealism, in short, fails because the primary objective of a sovereign nation is to pursue its interests, not to adhere to some abstract, universal ideal of right or justice. As George Washington said, "It is a maxim founded on the universal experience of mankind; that no nation can be trusted farther than it is bounded by its interests."[259]

The great failure of internationalist idealism and its pacifist corollary, a failure that helped make possible the policy of appeasement, derived from delusional beliefs about human nature as universally rational, kind, peace-loving, and desirous of the same goods, thus rendering divisive nationalist identities the avatars of a benighted past that humanity was progressing beyond. Labor Party leader and twice Prime Minister Ramsay MacDonald illustrated these beliefs: he "really was persuaded," diplomat Robert Vansittart wrote, "that 'our true nationality is mankind,'" that "men were naturally good," and that the human race was "eternally moving in a great surge towards righteousness."[260] So too Woodrow Wilson, who said on America's entry into the Great War, "National purposes have fallen more and more into the background; and the common purpose of enlightened mankind has taken their place."[261]

This dismissal of nationalism that underlay internationalist sentiment, however, was not founded on historical experience or a discovered truth about human nature, but rather was a philosophical idea developed in the Enlightenment and reflective of its assumptions about a universal, rational human nature more essential than local ethnic or national identities. However, the mass of people continued to find their identities and loyalties not in cosmopolitan internationalism but in their own particular culture and way of life shared with people like themselves. In 1918, G. K. Chesterton challenged the internationalist assumptions of a universal human identity supposedly created by the new technologies of global communication:

> What we call the modern world is more ancient than we thought; and its simplicities will survive its complexities. Men care more for the rag that is called a flag than for the rag that is called a newspaper. Men care more for Rome, Paris, Prague, Warsaw, than for the international railways connecting these towns; or for the international relations that are often as cold, as mechanical, and as dead as the rails. Nobody has any such ecstatic regard for the mere relations of different peoples to each other, as one would gather from the rhetoric of idealistic internationalism. It is, indeed, desirable that the men should love each other; but always with the recognition of the identity of other

peoples and other men. Now, too much cosmopolitan culture is mere praise of machinery. It turns ultimately upon the point that a telegram can be sent from one end of the earth to the other, irrespective of what is in the telegram.[262]

Indeed, the Great War, in its origins and conduct, had shown the primacy of nationalist loyalties and aspirations over abstract internationalism, whether liberal-capitalist or socialist. And the postwar settlement had acknowledged that primacy in the place it gave to national self-determination, at the same time it created a super-national institution like the League of Nations, whose purpose was to deter and restrain those same nations, many of them newly minted by the war, which would inevitably seek to pursue their interests, necessarily at the expense of other nations. The rise of fascism and its "passionate nation-alism," a phenomenon arising from powerful nationalist emo-tions and mystic ethnic identities, further exposed the feebleness of idealistic internationalism and its faith in a reasonable human nature.[263] Though a socialist sympathetic to internationalism, George Orwell realized the power of passionate nationalism and the necessity of force to resist its malign effects. Speak-ing of novelist H. G. Wells, one of the most well-known inter-nationalists of the times, Orwell wrote in 1941, "He was, and still is, quite incapable of understanding that nationalism, reli-gious bigotry and feudal loyalty are far more powerful forces than what he himself would describe as sanity. Creatures out of the Dark Ages have come marching into the present, and if they are ghosts they are at any rate ghosts which need a strong magic to lay them."[264]

The Triumph of "Unwarrantable self-abasement"

These questionable ideas—pacifism and idealistic internation-alism—were linked to a more general climate of thought and sensibility that helped make possible the policy of appeasement.

This climate was the increasing estrangement, if not active dis-like, that many in England, particularly among the political and cultural elite, felt toward their own country and its insti-tutions, a loss of faith in the goodness of their own way of life that made it more difficult for many to find the will to fight, kill, and die for those beliefs until it was nearly too late. Partly this feeling reflected the interpretation of the Great War as pointless and corrupt slaughter, as popularized in numerous novels and plays; disillusionment with the war, Theodore Dal-rymple writes, implied that "the culture of which this war was a manifestation must be a worthless one too."[265] The rise of communism and socialism, which opposed the democratic lib-eralism and free-market capitalism defining England by the late nineteenth century, attracted many and perforce turned them to some degree against their own country and its insti-tutions. Socialism, moreover, was an internationalist, antina-tionalist creed, and so reinforced the internationalist idealism discussed above.

Anti-imperialism was another movement that for many in England challenged the legitimacy of their country and its empire. The brutal Boer War (1899–1902)—fought not against benighted natives in need of Christian civilization but against fellow European colonists seeking self-determination—cost England 250,000 million pounds and 45,000 dead, and it involved scorched-earth tactics and novel brutalities, such as concen-tration camps, where one in three of those imprisoned died. These harsh realities caused many in England to question the moral integrity of the empire. As Niall Ferguson writes, "it was revulsion against the war's conduct that decisively shifted British politics to the Left in the 1900's, a shift that was to have incal-culable implications for the future of the Empire."[266] An impor-tant manifestation of this revulsion was a growing cynicism about the empire and its ideals, one expressed in J. A. Hob-son's influential *Imperialism: A Study* (1902). Hobson scorned the civilizing mission the Victorians claimed for imperialism, seeing it instead as economic exploitation that fostered great-power competition and ultimately war: "Thus we reach the conclusion that Imperialism is the endeavour of the great controllers of industry to broaden the channel for the flow of their surplus wealth by seeking foreign markets and foreign investments to take off the goods and capital they cannot sell or use at home."[267] A consequence of this "economic parasitism" was militarism, a hypertrophied armaments industry, and ultimately war as the great powers competed to control markets and resources. Hobson joined this anti-imperialism to anti-nationalism, as imperialism and colonialism were the projections of nationalist sentiment into alien territories beyond the nation's borders. Thus his critique bound together the various questionable ideals—anti-nationalism, pacifism, and disarmament—that looked to international institutions as the means for ensuring global peace and prosperity. Finally, the huge human and economic costs of the Great War exacerbated this "crisis of confidence" in the empire, and by the Thirties, the once heroic imperialist had been transformed into cartoonist David Low's caricature Colonel Blimp, the xenophobic war-monger who distrusted democracy and the League of Nations alike.[268]

Loss of faith in the empire, moreover, precipitated for many a loss of faith in England itself, particularly among its cultural and intellectual elites, for whom patriotism became something dangerous and disreputable, what poet and war-veteran Wilfred Owen called "The Old Lie" in his poem "Dulce Et Decorum Est," the most famous piece of literature to come out of the Great War. H. G. Wells, for example, protested against "the teaching of patriotic histories that sustain and carry on the poisonous war-making tradition of the past," and novelist J. B. Priestly considered patriotism "as a mighty force, chiefly used for evil."[269]

Nothing epitomizes this fashionable self-loathing better than the Bloomsbury group, a collection of writers, artists, intellectuals, and various hangers-on that influenced English culture for decades, starting during the Great War. Its philosophy was one of hedonism and loyalty to nothing other than one's own sensibilities and friends, seasoned with scorn for everything normal Englishmen valued, such as patriotism, faith, duty, decorum, self-sacrifice, and whatever else subordinated the self to something larger. This impulse to tear down the Victorian moral edifice was obvious in the work of Lytton Strachey, the draft-dodging guiding genius of the group, particularly his book *Eminent Victorians,* which ridiculed Victorian heroes such as Florence Nightingale and General Charles "Chinese" Gordon, who in 1885 had died in the siege of Khartoum by jihadists. *Eminent Victorians* was published in 1917, and thus was ready to feed the post-war angst, proving itself, as Paul Johnson writes, "far more destructive of the old British values than any legion of enemies."[270]

All of the interwar cultural pathologies that weakened England in the Twenties and Thirties characterized the "Bloomsberries": pacifism, "war guilt," internationalist idealism, hostility to the military, all the delusions that made a policy of appeasement seem not just expedient but a moral imperative. In early 1939, as Hitler's plans to swallow all of Czechoslovakia were becoming obvious, Clive Bell advised "uniting the continent under German leadership" and wanted the "warmonger" critics of Hitler censored.[271] But perhaps nothing better encapsulates the smug and narcissistic idealism of this sensibility than novelist E. M. Forster's famous statement, published in 1939 when a war loomed that would put England's very survival at stake: "If I had to choose between betraying my *country* and betraying my *friend,* I hope I should have the guts to betray my country."[272] This sort of mentality was positively suicidal in the face of the "bands of sturdy Teutonic youths," as Churchill had called them six years earlier, "marching through the streets and roads of Germany, with the light of desire in their eyes to suffer for their Fatherland."[273]

The moral bankruptcy of the Bloomsberries, particularly the distaste for the political and social order that made their freedom and leisure possible, was widespread among England's intellectuals, as George Orwell noted in *The Lion and the Unicorn* (1941): "England is perhaps the only great country whose intellectuals are ashamed of their own nationality. In left-wing circles it is always felt that there is something slightly disgraceful in being an Englishman and that it is a duty to snigger at every English institution." In the critical years before World War II broke out, "left-wingers were chipping away at English morale, trying to spread an outlook that was sometimes squashily [sic] pacifist, sometimes violently pro-Russian, but always anti-British." As a consequence, Orwell points out, the fascist powers judged the English to be "decadent," and this "systematic Blimp-baiting affected even the Blimps themselves and made it harder than it had been before to get intelligent young men to enter the armed forces."[274]

Winston Churchill had said much the same thing some eight years earlier in 1933, when he addressed the Royal Society of St. George: "Our difficulties come from the mood of unwarrantable self-abasement into which we have been cast by a powerful section of our own intellectuals. They come from the acceptance of defeatist doctrines by a large proportion of our politicians. But what have they to offer but a vague internationalism, a squalid materialism, and the promise of impossible Utopias?" Without the will to support one's own country based on a faith in its essential goodness, a policy of appeasement will become attractive, for why should one kill and die for something so reprehensible? This was the moral Churchill went on to draw in the same speech: "Nothing can save England if she will not save herself. If we lose faith in ourselves, in our capacity to guide and govern, if we lose our will to live, then indeed our story is told. If, while on all sides foreign nations are every day asserting a more aggressive and militant nationalism by arms and trade, we remain paralysed by our own theoretical doctrines or plunged into the stupor of after-war exhaustion, then indeed all that the croakers predict will come true, and our ruin will be swift and final."[275]

The "ruin" of which Churchill spoke did not come with World War II, but that victory was followed in a decade by the loss of England's empire and the global dominance and influence it had exercised for over two centuries. Fear, shortsighted national interests, and bad ideas such as idealistic internationalism and pacifism had done their work. Just as the ancient Athenians had lost sight of what they owed to Athens as citizens, seeing their city instead as a dispenser of entitlements, one to be managed and defended by others, so too in England the loss of faith on the part of many Englishmen in the rightness and superiority of their way of life had made it difficult to find the will to resist aggression until they had no choice. And even then, despite the incredible bravery, sacrifice, and endurance shown by the English people, the final victory was a consequence of America's entry into the war and Hitler's disastrous invasion of Russia, where the decisive battles of the war were fought.

The failure, then, of political virtues such as self-sacrifice, duty, and love of one's country—not because science proves they are superior, but because they *are* one's own, and the nation's values of political freedom, tolerance, equality, and the like are better than the alternatives—played its part in the policy of appeasement. The failure of this faith in and affection for one's political community was widespread in the Twenties and Thirties, and its pernicious effects are still with us today. The Austrian novelist Robert Musil, whose interwar epic *The Man Without Qualities* examined this phenomenon, put it in these terms:

> In love as in business, in science as in the long jump, one has to believe before one can win and score, so how can it be

otherwise for life as a whole? However well founded an order may be, it always rests in part on a voluntary faith in it, a faith that, in fact, always marks the spot where the new growth begins, as in a plant; once this unaccountable and uninsurable faith is used up, the collapse soon follows; epochs and empire crumble no differently from business concerns when they lose their credit.[276]

And when a civilization that has lost its faith in its country as something worth killing and dying for, is confronted with one that has a powerful belief in the righteousness and superiority of *its* way of life, then no amount of material power, whether economic or military, can compensate for that loss.

Chapter Three

America and Jihad

The spirit of Munich has by no means retreated into the past;
it was not a brief episode. I even venture to say that the spirit
of Munich is dominant in the twentieth century. The
intimidated civilized world has found nothing to oppose the
onslaught of a suddenly resurgent fang-baring barbarism,
except concessions and smiles. The spirit of Munich is a
disease of the will of prosperous people; it is the daily state of
those who have given themselves over to a craving for
prosperity in every way, to material well-being as the chief
goal of life on earth. Such people—and there are many of
them in the world today—choose passivity and retreat,
anything if only the life to which they are accustomed might
go on, anything so as not to have to cross over to rough
terrain today, because tomorrow, see, everything will be all
right. (But it never will! The reckoning for cowardice will
only be more cruel. Courage and the power to overcome will
be ours only when we dare to make sacrifices.)

ALEXANDER SOLZHENITSYN[1]

The Jihadist Challenge

The "fang-baring barbarism" Solzhenitsyn was alluding
to, the Soviet Union, has passed from history. But a
new threat has arisen to challenge the free West, one
that has been nurtured by the same "spirit of Munich" that at
times had put in doubt the eventual victory over communist

totalitarianism. This new challenge in fact is an old one, a descendent of the West's most powerful historical enemy, Islam, which in the seventh century burst forth from the Arabian peninsula to challenge and eventually destroy the Christian Byzantine empire, and to repeatedly attack Europe for another millennium until the Ottoman army was turned back at Vienna in September 1683. After that defeat, the world's greatest Islamic empire faced serial retreat and piecemeal reduction from a resurgent West and a newly expansionist Russia. For the next three centuries, the European powers that once trembled at the approach of Allah's warriors increasingly dominated the Ottomans and the Middle East until the final "humiliation and disgrace," as Osama bin Laden called it, came after World War I, when Kemal Atatürk's abolishing of the caliphate in 1924 ended thirteen hundred years of Islamic imperial domination.[2]

The magnitude of that historical reversal helped spark an Islamic revival that looked back to the idealized early centuries of Islam and its extraordinary military and cultural hegemony, an achievement wrought by the intensity and doctrinal purity of the Islamic faith. To the Islamists, despite the transient appeal of Western ideas such as socialism, fascism, democracy, or nationalism to some Muslim elites, only a renewal of that religious faith can turn back and reverse the Western dominance of the Islamic world. "From the beginnings of Western penetration in the world of Islam," Bernard Lewis writes, "until our own day, the most characteristic, significant, and original political and intellectual responses to that penetration have been Islamic. They have been concerned with the problems of the faith and the community overwhelmed by infidels."[3] In the view of Islamic revivalist sects such as Wahhabism, Salafism, Deobandism, the Muslim Brothers, and terrorist organizations like al Qaeda, a return to the uncorrupted Islam of the seventh century and a rejection of various un-Islamic Western cultural, social, and political ideas would restore the Islamic world to the preeminence it deserved as the caretakers of the true faith. "The last great Muslim empire may have been destroyed," historian Ephraim Karsh writes, "and the caliphate left vacant, but the Islamic imperial dream of world domination has remained very much alive in the hearts and minds of many Muslims."[4] And jihad against the infidel is the traditional means for achieving that domination.

America's first direct encounter with modern jihad came with the Iranian revolution that deposed Shah Mohammed Reza Pahlavi in February 1979 and the kidnapping in November of the U.S. embassy personnel in Tehran. That crisis, along with the *mujahidin* resistance to the Soviet invasion of Afghanistan that began in December 1979, emboldened, legitimized, publicized, and globalized modern jihadism, and seemingly confirmed the superiority of pure religious faith over modern military power. Before then, modern jihad had existed in the writings of Islamist theorists such as Sayyid Qutb, in the various Islamist organizations, such as the Muslim Brothers, that harassed secular Middle Eastern governments, and in the Arab attacks on Israel, where the religious foundations of Palestinian terrorism were obscured for many in the West by nationalist, anti-colonialist, and Marxist rhetoric. After the Iranian revolution, Islamic jihad was poised to expand its dreams of renewed hegemony throughout the world.

The Malign Legacies of Vietnam

The failure of America's appeasing response to the Iranian crisis cannot be understood without first tracing the fallout of the disaster of Vietnam. It should be remembered that the debacle in Southeast Asia was not the consequence of military defeat, but of a political failure of nerve. Under the leadership of General Creighton Abrams, after 1968 American and South Vietnamese forces had rocked the communist North back on its heels and thwarted its subsequent offensives with huge losses of men and materiel. By 1972, as both U.S. Ambassador to South Vietnam Ellsworth Bunker and British adviser Sir Robert Thompson said, the war was as good as won: the guerillas in the South had been neutralized, the countryside was stable, U.S. troops were going home, and the South Vietnamese were in a position to hold their own as long as they continued to have American air support and military resources. When in August 1973 the Democratic-controlled Congress cut off that support and drastically reduced military aid, a North Vietnam armed and backed by the Soviet Union and China overran the South. The cost of snatching defeat from the jaws of victory was of course most grievous for the South Vietnamese: In addition to the 750,000 killed during the war, a million "boat people" fled their so-called liberators, 65,000 political enemies were executed, and another 250,000 died in "reeducation" camps.[5]

For the United States as well, the cost went beyond the more than 58,000 lives lost in achieving a victory that politicians and many voters threw away. The damage to U.S. prestige following the abandonment of an ally for whom much blood and treasure had been sacrificed was enormous. For many allies and enemies alike, America had become what President Richard Nixon feared—a "pitiful, helpless giant" whose weakness would encourage "the forces of totalitarianism and anarchy."[6] The debacle in Vietnam, moreover, seemingly validated the self-loathing, Marxist narrative of America's role in the world that increasingly had come to dominate the media, universities, popular culture, and many in Congress. In this view, rather than a beacon of freedom and a force for global good, the United States was a neo-imperialistic, neo-colonialist rogue state run by a "military-industrial complex" serving capitalist interests that, under the camouflage of resisting communist tyranny, at home crushed dissent and abroad subverted nationalist liberation movements threatening corporate markets and profits. In this climate of opinion, the use of military force to advance U.S. interests and protect national security was politically and morally discredited. These attitudes

comprised the "Vietnam syndrome"—doubt about America's
goodness and power, and fear of casualties and foreign "quag-
mires"— that made the U.S. hesitant to act abroad in support
of its national interests and international commitments, just
as memories of the Great War's carnage had had a "paralyzing
effect" on British generals in the decades before World War II.[7]

This view of U.S. foreign policy, when it was not serving
the leftist agenda, marked as well the resurgence of the "moralizing internationalism" that, as we saw in the previous chapter, had facilitated the appeasement of Nazi Germany. Indeed,
those holding this view were explicitly rejecting, as did many
Englishmen in the Twenties and Thirties, a foreign policy based
on national self-interest and an "amoral" balance of power. In
the United States, liberal idealists associated such foreign policy realism with the despised Richard Nixon's Secretary of State
Henry Kissinger, and blamed it for the debacle in Vietnam and
the depredations of various authoritarian regimes supported
because they were bulwarks against a Soviet international
aggression that many liberals believed realists had exaggerated
or invented. But American reverses and Soviet expansion in
the Seventies showed that a foreign policy based on moral idealism carried significant risks. As Kissinger wrote in his memoirs, "A nation and its leaders much choose between moral
certainty coupled with exorbitant risk, and the willingness to
act on unprovable assumptions to deal with challenges when
they are manageable," action that "carries with it the burden
that it can never be proved whether the sacrifices it demands
are in fact necessary."[8] After Vietnam, a foreign policy of "moral
certainty" was indeed endorsed by many Americans, one that
gratified its adherents' sense of their own moral superiority and
utopian idealism but that also subjected the nation to "exorbitant risk."

This moralizing foreign policy increasingly defined the
Democratic Party and its leaders, such as Senator George
McGovern. After the debacle of McGovern's defeat in the 1972

presidential election, the views and Senate investigations of
Senator Frank Church became the most prominent example
of this moralistic foreign policy. The Democrat from Idaho was
a relentless critic of the war in Vietnam and a fierce advocate
of withdrawal from that conflict, in addition to harboring ambitions to run for President in 1976. In the words of his admir-
ing biographers, Church thought of himself as "a modern-day
political evangelist, infusing the old democratic faith with new
energy, strengthening the moral dimension of public life."[9] The
policies he advocated reflected the revisionist view of American foreign policy sketched above: "The sad truth, [Church]
argued, was that U.S. policies often hinged far less on the real
issues of national security than on inflated views of America's
role abroad, exaggerated Cold War fears, and the desire to
shield powerful interest groups."[10] Church's 1975–76 Senate
investigations into corporate bribery abroad and the domestic
activities of the FBI and the CIA reflected both this narrative
of America's moral failure, and the naïve, quasi-religious idealism that people like Church thought should guide foreign
policy. An "America doped on *hubris,* playing God in the world,"
as one Church associate described the Senator's views, had
manipulated a spurious patriotism and national security fears
in order to magnify the power of the state and curtail individual liberty for the benefit of arms manufacturers and other
corporate hegemons. Central to this assault on freedom was
the CIA, which Church characterized as behaving "like a rogue
elephant rampaging out of control."[11] Anticipating many of the
current criticisms of policies and practices in the war against
jihad, Church believed that the necessarily rough practices
employed in a world of dangerous regimes bent on our destruction harmed the national interest by diminishing America's
image abroad.

In addition to legitimizing this more idealistic view of foreign relations, the Church committee investigations ultimately
led to Congressional legislation and Presidential executive

orders that, while correcting some real abuses, such as domestic counterintelligence programs, in the long term complicated the mission of our intelligence agencies and compromised their effectiveness.[12] Even before Church's hearings, in 1974 Congress passed the Hughes-Ryan Amendment to the Foreign Assistance Act, which required the Director of the CIA to brief eight Congressional committees before undertaking any covert action. A consequence of these briefings was that committee members or staffers leaked details of CIA operations to the press.[13] A few years later, the establishment of the Senate Intelligence Oversight Committee and a similar House version meant that the odds of any planned covert operation remaining secret plummeted even further, given that nearly 200 people were potentially involved in the briefings. President Gerald Ford later noted the inhibiting effect of this possibility: "Rather than risk exposure [in the media] and embarrassment, the intelligence agency will simply decide not to undertake the operation it planned. That's what happened to the CIA."[14]

Other consequences followed the Congressional investigations of the CIA and FBI. In 1976, President Ford signed Executive Order 11905, which added more layers of bureaucratic oversight onto the activities of the national security agencies, and codified in Section 5 a whole host of "restrictions on intelligence activities," including a prohibition of political assassination, hampering further the agency's ability to gather intelligence and take action abroad in defense of America's national security. A more far-reaching consequence of the attack on America's clandestine intelligence-gathering agencies was the Foreign Intelligence Surveillance Act (FISA), passed in 1978. The FISA act required a court order from special FISA judges for the surveillance of foreign agents, physical searches, and monitoring of electronic communications in the United States.[15] The establishment of the FISA court created more difficulties that compromised our intelligence agencies' ability to keep track of hostile agents and activities, as would become clear in the years leading up to 9/11. "The FISA rules," Arthur Herman writes, "would seriously hamper efforts to learn the degree to which foreign espionage services including the KGB—or later, groups like al-Qaeda—were operating within American borders."[16]

The election of Jimmy Carter as President in 1976 put into the White House this new vision of America's place in the world as less reliant on military power and clandestine activities in order to protect the national interest, and more committed to open diplomacy, negotiation, and a moralizing posture in international affairs. The governor of Georgia for only two years before being elected, Carter had little direct experience with foreign policy, but he did have an idealistic view of what should be America's behavior toward other countries, including our enemies. Like the moralizing internationalists of the interwar years, Carter believed in the power of principled example to affect the behavior of other nations, even those bent on our destruction and utterly contemptuous of our political principles. Thus defending and promoting human rights, acting abroad in accord with the principles of the U.S. Constitution, and disarmament became the foundations of his foreign policy, all predicated on an acceptance of American limitations and guilt seemingly validated by the fiasco of Vietnam and the depredations of the CIA, both at home and abroad.

These were the ideas Carter laid out in his inaugural address, where he acknowledged the nation's "recent mistakes," counseled Americans not to "dwell on remembered glory," and reminded his fellow citizens that "even our great nation has its recognized limits" and can only "simply do its best." Conflicting somewhat with this hesitant tone of American retreat— reprised a few years later in the infamous "crisis of confidence" or "malaise" speech— Carter stressed that "our commitment to human rights must be absolute," promised that "we will not behave in foreign places so as to violate our rules and standards here at home," and pledged "perseverance and wisdom in our efforts to limit the world's armaments to those necessary for each nation's own domestic safety."[17] In his memoirs Carter would assert again this fundamental belief in the power of example and fidelity to principle to achieve our foreign policy aims: "To me, the demonstration of American idealism was a practical and realistic approach to foreign affairs, and moral principles were the best foundation for the exertions of American power and influence."[18] Left unexplained was how these lofty goals and the acceptance of America's limits could be squared with international disarmament or advancing human rights, ideals that required some level of interference in the business of other nations; or with keeping America safe in a world where a nuclear-armed aggressive enemy pursued its aims with none of America's inhibitions and with complete indifference to the persuasive power of what we saw as our superior "moral principles."

The impact of Carter's foreign policy idealism and aversion to covert activities became apparent during his presidency. At the CIA, under Director Stansfield Turner, Herman writes, "secrecy as well as human intelligence was passé; openness was the new catchphrase."[19] Covert actions and counterintelligence—the attempt to thwart the enemy's intelligence-gathering operations—were abandoned or severely reduced. Rather than developing human intelligence assets, Turner "concentrated on technical intelligence and attempts to run the intelligence community, ruthlessly disbanding what remained of the clandestine service: 820 positions were abolished, including those of approximately 200 experienced covert operation staffers and more than 311 backup officers and staff in covert action and espionage."[20] Intelligence files were destroyed, and human assets and intelligence networks were abandoned. In addition, Carter issued Executive Order 12036, which expanded the already cumbersome bureaucratic surveillance of the CIA initiated in Gerald Ford's earlier order and increased the number of activities forbidden to the agency.[21]

This neutering of the CIA under Carter accompanied the privileging of human rights and arms reductions over national interests and security in American foreign policy, following the post-Vietnam script that American power and arrogance posed the greatest danger for the United States and the world. Regimes now were to be supported not because they served American interests in countering Soviet aggression, but rather on the basis of their "progressive" posture and anti-colonialist, liberationist rhetoric. The international face of this policy was Carter's United Nations Ambassador Andrew Young, "whose frequent ideological sorties on behalf of radical Third World regimes were sometimes indistinguishable from the pronouncements of Cuban dictator Fidel Castro."[22] While still acknowledging the need to contain the Soviet Union, Carter himself rejected the Cold War view of the communist regime as America's inveterate ideological enemy, announcing in June 1977 that the United States was "now free of that inordinate fear of communism which once led us to embrace any dictator who joined us in that fear."[23] As a consequence, Carter would reduce weapons exports as a means for achieving the utopian aims of universal peace and respect for human rights, aims supposedly compromised by America's numerous past foreign policy sins. More dangerously, he pursued arms control treaties with the Soviet Union at the same time he ordered unilateral cutbacks in American weapons development in the hope the Soviets would reciprocate. However, just as British reductions in armaments were met by clandestine German rearmament even before Hitler came to power, Carter's delays and cancellations of weapons such as the B1 bomber were met with a Soviet military buildup rather than reciprocal reductions.

Such policies may have made some Americans feel righteous and redeemed from the presumed sins of recent history, but they were as contradictory and dangerous to American security and interests as the similar ideals were in England during the interwar years. For one thing, if America was really serious about promoting human rights, then it was difficult to see how it could achieve that aim without serious interference in the affairs of other nations by linking U.S. economic or other support to those nations' performance on improving human rights, or ultimately employing force to prevent actions by the bloodiest offenders, which requires a strong military capability and the will to use it.

Yet wasn't this preaching about human rights just another version of American arrogance based on its sense of moral superiority, the crime of "playing God in the world" that according to liberals lay behind earlier foreign policy misadventures? And if military force and covert action were off the table, what further weapons did the U.S. have to compel illiberal regimes to change their ways? Non-lethal sanctions and trade restrictions might be effective with allies dependent on American support, or with international pariahs like Rhodesia or South Africa, but absent the credible threat of force, powerful regimes like China and the Soviet Union, along with their satellites the most egregious violators of human rights, would simply brush aside these attempts at pressuring them into liberalizing and denounce them as "imperialist" interference. Such a human rights policy, dependent on moral suasion and sanctions, as we still see today 30 years later with nations such as China and Iran, resembles the laws in the Spanish proverb: They are cobwebs that catch the fly and let the hawk go free. Finally, Carter's focus on human rights created the perception that the United States had abandoned the policy of containment regarding the Soviet Union, and so smaller countries faced with communist aggression could no longer depend on American support unless they conformed to American moral standards no matter how dangerous or inappropriate those might be for any particular country's security—or for America's own security and interests.

The Iranian Revolution Begins

What Henry Kissinger called the "disintegration of the Central Intelligence Agency," coupled with Carter's moralizing foreign policy, contributed to America's disastrous response to the Iranian revolution, the fall of the Shah, and the kidnapping of the embassy staff in 1979.[24] Most obviously, the dearth of clandestine intelligence assets in Iran left our government in the dark about the true import of the brewing resistance to the Shah and the fragility of his regime, not to mention the religious origins of the Islamic revolution. This failure of intelligence was worsened by the absence in the CIA of experts on Iran; during the crisis of 1977–78, only two analysts were working on Iran, and they were not Persian specialists.[25] More important, Carter's much-publicized human rights idealism hamstrung both the Shah, who was unsure how much public support, if any, a military crackdown on the brewing revolution would receive from the United States; and the response of the Carter administration, which was unwilling to vigorously encourage the Shah to restore order, despite a recognition of the geostrategic importance of Iran—the second-largest state in the Middle East and possessor of the second largest oil reserves— for containing the Soviet Union and providing oil to the West. "Throughout the long crisis," Ledeen and Lewis write, "the Americans were hobbled by their own doctrines. To support the shah was viewed in many quarters as a betrayal of the human rights campaign, especially if the shah used American support as an excuse to use military force against his enemies. But to permit the shah to be toppled was a geopolitical risk of vast dimensions"[26]

Given this vacillation, the Islamists in Iran and America's allies alike assumed that there was a new policy in place, one that left the Shah—already dying of lymphoma and increasingly uncertain whether to make more concessions or employ the "iron fist"— alone in confronting the challenges to his regime. The Shah's uncertainty was reinforced by U.S. warnings about respecting human rights and by delays in providing riot-control materiel such as tear gas and rubber bullets, even as protestations of support kept being issued from Washington. As Barry Rubin summarizes, "By mid-December [1978] the United States did not have any coherent Iran policy nor was there even a system of coordination between the different policymaking groups. . . . Consequently, each step was dictated partly by chance, partly by the relative strength of various personalities in the administration, and very much by whatever turn events might be taking at the moment in Iran."[27] Carter vacillated between his foreign policy idealism and commitment to human rights, both of which left him hesitant to directly encourage a brutal crackdown by the Shah; and his recognition of Iran's importance for America's interests in the Gulf and the containment of the Soviet Union. Unable to commit fully to one course or the other, in effect he left events to take their own course, one ultimately determined by Khomeini and the Islamists. "At a time when the shah needed clarity," Patrick Tyler writes, "America was speaking with multiple voices."[28]

The Failure to Take Religion Seriously

The most important failure, however, and one still evident today in our understanding of jihad, lay in missing the true nature of the Islamic revolution and the role that religion played in the overthrow of the Shah.[29] In the view of many in the foreign policy establishment, the keys to hatred of the Shah and his regime were not Islam, but anti-colonialism, anti-imperialism, liberal aspirations, and resistance to an oppressor seen as the puppet of American corporate and nationalist interests. Partly this assessment reflected the post-Vietnam narrative of U.S. foreign policy behavior, in which brutal dictators who oppressed their own people's rights and aspirations for self-determination and civil liberties were nonetheless supported as useful stooges for protecting America's corporate interests. Thus the Shah was presented as another such oppressor, whose depredations had awakened a justified attempt at liberation and nationalist self-determination, a bit of leftist received wisdom that Teddy Kennedy exploited in his brief run against Carter in the 1980 presidential primaries: "The shah ran one of the most violent regimes in the history of mankind," the historically challenged Senator said at a press conference, decrying the "umpteen billion dollars stolen from Iran" and calling for an "open debate" to examine America's support of the Shah's regime.[30]

In fact, the Shah's problems were a result not so much of his brutality, which in the context of the Middle East was much less severe than that of many other regimes, and far less brutal and lethal than the tyranny of the mullahs who replaced him. Khomeini and his clerics killed more people in one year than the Shah's dreaded secret police, the Savak, had in 25. More important was the Shah's intemperate modernization and secularizing programs, which had long collided with more devout Iranians' religious beliefs by emancipating women and empowering minorities like the Jews and Baha'is. In 1962, when the Shah proposed a law that extended the franchise to minorities and women, Khomeini preached that the law "was perhaps drawn up by the spies of the Jews and the Zionists ... the Qur'an and Islam are in danger."[31] More important, these programs challenged the power of the clerical establishment. "We have come to the conclusion," Khomeini said in 1963, "that this regime also has a more basic aim: they are fundamentally opposed to Islam itself and the existence of a religious class."[32] For many other Iranians, Rubin writes, modernization "became associated with negative things—anomie, disorganization, waste, corruption, incompetent administration, dependence on foreigners, inflation, and uncomfortably dizzying change."[33] These changes were seen as stalking horses for foreign, which is to say, anti-Islamic ideas like a secular government and the emancipation of women, and the technologies such as television, cassette tapes, and movies that were the vehicles of those corrupting influences.

However, the response of many in the foreign policy establishment was to diminish the religious dimension of the growing resistance to the Shah's regime, even though this dissatisfaction of the faithful had been brewing for decades. This clash with the clerics dated back to the rule of the Shah's father, Reza Shah Pahlavi, who initiated in the 1920s a secularizing program that included women's rights and the reduction of tribal and clerical power. Proscribing turbans and veils and forbidding the faithful to make the pilgrimage to Mecca were other policies that attempted to lessen the role of Islam in Iranian society. These assaults on traditional Islam aroused violent opposition among the faithful. An organization called the Devotees of Islam assassinated the Prime Minister in 1951. They were popular with the people and terrorized politicians, suffering brutal suppression until they were vindicated in the 1979 revolution.[34] An influential cleric who resisted the elder Shah's program was Sayyid Mahmud Taleqani. Taleqani railed against "the infidel materialists of this century," and blamed Jews and Christians for facilitating godless modernization.[35] Moreover, he asserted, these anti-Islamic ideas had their origins in the West, the historical rival that had destroyed the caliphate and now dominated the Muslim heartland. Another Iranian critic of the Shah, Al-e Ahmed, would later dub this malign influence "Westoxification."[36] The Ayatollah Ruhollah Khomeini, who became the driving force of the revolution, was the latest in this decades-long clerical resistance to Westernization.

Despite this context of religious-based opposition to the Shah, Carter's advisers continued to underestimate the impact of religious fervor on events. After the Ayatollah Khomeini returned to Iran from France in February 1979, National Security Adviser Zbigniew Brzezinski prepared a briefing for Carter on Islamic fundamentalism. According to Farber, Brzezinski "soft-pedaled the specific threat of 'Islamic fundamentalism' to American interests." He predicted that the Islamic revolution would falter when faced with the daily practicalities of governance, which would require secular technicians and experts whose presence would dilute the purely religious nature and aims of the regime in order to fulfill the liberal aspirations of the people. Finally, he advised that the U.S. should "pursue our relations with individual Muslim countries on the basis of shared interests, but our emphasis on moral as well as material values, our support for a world of diversity, and our commitment to social justice should place us in a strong position to deepen our dialogue with the Muslim world."[37] Evident in this assessment are the priority given to material, secular interests, such as running a government and delivering material boons and personal freedom to the people, and the naïve belief that because the Islamists were "religious," they shared the same moral values as the West and the same view of "social justice," and that this commonality could provide the foundation for mutually beneficial "dialogue." Missing, however, was any understanding of Islamic doctrine and its totalizing reach over social and political life, at the same time that Islam's chauvinistic and expansionist spiritual aims—epitomized in the Koranic verse that proclaimed Muslims "the best of nations raised for (the benefit) of men"[38]—were incompatible with rival Western political ideals such as human rights or social values such as mutual tolerance and a respect for diversity, particularly of religion. Given these Western materialist and political biases of Carter's advisers, Rubin writes, "Islamic rhetoric was seen as a mask, as a convenient vehicle for expressing accumulated economic, political, and social grievances."[39]

Such a mistake was possible because in the dominant model of national development endorsed by Western political thought and reflecting its Enlightenment roots, religious faith and priestly castes were assumed to be relics of the past, doomed to marginalization as a society progressed and modernized. In times of revolutionary crisis, the true movers of change, such as middle-class intellectuals, students, and technical elites, could use people of faith and their leaders as allies, but in the end these modernizing elements would comprise the new regime. Thus "throughout 1977," Ledeen and Lewis write of the growing opposition to the Shah, "no one seemed to believe that the opposition was fundamentally religious, or to appreciate the power of the mullahs and ayatollahs."[40] This dismissive view of religion missed the significance of the numerous demonstrations, protests, and riots that began to escalate in 1977, all calling for an Islamic government or a rollback of the Shah's programs of secularization and modernization, the latest in a long tradition of protest against secularism. Indeed, so deaf was the State Department to the religious fervor roiling Iran that an Assistant Secretary of State testified to the Senate in June 1978, "We believe a large majority of Iranians thoroughly approve of the very substantial improvements that have been made in living standards and economic and social opportunities during the last three decades."[41] But as the Ayatollah Khomeini would say later, "We did not create a revolution to lower the price of melons."[42]

Misunderstanding Khomeini's Jihad

This slighting of the power of religious aims in favor of material and political ones was most dangerous in the misunderstanding of the revolution's prime mover, the Ayatollah Khomeini, whom many Americans considered a "crazy fanatic living in a time warp,"[43] a "ghost from the Middle Ages,"[44] a bearded and turbaned combination of cult leaders Jim Jones and Charles Manson, replete with the latter's piercing gaze. *Time* magazine wrote that to many people Khomeini was "a fanatic whose judgments are harsh, reasoning bizarre and conclusions surreal," a medieval throwback who taught the world a "frightening lesson in the shattering power of irrationality."[45]

President Carter, a religious man himself, responded to an interview with Khomeini in *Le Monde* with the one-word assessment, "Nutty," and during the hostage crisis wrote in his diary, "It's almost impossible to deal with a crazy man."[46]

But this secularist, ethnocentric view of Khomeini as a crazy fanatic was dangerously far off the mark. In reality, the charismatic cleric, a descendent of the Prophet Mohammed, was a highly trained and respected Islamic scholar educated in Qom, the "Oxford and Harvard of Iranian Shi'ism."[47] So extensive was his knowledge of Islam that his teachers anointed him a *mojtahed,* someone capable of applying Islamic law to all aspects of human life. Later he became known as an *ayatollah al-ozma,* a "grand sign of God," an honor given to highly learned religious leaders.[48] In addition, Khomeini had shrewdly taken the measure of the self-loathing West, and so he salted his Islamic revivalism with anti-colonial, anti-imperialist, and Third World revolutionary rhetoric drawn from the Psalter of Third World anti-colonialism, Frantz Fanon's 1963 *Wretched of the Earth,* a synthesis sure to win him allies among leftist and liberal Westerners.[49] Nor were Khomeini's ideas a mystery: in two books and in numerous audiocassettes smuggled into Iran, his anti-Western, Islamist philosophy was obvious. But American analysts did not have copies of Khomeini's works. Indeed, when three journalists published long excerpts from Khomeini's writings, Ledeen reports, they "were subjected to heated criticism from government and academic experts who either denied the existence of the books, or denied that they said" what the journalists had published. The CIA concurred with the criticism, telling Senator Henry Jackson that the books were not written by Khomeini and had possibly been forged by the Israelis.[50]

Close attention to Khomeini's writings would have revealed their uncompromising radicalism grounded in his Islamic faith. They were permeated by hatred of a corrupt West, particularly the United States, the "Great Satan" that had usurped Islam's divinely sanctioned role as the best social-political order for the whole human race. Western political ideals such as freedom and the separation of religion from government were dismissed as camouflage for hedonism and atheism. In a speech given in August 1979, for example, Khomeini heaped scorn on Western notions of freedom, a "freedom that will corrupt our youth, freedom that will pave the way to the oppressor, freedom that will drag our nation to the bottom. This is the freedom you [secular intellectuals] want; and this is a dictate from abroad that you have imposed. You do not believe in any limits to freedom. You deem license to be freedom."[51] Khomeini particularly condemned the trappings of this corrupt freedom introduced by the Shah's liberalizing programs: mixed-sex education and recreation, bars, discos, television, movies, popular music, Western fashion, divorce for women, secular law and government—all were symptoms of "Westoxification."

And this malign process, begun by the first Shah, had been intensified by his son—the "puppet" of the Americans and the Jews, the "enemies of Islam"—whose programs of secularization and Westernization were motivated by the desire to achieve "the abolition of the laws of Islam" and their replacement by Western judicial notions.[52] Hence Khomeini's solution was first to overthrow the apostate Shah and then replace him with a government grounded in traditional Islam, that is, a virtual theocracy consisting of a "Guardianship of the Islamic Jurists" and a clerical "Supreme Guide," one whose laws and justice system would be based on shari'a, the Islamic code of justice and behavior applicable to every dimension of social, political, and private life: "We want a ruler," Khomeini wrote, "who would cut off the hand of his own son if he steals, and would flog and stone his near relative if he fornicates," just as shari'a law dictates.[53] By this means, Iran would not only achieve greatness but also become the vanguard in the restoration of the global power that Islam once wielded and that the infidel West had usurped in order to impose its idolatrous culture on the faithful.

Even more troubling than the U.S. dismissal of the religious origins of the revolution was the failure to understand the role of violent jihad in Khomeini's program to battle the forces of Western idolatry and materialism and restore the global greatness of Islam. In 1942, Khomeini had written, "Those who study *jihad* will understand why Islam wants to conquer the whole world. All the countries conquered by Islam or to be conquered in the future will be marked for everlasting salvation." Khomeini explicitly identifies this process as a violent one: "Those who know nothing of Islam pretend that Islam counsels against war. Those [who say this] are witless. Islam says: Kill all the unbelievers just as they would kill you! ... Islam says: Whatever good there is exists thanks to the sword and in the shadow of the sword! People cannot be made obedient except with the sword! The sword is the key to paradise, which can be opened only for holy warriors!"[54] After he took power, Khomeini reiterated his jihadist program: "The great prophet of Islam carried in one hand the Koran and in the other a sword; the sword for crushing the traitors and the Koran for guidance.... Islam is a religion of blood for the infidels but a religion of guidance for other people."[55] The goal of this jihad, moreover, was the global triumph of Islam: "We shall export our revolution," Khomeini promised, "to the whole world. Until the cry 'There is no God but God' resounds over the whole world, there will be struggle."[56]

Ignorant of Khomeini's Islamist ideology, the Carter administration attempted to deal with the Ayatollah in terms of Western materialist and political assumptions. Anti-Americanism, for example, was not a transient passion and rhetorical device in response to America's support of the Shah, one to be abandoned once the regime got down to the pragmatic business of creating a government, consolidating rule, and entering into international relations. On the contrary, anti-Americanism lay at the heart of Islamist ideology.[57] Hatred of the "Great Satan" was necessary for definitively ending Iran's subservience to a foreign hegemon and establishing the Islamic bona fides of the new regime, one founded on Islamic doctrine and hence necessarily hostile to an infidel power. Also not coming to pass was Brzezinski's prediction that, as Farber puts it, "experts and secularists of various stripes would replace Islamic fundamentalists in key decision-making posts." [58] Yet diplomatic contacts were pursued in order to normalize relations,and American diplomats attempted to be understanding and flexible, as though they were negotiating with like-minded, pragmatic counterparts eager to find a mutually beneficial accommodation. Thus an Assistant Secretary of State reported, "the Iranian suspicions of us were only natural in the post-revolutionary situation but that after a transition period common interests could provide a basis for future cooperation."[59] However, what "common interests" could a true Muslim have with the infidel minion of Satan? As a Revolutionary Council member put it a few months after the seizure of the American embassy, "No individual, no official and no Muslim has the right to show forbearance or compromise toward an enemy who is not defeated and is not overthrown."[60] Carter's belief that rational negotiations and compromise could establish peaceful relations with the infant Islamic Republic was as delusional as Chamberlain's notion that Hitler's grand aims for a German empire based on racial purity would be satisfied by the negotiated sacrifice of Czechoslovakia.

The Hostage Crisis and the First Appeasement

The wages of Carter's incoherent foreign policy became obvious with the seizing of the American embassy on November 4, 1979, and the taking of 66 American hostages, 52 of whom were held for 444 days.[61] The "pretext," as Thucydides would put it, of this aggression was Carter's decision to allow the dying Shah into the United States for medical treatment. The real cause was the need to consolidate the Islamists' power, marginalize the secularist nationalists and socialists, and humiliate a super-power in order to demonstrate to the world the superior power of Islam. The magnitude of this affront to international law—a government-sanctioned seizure of another sovereign nation's territory and diplomatic personnel—and the damage to American prestige that such unpunished aggression would leave in its wake seemingly did not register on Carter enough to shape his response. "Not eager for a direct confrontation," Rubin writes, "President Carter embarked on a course that combined conciliatory gestures and a gradual escalation of pressure."[62] The whole repertoire of appeasing evasions familiar from the 1938 Czechoslovakia crisis—diplomatic negotiation, a United Nations Security Council resolution, a U.N. commission of inquiry into America's "crimes," secret negotiations through third-party countries, and other excuses to substitute talk for action—were employed, all to no avail, since the real power in Iran, Khomeini, had no intention of reaching an agreement, since that did not suit his political interests or Islamist ideology. Particularly groveling was the letter to Khomeini Carter sent via leftist former Attorney General Ramsay Clark and Senate staffer William Miller. In it Carter assured the Ayatollah of his desire for good relations "based upon equality, mutual respect and friendship." Khomeini refused even to meet with the envoys, although later Clark would go to Tehran to participate in a "crimes of America" conference.[63] These and other "conciliatory" gestures did nothing but confirm the Islamists' contempt for a corrupt, hedonistic civilization whose spiritual poverty rendered its military and economic power impotent.

As for the "pressure," it comprised actions such as freezing Iranian asserts in the U.S. and imposing economic sanctions, including an embargo on trade with Iran. A U.N. Security Council resolution to this effect was vetoed twice by the Soviet Union: "Thus did the world organization," Mark Bowden writes, "dedicated to diplomacy acquiesce in the kidnapping of diplomats."[64] An appeal to our NATO allies for an embargo was met with equivocation and delay. Finally, the threat of Iran's President Bani-Sadr to cut off oil to the Europeans if they signed on to an embargo demonstrated the primacy of national self-interest over fealty to international law and support for an ally: the Europeans eventually agreed to impose an embargo only on contracts signed *after* the seizure of the embassy on November 4, 1979, which made the agreement meaningless.

However, even successful material punishments would likely have meant little to the faithful. "The denial of material things," the *Economist* pointed out, "is unlikely to have much effect on minds suffused with immaterial things."[65] Indeed, the primary reason for the student takeover of the embassy was to demonstrate that "God is the ultimate power." The student leadership group was called "Muslim Students Following the Line of the Imam [Khomeini]," and it had expelled communists and other secularists from leadership positions. And when the students overran the embassy, they raised a banner inscribed with the traditional Islamic cry of triumph: "God is Great."[66] Confronted with such spiritual power, America's overwhelming military power was irrelevant: as Khomeini would say three years after the takeover, "Victory is not achieved by swords; it can be achieved only by blood. Victory is not achieved by large populations; it is achieved by strength of faith."[67] The abject and humiliating failure of an overly complex and half-hearted attempt to rescue the hostages in April 1980—with its televised spectacle of mullahs gleefully poking their canes into the charred remains of eight American soldiers—merely confirmed the Islamists in their belief that indeed "God is the ultimate power." To many Iranians, evidence of God's favor could be seen in the sandstorm that caused the helicopter crashes dooming the rescue mission: "Those sand particles," Khomeini preached, "were divinely commissioned. . . . Carter still has not comprehended what kind of people he is facing and what school of thought he is playing with. Our people is the people of blood and our school is the school of *Jihad.*"[68]

In the end, Iran was lost, "a calamity," Niall Ferguson writes, "whose ramifications were and are incalculable."[69] Carter negotiated a humiliating agreement for the release of the hostages. In a series of Executive Orders, he agreed to return billions of dollars of frozen Iranian assets in American banks, in effect paying ransom to hostage takers. In addition, he promised not to overthrow the Iranian revolutionary government and prevented Americans from suing the regime for the destruction of American property and the abuse of the diplomats. Worse, however, than these rewards for aggression were the international ramifications of America's humiliation, proving prophetic a German newspaper's observation at the time of the embassy takeover: "[A] Lilliputian is binding a giant. Such an example invites followers."[70] The Soviet Union had already embarked upon a "campaign of geopolitical opportunism in the Third World," as Peter Rodman puts it, hard on the American debacle in Vietnam.[71] More significant for the later development of global jihad, the Soviets invaded Afghanistan in December 1979, a month after the embassy takeover. The Soviets were defending their Afghan communist clients against an Islamist resistance fired up by the Islamic revolution unfolding next door in Iran. The difference between the two conflicts, as Farber points out, was that "the Soviets had done for their closely allied communist friends (less charitably, puppet regime) what the Carter administration had chosen not to do in Iran."[72] The contrast between the Soviets, who ignored earlier U.S. warnings not to interfere in Afghanistan, and the Americans, who appeared to be deterred by Soviet warnings not to intervene in Iran, no matter how simplistic or misleading, nonetheless gave force to the global perception of American weakness and timidity. This perception was strengthened when Libya's strongman Muammar Qaddafi fired a missile at an American reconnaissance aircraft and Carter did nothing in response.

The Jihad Metastasizes

More important for America's conflict with Islamic jihad, defeat in Iran encouraged Islamist aggression elsewhere, much of it directly supported by the new Iranian Islamic regime, which as one ayatollah put it was merely "the start of the story. An Islamic and divine government, much like Iran and better, will be created" in other Muslim nations.[73] Indeed, the Iranian revolution and the establishment of an Islamic regime was a catalyst for Islamists everywhere. "For the Iranian revolution," Paul Berman writes, "was large and deep and inspiring, and, with the Iranian example in everyone's eyes, the Islamist movement became a greater phenomenon than ever before, and the newly mass movement began to achieve success across the wide arc from Afghanistan to Algeria, and beyond."[74] A few weeks after the embassy takeover, inspired by the Iranians, Muslim radicals in Pakistan and Libya attacked and burned the American embassies, killing two Americans in Tripoli. More significant was the still continuing material support the Iranian regime began to provide for other Islamist jihadists, including numerous terrorist organizations. Yasser Arafat, leader of the terrorist Palestinian Liberation Organization, celebrated Khomeini's return to Iran with gunfire, and was the first state visitor to the Islamic Republic: "Khomeini declared that Iran's revolution would not be complete until the Palestinians won the Holy Land."[75] Even if Western observers, misdirected by Arafat's nationalist and anti-colonialist rhetoric, saw no link between the PLO and Islamism, Khomeini certainly did.

More material Iranian support for terrorism quickly developed in the 1980s, making good on Khomeini's threat that "We shall export our revolution to the world." The deadliest and still dangerous manifestation of Khomeini's program of global jihad was the support Iran gave to an underground Shiite terrorist organization eventually known as Hezbollah. This organization was explicit about its loyalties and jihadist aims: its 1985 "program" acknowledged Khomeini as its "one leader, wise and just" and set as its objectives driving all foreigners out of Lebanon, except, of course, the PLO and the Syrians; combating "abomination" and "its very roots, its primary roots, which are the United States"; destroying Israel, the "Zionist entity"; and exhorting all to "embrace Islam."[76] Iran's sponsorship began in 1982, when Iranian Revolutionary Guardsmen established a base in Lebanon's Bekaa Valley, which came to be known as "Little Tehran." There the Iranians, according to Robin Wright, "acted as missionaries more than fighters . . . systematically mobilizing the Shiite community and establishing small cells of activists under the leadership of radical local clergy for possible action."[77] Later, a National Security Council staff member, commenting on U.S. indifference to the Iranian activity in Lebanon, said, "We had no idea that this action would inevitably lead to the radicalization of large elements of the Lebanese Shiite community, the widespread taking of hostages, a dramatic upsurge in international terrorism and the Iran[-Contra] Affair."[78] Just as British indifference to Hitler's plans outlined in his memoir *Mein Kampf* paved the way for the debacle of Munich, so too a failure to take seriously Khomeini's religious motivations and publicized jihadist doctrines facilitated the wave of terrorist assaults against Americans in the 1980s, 1990s, and beyond.

The deadliest Iranian-sponsored attack on America was the October 23, 1983, suicide bombing of the Marine barracks in Beirut, which killed 241 American marines and military personnel who had been sent as "peacekeepers" into the maelstrom of an Israeli-Lebanese-PLO-Syrian conflict; 59 French soldiers were killed in a similar attack two minutes later. This was the second bombing attack that year by Islamic Jihad, one of the many terrorist organizations nurtured by Iran. The first attack was in April, when a suicide car bomber blew up outside the U.S. embassy, killing 17 Americans, at that time the worst terrorist attack ever against the United States, a record that would stand a scant five months. Even before the October bombing, since July the American headquarters, checkpoints, and outposts had been subjected to continual fire from snipers, mortars, rockets, artillery, and a variety of small arms. The Marines were taking casualties, including several dead, and as the summer wore on they were slowly being sucked into a conflict whose complexity was far beyond the peacekeeping objectives and finely calibrated rules of engagement that had defined the Marines' original mission. Headquartered at the Beirut International Airport in the heart of the war, the U.S. troops were "sitting ducks," as Commander Timothy Geraghty put it to Ambassador Robert McFarlane, for the Iranian and Syrian-backed Islamist terrorists seeking to influence American policy in the Middle East.[79]

Those terrorists, however, were acting in concert with the Iranians and the Syrians. Before the Marine headquarters bombing, Syrian and Iranian troops had participated in and directed some of the attacks.[80] Later, a high Iranian official would admit that Iran had trained the bombers: "In Lebanon, we trained the people who drove a bomb into the American Marine barracks, but we didn't tell them to do such an act.... When we heard about the bomb, we were happy."[81] Yet even at the time of the bombing, there was ample evidence of Iranian complicity in the attack. Seven messages intercepted by American intelligence revealed Iranian officials prodding Shiite terrorists to attack American targets, and the Iranian ambassador in Damascus had instructed the Islamic Amal organization to "undertake an extraordinary attack against the U.S. Marines." Islamic Amal was one of the Shiite terrorist groups under the command of the Iranian Revolutionary Guard force in the Bekaa Valley. The man believed to have masterminded the attack, Imad Fayez Mugniyah, had also been part of the Iranian-sponsored terrorist network.[82]

Despite President Reagan's assertion that "We will not yield to international terrorism," his administration's response to this vicious assault, one orchestrated by a regime that had declared war on the United States and already attacked it, was muddled and, in the end, as appeasing as Carter's failure to punish the takeover of the embassy in Tehran.[83] Three weeks after the attack on the Marine barracks, a punitive raid against the Hezbollah and Iranian fighters based in the Bekaa Valley was planned and approved by Reagan—then vetoed by Secretary of Defense Caspar Weinberger, who feared the international repercussions of any American retaliation and claimed that the attackers were "unknown," a dubious assertion.[84] Reagan did not overrule his insubordinate Secretary of Defense, and in the end never retaliated against those responsible for the murder of hundreds of Americans.[85] Meanwhile, the Israelis and French, also victims of suicide bombing attacks, sent their jets to bomb and strafe the Bekaa Valley and the nearby hills. For three more months, the Marines were bombed, sniped, and shelled, while offshore the battleship *New Jersey* responded with its 16–inch guns, and domestic and Congressional opposition to continuing the mission intensified. As Secretary of State George Shultz wrote later, Washington had "pullout fever." By February 1984, there was a "virtual stampede just to 'get out' of Lebanon." The Marines "left in a rush," Shultz writes, "amid ridicule from the French and utter disappointment and despair from the Lebanese."[86] The terrorists were left unpunished, and they fulfilled their vow "that not a single American or Frenchman will remain on this soil."[87] Tyler summarizes the disastrous consequences of this unwillingness to respond to aggression: the "failure to retaliate for the marine barracks bombing, the worst terrorist attack on the United States up to that time, probably emboldened the Iranian-Syrian alliance against the United States that would radiate violence for decades. For [Syrian president] Assad and the Hezbollah militants, America was risk averse; it had wilted in the face of casualties. It *was* susceptible to terrorism."[88]

The retreat from Beirut was followed in the next few years by more attacks on American citizens and embassies, including bombings of the embassies in Kuwait and Beirut, the killing of 18 U.S. servicemen in Spain, and the murder of several Americans in plane hijackings and attacks on airports in Rome and Vienna. Convinced that the United States could be bullied and blackmailed with impunity, in 1984 Islamist terrorists kidnapped four Americans in Lebanon, including CIA station chief William Buckley, who would eventually be beaten and tortured to death by the Marine barracks bomber Mugniyah. The next year, a truck bomb attack in Beirut near the headquarters of a Shiite cleric considered the spiritual leader of Hezbollah was blamed on the United States, so terrorists seized three more Americans. The Reagan administration's response was another ill-conceived act of appeasement that would become known as the Iran-Contra affair, which unfolded over 1985–86. This operation involved ransoming the American hostages by selling nearly 2,211 TOW anti-tank missiles and over 100 HAWK anti-aircraft missiles to Iran in violation of an arms embargo, at first through Israel, then directly, and using the proceeds to fund the Contra insurgents battling the Sandinista regime in Nicaragua. The scheme secured the release of only three hostages, who were immediately replaced by three other Americans kidnapped in Lebanon.

In the end, apart from the "moral hazard" of paying ransom to terrorist kidnappers, Iran-Contra revealed the continuing failure to understand the Khomeini revolution in Iran. In addition to securing the release of the hostages by selling weapons to Iran, the arms sales had been considered a way to improve relations with Iran and prevent it from moving closer to the Soviet Union. On one trip to Iran in May 1986, American emissaries had brought along with military equipment a cake in the shape of a key, apparently symbolizing the "key" to Iranian-American friendship. An accurate understanding of Islamist ideology, however, would have shown that the mullahs had no interest in improving relations with America, no matter how many tactical diplomatic feints suggested otherwise. Rather

than effecting a rapprochement with Iran, the scheme reinforced the Islamists' perception that America had no stomach
for a fight and would appease its enemies to avoid harm to its
citizens, even selling advanced weapons to a regime that had
explicitly declared itself a mortal enemy and that had American blood on its hands.

Blindfolding and Handcuffing the CIA

Another consequence of Iran-Contra, Herman writes, was that
it "represented for liberal CIA critics the greatest target of
opportunity since the Church hearings."[89] The subsequent
Congressional investigation conjured up the old CIA bogeyman once again running amok in defiance of the law. So it was
no surprise that under President Clinton, restrictions on the
CIA were tightened. The prohibition on assassination was now
interpreted to forbid even making contact with groups plotting
a regime change. Indeed, CIA lawyers argued that the agency
had "a duty to warn" targeted foreign leaders.[90] The most notorious blowback from this policy came in 1995, when the White
House ordered an FBI investigation of CIA field officer Robert
Baer for his involvement in a coup to overthrow Saddam Hussein in the mid-1990s. Also in 1995, CIA Director John Deutch
issued the "Deutch Guidelines," new rules concerning the
recruitment of foreign assets, or spies, that excluded those with
criminal records. Existing assets with sketchy records were
fired. As a consequence of this "asset scrub," by 2000 the CIA
had no human assets in Iraq and Iran, and so had become
increasingly reliant on other countries' intelligence services.
More important, these restrictions on recruiting foreign assets
perforce forbade the cultivation of anyone belonging to al
Qaeda as a source of intelligence.

Equally harmful to our ability to uncover terrorist plots
was Attorney General Janet Reno's 1995 interpretation of the

FISA Act, which led to regulations creating an artificial divide between national security and criminal investigations out of a fear that criminal prosecutions would be contaminated by the illegal use of intelligence gathered by the CIA. This interpretation created difficulties for those investigating terrorists who have committed crimes and thus are of interest both to national security agencies and criminal prosecutors.

According to former federal prosecutor Andrew C. McCarthy, this distinction between national security and criminal intelligence gathering should not have caused any difficulties in the investigation of suspected terrorists, the correct strategy being a cooperative effort between national security and criminal investigations. But "prior to 9/11," McCarthy writes, "development of such a strategy was hamstrung by a hypothetical and wrong-headed concern: *viz.,* that permitting use in criminal cases of FISA-generated evidence might induce agents to resort to FISA when their 'real' purpose was to conduct a criminal investigation." Soon FISA required a "certification" from an executive branch official that the information being sought was for the purpose of gathering intelligence rather than for a criminal prosecution. Though contrary to the intention of the certification requirement, "the Justice Department began construing the certification not as a mere *announcement of purpose* but as something more restrictive: a *substantive limitation* on the use of FISA evidence in criminal cases." This interpretation bred others, such as the "primary purpose" test, which barred the use of evidence gathered from a FISA controlled investigation in a criminal prosecution unless the government could demonstrate that the primary purpose of the investigation was to gather intelligence. The final outcome of such metastasizing bureaucracy, McCarthy explains, was the infamous "wall," an interpretation of the FISA rules that "instructed 'the FBI and Criminal Division [to] ensure that advice intended to preserve the option of a criminal prosecution does not inadvertently result in either the fact or the appearance of the Criminal Division's directing or controlling the [foreign intelligence (FI) or counterintelligence (FCI)] investigation toward law enforcement objectives.'" The result, McCarthy goes on, was to "prevent the FBI intelligence officials from communicating with the Criminal Division regarding ongoing FI or FCI investigations. This effectively cut intelligence investigators off not only from criminal agents but also from Assistant United States Attorneys who, by virtue of investigating and prosecuting several terrorism cases in the 1990s, were among the government's best resources regarding al Qaeda and its affiliates."[91]

Two decades of such oversight and institutionalized second-guessing bred timidity and risk-aversion among those intelligence officers responsible for investigating and exposing terrorist plots. According to one CIA agent, "We understood that if things went wrong, we were on our own. . . . Inspector general investigations after a flap became the norm, and finger-pointing was a defensive survival tactic."[92] The fate of agents such as Keith Hall, who was fired from the CIA for the rough interrogation of a suspect after the Beirut embassy bombing in 1983, led to programs like "extraordinary rendition," in which suspects are shipped off for brutal interrogation in foreign countries unhampered by our regard for human rights and with their own national interests often different from our own. For many CIA officers, Thomas Powers wrote in 2002, "The Clinton years . . . saw a crippling erosion of the agency's position in Washington. Its leadership is now timid and its staff demoralized. Top officials . . . worry more about the vigilantes of political correctness than the hard work of collecting intelligence in the field."[93]

The CIA was reduced to another politicized Washington bureaucracy that rewarded careerist jockeying, while operations in the field, along with skills such as language fluency and the requisite cultural knowledge, became less important, leaving the Agency dependent on foreign intelligence services and their own national agendas. "Years of public criticism," Powers summarizes, "attempts to clean house, the writing and rewriting of rules, and efforts to rein in the Directorate of Operations have all conspired to make the agency insular, risk-averse, and gun-shy."[94] Worsening these problems, foreign intelligence budgets were cut in fiscal years 1990–1996 and remained flat in 1996–2000, and there were more staff reductions. Finally, after the arrest in 1994 of CIA agent Aldrich "Rick" Ames, who had been selling classified information to the Russians, internal investigations intensified the institutional paranoia that made the agency even more "insular, risk-averse, and gun-shy." On the eve of 9/11, Mark Riebling writes, the CIA was "put out of business. . . . Its key divisions had been stripped and plundered in a hostile takeover. It no longer *had* any big secrets to steal. Counterintelligence and counterterrorism, in the conventional senses, no longer existed. The Agency's work in those areas was merely an adjunct to law enforcement."[95] Terrorism now was considered a criminal more than a national security problem, a misapprehension still bedeviling our efforts to root out terrorists.

The downplaying of the religious roots of Islamism, the damage to American prestige that followed the failure to punish attacks on American interests, the continuing force of a foreign policy based on American self-doubt and moralizing internationalism, and the gutting of the CIA had all set the stage for the sequence of jihadist attacks in the 1990s and the rise to prominence of al Qaeda. The trajectory of appeasement that had begun in Saigon in 1975 and then proceeded through Tehran in 1979 and Beirut in 1983 was now pointing to New York in 2001.

The Emergence of Bin Laden

If the Iranian revolution's successful attack against a more powerful West and its creation of an Islamic state provided Islamists with an inspiring model, the ten-year guerilla war against the Soviet Union in Afghanistan added practical military experience and training, plus even more prestige following the defeat of the other superpower impediment to renewed Islamic hegemony. Thousands of Muslims from across the world flocked to the jihad against communist atheism, including a 23-year-old Saudi engineer named Osama bin Laden, who had studied with Mohammed Qutb, brother of the martyred Islamist theorist Sayyid Qutb. After the defeat of the Soviets in 1989—thanks in the main to the financial and materiel support of the United States—bin Laden began to put into operation the larger jihadist goal of attacking and defeating the enemies of Islam, which included both the United States and those Middle Eastern regimes allied with the "Great Satan," thus globalizing the project that Khomeini had successfully started in Iran. Ultimately, bin Laden's jihad, like Khomeini's, was part of the 14-centuries-long conflict between Islam and the West. As bin Laden said in November 2001, "This war is fundamentally religious. Under no circumstances should we forget this enmity between us and the infidels. For the enmity is based on creed."[96] Khomeini had said much the same thing in November 1979: "The Muslims must rise up in this struggle, which is more a struggle between unbelievers and Islam than one between Iran and America: between all unbelievers and the Muslims. The Muslims must rise up and triumph in this struggle."[97]

The pretext of bin Laden's war against America was the stationing of troops in Saudi Arabia during the 1991 Gulf War. In 2004, bin Laden claimed that American involvement in Lebanon in 1983 created his hatred of the United States, even though at the time he told the Saudi ambassador to the U.S. how grateful he was for the aid in defeating the "secularist, atheist Soviets."[98] Elsewhere he asserted that the U.S. had waged "a war against Muslims" since 1945.[99] After 9/11, he mentioned the "humiliation and disgrace" inflicted on Muslims by the dissolution of the caliphate in 1924. In fact, such varying pretexts publicized by bin Laden, in addition to casting the jihad as "defensive" for the benefit of Muslims, are also directed at audiences in the West, in order to exploit Westerners' failure of nerve and self-loathing, their perennial eagerness to don the hair shirt of guilt for various crimes against the Third World "other," such as colonialism or imperialism. This use of rhetoric tailored to Western assumptions is a hallmark of all al Qaeda's communications to the West. "In their political speeches," Raymond Ibrahim writes, "bin Laden and [Ayman al-] Zawahiri [al Qaeda's theorist and bin Laden's second in command] insist that they are waging a 'Defensive Jihad' against an oppressive West. When discussing the tenets of Islam, however, they argue to Muslims that Muslims should battle the West because it is the infidel."[100]

Just as the Carter administration could not grasp the religious sources of the Iranian revolution, neither did the Clinton administration—and many in government down to the present—see how rooted in traditional Islam are bin Laden's motives, misdirected as Westerners are by their inability to take religion seriously. Thus, rather than being a devout Muslim, bin Laden is simply "insane," as Thomas Friedman wrote.[101] Or he is considered a fringe fanatic, "a trigger-happy nut, psychopath, or violence-prone youngster who never grew up." Scheuer goes on to survey some of the Western analyses that totally ignore or rationalize bin Laden's religious motives: he is "neither a mainstream Muslim nor a paragon of sanity," according to *Newsday*; a "malignant narcissist," in the estimation of a U.S. government psychologist; a "fringe character," as the Arab-American Anti-Discrimination Committee claims.[102] However, as bin Laden's global support from millions of Muslims demonstrates, like Khomeini the Saudi is an admired

Muslim knight continuing the millennial battle against the Western infidels that have marginalized and humiliated Islam for three centuries.

Theorists of Jihad

Rather than a "beard from the fringe," then, bin Laden was commencing the jihad against the U.S. based on the same Islamist doctrines earlier developed by other Islamists, such as Sayyid Qutb, the Egyptian Islamist theorist executed by Egyptian strongman Gamal Nasser in 1966.[103] After Khomeini, Qutb is the most important figure for modern jihad, "al Qaeda's intellectual godfather," as Lee Smith puts it.[104] Like the Ayatollah, Qutb was opposed to the whole modern liberal ideology, viewing it as anti-Islamic. In his influential tract *Milestones,* Qutb wrote, "It is necessary to revive the Muslim community which is buried under the debris of the man-made traditions of several generations, and which is crushed under the weight of those false laws and customs which are not even remotely related to the Islamic teachings."[105] All the trappings of Western socio-political order, though not its science and technology, were to be rejected, particularly secularist government and its dismissal of religion's role in society, for "the only principle on which the totality of human life is to be based is God's religion and its system of life."[106] Again like Khomeini, Qutb despised the Western notions of democracy and freedom, which is nothing more than license, an Islamist theme running throughout al Qaeda's writings: "The freedom we want," writes al Qaeda theorist Ayman al-Zawahiri, "is the not the freedom to use women as commodities . . . it is not the freedom of AIDS and an industry of obscenities and homosexual marriages."[107]

To Qutb, true freedom, the freedom that comes from obedience to God's commands, would follow the rejection of Western political ideals and the institution of shari'a law in an Islamic state. And the way to achieve this utopian restoration of Islam's dominance would be jihad, for, as Qutb writes, "Islam came into this world to establish God's rule on God's earth, to invite all people toward the worship of God, and to make a concrete reality of its message in the form of a Muslim community in which individuals are free from servitude to men and have gathered together under servitude to God and follow only the Shari'ah of God. This Islam has a right to remove all those obstacles which are in its path so that it may address human reason and intuition with no interference and opposition from political systems."[108] Nor will these obstacles be removed "through sermons or discourse," Qutb warns. "Those who have usurped the power of God on earth and made His worshippers their slaves will not be dispossessed by words alone."[109]

Hasan al-Banna, the founder of the Muslim Brothers in 1928, whose weekly newspaper *Al-Ikhwan al-Muslimin* Qutb would edit in the 1950s, agreed with Qutb. The Muslim Brothers also opposed Western political and social ideals such as democracy and secularization, and saw jihad as the means of restoring Islamic global hegemony. "It is the nature of Islam," Al-Banna wrote, "to dominate not to be dominated, to impose its laws on all nations, and extend its power to the entire planet."[110] Given this Islamist context, the American forces stationed in Saudi Arabia, like the creation of Israel, were merely a symptom of the religious corruption that allowed the infidel West to dominate and marginalize the true believers for decades, prevent the restoration of true Islam in the Middle East, and interfere with Islam's global destiny. Only jihad against the infidels and the "apostate" Muslim regimes that groveled before unbelievers could reverse this injustice and restore Islam to its rightful global place as the one true faith.

The Islamist dreams of Qutb, al-Banna, and bin Laden seemed closer to realization after Khomeini's establishment of the Iranian Islamic regime at the expense of one superpower, and after the *mujahidin*'s defeat of the other in Afghanistan.

In August 1988, as the Soviets were withdrawing from Afghanistan, al Qaeda was created in Pakistan by various Islamists and *mujahidin,* including bin Laden. Their goal, according to the minutes of the meeting, "is to lift the word of God to make His religion victorious."[111] Bin Laden then returned to Saudi Arabia, where he enjoyed some measure of prestige based on his exaggerated exploits in the jihad against the Soviets. Back home, according to Lawrence Wright, bin Laden "offered a conventional, Muslim Brothers critique of the plight of the Arab world: The West, particularly the United States, was responsible for the humiliating failure of the Arabs to succeed."[112] America was targeted not so much for its alleged crimes against Muslims as for its role as the dominant Western power responsible for lost Islamic glory, the power that had given the despised Jews their own state in the Muslim heartland.

Moreover, bin Laden perceived that since the abandonment of Vietnam, the United States was spiritually impoverished and hence vulnerable to terrorist intimidation. "The Americans did not get out of Vietnam," bin Laden preached, "until after they suffered great losses. Over sixty thousand [sic] American soldiers were killed until there were demonstrations by the American people. The Americans won't stop their support of Jews in Palestine until we give them a lot of blows. They won't stop until we do jihad against them."[113] A few months after 9/11, bin Laden returned to this theme, demanding "the American people to take note of their government's policy against Muslims. They described the government's policy against Vietnam as wrong. They should now take the same stand that they did previously."[114] Bin Laden shrewdly understood that he could weaken American resolve by casting his struggle as legitimate resistance against a neo-imperialist aggressor, exploiting simultaneously the "Vietnam syndrome," liberal guilt, and the fear of a terrorist attack. And he knew that furthering the damage to American prestige inflicted by Vietnam and Iran could help al Qaeda achieve its aims by eroding global support: "When people see a strong horse and a weak horse, by nature they will like the strong horse," he said in December 2001.[115]

The Road to 9/11 . . .

In the 1990s, al Qaeda began a series of attacks on American interests as part of its program to demoralize the United States and intimidate it into changing its foreign policy no matter how detrimental to its own interests. As part of this program, after his exile from Saudi Arabia and during his residence in Sudan, bin Laden created the "Islamic Army Shura," a "coordinating body for the consortium of terrorist groups with which he was forging alliances."[116] The goal was to support all organizations waging jihad against both apostate Arab regimes and the United States. At his camp near Khartoum, bin Laden mixed training in weapons and explosives with sermons about the degeneracy and weakness of the United States, evoking the past examples of Vietnam and Lebanon. "Whenever soldiers start coming home in body bags," Wright summarizes bin Laden's theme, "Americans panic and retreat. Such a country needs only to be confronted with two or three sharp blows, then it will flee in panic, as it always has. For all its wealth and resources, America lacks conviction. It cannot stand against warriors of faith who do not fear death."[117] In bin Laden's view, American fear bred of spiritual poverty would in turn produce American appeasement.

Another dimension of bin Laden's jihadist activities was his participation in 1991 at a conference organized by Sudanese Islamist Hasan al-Turabi, whose efforts focused on getting Sunnis and Shiites to coordinate against the common infidel enemy. As a result, al Qaeda operatives received explosives training in Iran, and in the fall of 1993 other al Qaeda members were instructed in explosives, security, and intelligence in Lebanon's Bekaa Valley, the long-standing locus of Iranian support for terrorism.[118] One of their instructors was Imad Mugniyah, the Hezbollah architect of the 1983 bombing of the U.S. marine barracks in Beirut. Iranian support for al Qaeda has continued in subsequent years: according to the *9/11 Commission Report,* "there is strong evidence that Iran facilitated the transit of al Qaeda members into and out of Afghanistan before 9/11, and that some of these were future 9/11 hijackers."[119] The recent attack on the U.S. embassy in Yemen in August 2008 was aided by Iran, as revealed by a letter from Ayman al-Zawahiri to the leader of the Iranian Revolutionary Guards.[120] And today in Afghanistan and Iraq, the Iranian Revolutionary Guards have supplied insurgents with Russian anti-aircraft missiles and the roadside bombs engineered to pierce the protective armor on vehicles.[121]

The first of bin Laden's "blows" to rout the United States was the attempt made in 1992 against U.S. troops on their way to Somalia to participate in another ill-planned U.N. humanitarian and peacekeeping effort. Bombs were detonated at two hotels in Aden, Yemen, where American troops were mistakenly believed to have stopped on their way to Somalia. An Australian tourist and a Yemeni waiter were killed. Although no Americans died, bin Laden inflated this botched attack as "the first al Qaeda victory scored against the Crusaders."[122] A year later, al Qaeda trainers were sent to the Somali warlords locked in a gruesome Darwinian struggle with one another and against the international peacekeeping forces. These trainers later boasted, falsely as it turns out, that they had helped bring down two American Black Hawk helicopters in October 1993, an incident made famous in the book and movie *Black Hawk Down.* The globally televised scenes of dead American servicemen dragged through the streets of Mogadishu—an image reminiscent of the charred helicopters and corpses of Carter's botched attempt to rescue the Iranian embassy hostages—and President

Clinton's subsequent withdrawal of American forces a few months later added one more humiliating entry to the catalogue of American appeasement.

Bin Laden later linked this event to his larger interpretation of America's degeneracy and weakness. In Somalia, he told an interviewer in 1997, the *mujahidin* "were surprised to see the low spiritual morale of the American fighters in comparison with [Russian fighters]. The Americans ran away from those fighters who fought and killed them, while the latter [Russians] stayed. If the US still thinks and brags that it still has this kind of power, even after all these successive defeats in Vietnam, Beirut, Aden, and Somalia, then let its troops go back to those who are awaiting its return."[123] The facts of the incident, of course, were very different from bin Laden's narrative, given how superbly the American forces fought to rescue their comrades and the enormous casualties they inflicted on the enemy. As with Vietnam, it was not the military but the subsequent political failure of nerve that created the perception of American weakness and fear exploited by bin Laden, who several times referred to the events in Somalia as demonstrating American "cowardice and feebleness."[124] As the decade progressed, this perception, though based on a skewed version of the actual events, was reinforced by the flaccid U.S. responses to further attacks.

We are all now familiar with the grisly catalogue of terrorism before 9/11. In November 1995, a car bomb exploded at a U.S.-Saudi training facility in Riyadh, killing five Americans. The perpetrators had trained with al Qaeda in Afghanistan, and before they were beheaded by the Saudis admitted bin Laden's influence. In June 1996 a huge truck bomb exploded in front of the Khobar Towers residential complex housing U.S. Air Force personnel near Dhahran. Nineteen Americans died, and 372 were wounded. This attack was a joint project of Hezbollah, Iran, and al Qaeda. Bin Laden attributed the subsequent reductions of U.S. troop numbers in Saudi Arabia to

what he called this act of "praiseworthy terrorism."[125] A few
months later, bin Laden issued his "Declaration of War Against
the Americans Occupying the Land of the Two Holy Places,"
which rehearsed the usual pretexts for Islamist aggression
against apostate Muslim regimes and their infidel American
enablers, particularly the "occupation" by American troops of
the "holy places of Islam," the liberation of which "is the right
step towards unification of the word of our *umma* [the global
Muslim community] under the banner of God's unity."[126] Notice
that the ejection of infidels from Muslim lands, the pretext frequently assumed to be bin Laden's purpose in attacking America, is not the goal of jihad but merely a "right step" toward
the larger end of globally unifying and exalting Islam.

Also during this period, al Qaeda was involved in the first
World Trade Center bombing on February 26, 1993, in which
six people died and 1,042 were wounded. The leader of the cell,
Omar Abdel Rahman, the "Blind Sheikh," had spent time with
bin Laden in Afghanistan, and the al Qaeda chief had paid the
legal bills of El Sayyid Nosair, another member of the cell, who
had murdered the extremist rabbi Meir Kahane in 1990. The
designer of the bomb, Ramzi Yousef, the nephew of 9/11 mastermind Khalid Sheikh Mohammed, had entered the U.S. with
an al Qaeda bomb-making manual in his possession. While
living in America, Rahman made no secret of his jihadist beliefs.
A few weeks before the World Trade Center bombing, the Blind
Sheikh appeared at an event in Brooklyn, where he preached
that "God has obliged us to perform jihad," and that "we wel-
come being terrorists," for "the Quran makes it among the
means to perform jihad for the sake of Allah, which is to ter-
rorize the enemies of God and our enemies too."[127] Further
investigations of the cell that year uncovered a plot to destroy
New York landmarks like the Lincoln and Holland Tunnels and
the United Nations building; discovered later were al Qaeda's
1995 "Bojinka" plot to assassinate Pope John Paul II and simultaneously blow up 12 U.S. airliners over the Pacific. There were

also attacks planned against other U.S. embassies all over the world and plots to assassinate President Clinton and his National Security Adviser Tony Lake.

These are just al Qaeda's operations targeted directly at American interests: worldwide, between 1991 and 1996, 26 various attacks were connected to bin Laden and like-minded Islamists as part of the global jihad against the enemies of Islam.[128] For the next five years after 1996, violent assaults on American interests continued, all met with half-hearted and ineffective responses that confirmed the lesson first taught by the Ayatollah Khomeini: a corrupt America's material power was no match for the spiritual resources of the faithful. On August 7, 1998, al Qaeda pulled off its most complex and devastating attack to that point: simultaneous bombings at two U.S African embassies, in Nairobi and Dar es Salaam. The latter bomb was outfitted with oxygen tanks or gas canisters to intensify the explosion and create more shrapnel. No Americans died in Dar es Salaam, but 11 Africans were killed. In Nairobi, 213 died, including 12 Americans. The attacker dropped a stun grenade before the bomb went off so that people inside would be drawn to the windows, where flying glass shredded, decapitated, and blinded many.

Bin Laden offered several preposterous pretexts for the bombings, including the American "invasion" of Somalia, a plot to partition Sudan, and the Rwandan genocide, which he claimed the two embassies had had a hand in planning.[129] These attacks had been preceded in February by a fatwa from the World Islamic Front calling for "Jihad against the Jews and Crusaders." Signed by bin Laden and representatives from four other Islamist groups, the statement rehearsed the pretexts of American and Israeli "occupation" of Islamic territory and justified their terrorist war as a "defensive" jihad: "The ruling to kill the Americans and their allies—civilians and military—is an individual obligation incumbent upon every Muslim who do it and in any country," following the Koranic commands to "'fight the pagans all together as they fight you all together'" (9:36), and the Word of the Most High, 'Fight them until there is no more tumult or oppression, and [all] religion belongs to Allah' [8:39]."[130] That last Koranic injunction reveals bin Laden's larger Islamist ambitions, which go far beyond the expulsion of Americans from the Middle East.

The last successful major attack on American interests before 9/11 was the bombing on October 12, 2000, of the Navy destroyer *Cole* as it was docked at a fueling buoy in Aden, Yemen. [131] A small fishing boat loaded with explosives blew up amidships, tearing a 40- by 40-foot hole in the ship. Seventeen sailors died and 39 were wounded. "The destroyer represented the capital of the West," bin Laden said, "and the small boat represented Mohammed."[132] He also memorialized the attack in a poem. Later, in a sermon taped in February 2003, bin Laden summed up a decade of attacks, starting with the Beirut bombing: "We can conclude that America is a superpower, with enormous military strength and vast economic power, but that all this is built on foundations of straw. So it is possible to target those foundations and focus on their weakest points which, even if you strike only one-tenth of them, then the whole edifice will totter and sway, and relinquish its unjust leadership of the world."[133] By now it should have been clear that bin Laden was no fringe lunatic but rather the most visible and effective representative of a far-flung consortium of Islamist jihadists, one who had declared war on the United States in the service of restoring Islam to its rightful place of global dominance.

... Is Paved With Appeasement

In every case, the American response to these attacks confirmed bin Laden's estimation that U.S. power was "built on foundations of straw." The reasons for these failures to adequately punish aggression lay in many of the same naïve ideas

promulgated by Jimmy Carter. Particularly inhibiting of punitive action was the "moralizing internationalism" that eschewed
the use of force except within narrow parameters designed to
minimize American casualties and the danger of "mission creep"
that could drag the U.S. into a Vietnam-like "quagmire." Such
idealism also elevated human rights and multilateral diplomacy through transnational institutions like the United Nations
as the primary instrument for defending America's security and
interests. "Although lacking any dominating interests in foreign policy," Richard Sale writes, "Clinton was an internationalist and a liberal to whom foreign markets and the expansion
of trade were the critical determinants of policy, their end being
the spread of democracy and the betterment of human welfare around the world."[134] Two members of Clinton's foreign
policy team, Secretary of State Warren Christopher and
National Security Adviser Anthony Lake, "had been members
of the Carter administration, and they and their President were
widely seen as 'soft' on foreign affairs and reluctant to use force
when needed." Like Carter, they took a "cautious, minimal
view of America's role in the world."[135] As such, Clinton's team
looked to "dialogue" and "outreach" to Islamists, making a false
distinction between jihadists who claimed to oppose violence
and those who didn't. To the Clinton foreign policy team, Daniel
Pipes writes, "most Islamists were seen as decent people, serious individuals espousing [according to an Assistant Secretary
of State for the Middle East] 'a renewed emphasis on traditional values.'"[136] Unfortunately, the "traditional values" included
a return to the illiberal shari'a law code and a renewal of jihad
against the infidel.

Moreover, the collapse of the Soviet Union had created
the so-called "peace dividend," the notion that a leaner military, more reliant on sophisticated technology and air power,
could adequately defend America, justifying cuts in defense
budgets. However, like England during the interwar period,
the United States still had extensive international

commitments and interests, which, along with the high value put on human rights, global trade and development, and the promotion of democracy, meant that global intervention would at times require lethal force and "boots on the ground." However, in response to the crises challenging those commitments and interests, as Kagan and Kagan write of the Clinton years, "leaders hesitated to commit military forces, sought 'peaceful' resolution to crises, preferred 'economic leverage' and 'negotiated settlements' to the effective and necessary use of armed might."[137] Fear of the political costs of casualties and expanding involvement abroad, coupled to a reliance on air power and cruise missiles when some sort of action was politically unavoidable, inhibited the sort of vigorous and mind-concentrating military response to al Qaeda's attacks that could have disabused bin Laden of his belief in America's weakness and corruption.

Clinton's ineffective responses to the attacks on his watch confirm this estimation. After the disaster in Somalia, Clinton pulled U.S. forces out six months later, leaving behind snipers to kill any Somalis who ventured near U.N. compounds, a transient gesture akin to the *New Jersey*'s lobbing shells into the hills above Beirut in 1983. The attacks in Riyadh and on U.S. Air Force personnel in Saudi Arabia were treated as criminal matters to be investigated by the FBI. Military retaliation against Iran for its complicity in the Khobar Towers bombing was discussed and planned in the immediate aftermath, but in the end, as one former White House official said, "The anger was never fortified by any coherent depth of thought or planning. Every tactic brought up soon ran out of support or was forgotten. It was all momentary."[138] Clinton's aversion to the risks of using force inclined him instead to noisy but pointless displays, like the firing of twenty Tomahawk cruise missiles at the Iraqi intelligence headquarters in Baghdad in response to Saddam Hussein's plot to assassinate former president George H.W. Bush in 1993—but attacking at night in order to minimize Iraqi casualties. The administration's fear of force and its political costs; the delusion that diplomatic overtures to the supposed moderate Iranian Mohammed Khatami, elected president at this time, would improve relations with the Islamic Republic; and Clinton's domestic troubles caused by the Monica Lewinsky scandal, all left unpunished yet another Iranian and Islamist attack.

After the African embassy bombings, Clinton did respond—with another glorified fireworks display that merely confirmed the Islamist view of American weakness and fear. In August 1998, a pharmaceutical plant in Sudan, incorrectly suspected of manufacturing chemical weapons, was bombed with 13 cruise missiles, killing a night watchman and putting 300 Sudanese out of work. Equally ineffective were the 66 cruise missiles fired on two camps near Khost, Afghanistan, killing six militants but not bin Laden, who had decided at the last minute to go to Kabul, adding yet another "miracle" validating the righteousness of the Islamist cause. Seventy-five million dollars' worth of cruise missiles had, as Michael Scheuer put it, done "the work of day laborers armed with thirty-dollar sledgehammers."[139] But even if bin Laden had been in the camp, the administration's planners took off the table the best chance of killing him—while he was in the mosque for evening prayers—for fear of offending the Muslim world and killing other militants not involved in the embassy bombings.[140] The blowback of this failure, once again caused by the reluctance to send U.S. troops in to do the job, went beyond missing bin Laden. Several unexploded cruise missiles were recovered by bin Laden and sold to China for over $10 million. More important, bin Laden emerged as a global "symbolic figure of resistance," one "whose defiance of America now seemed blessed by divine favor."[141]

Before the embassy bombings, the Clinton administration had indeed recognized that bin Laden was a threat that needed to be dealt with. But fear of the political costs that would attend U.S. military casualties and any civilian deaths inclined the

administration to provide political cover by using covert operations. However, even these responses were vitiated by risk
aversion and bureaucratic infighting. A CIA plan to capture
bin Laden using tribal proxies in Afghanistan was developed
for several months in early 1998, only to be abandoned out of
fear of casualties, including bin Laden himself: one CIA officer involved in the operation was told there were worries that
"the purpose and nature of the operation would be subject to
unavoidable misinterpretation and misrepresentation—and
probably recriminations—in the event that Bin Ladin, despite
our best interests and efforts, did not survive."[142] The worry
over whether a murderer who had declared war on America
might die indicates the chronic failure of nerve that afflicted
government officials who were more concerned with international public relations and avoiding professional liability than
with the security and lives of the citizens for whom they worked.
Ultimately, however, the responsibility lay with President Clinton, who "wilted," as Patrick Tyler puts it, in the face of a difficult decision. Embroiled in a battle with special prosecutor
Kenneth Starr, who at the time was investigating the Monica
Lewinsky scandal, Clinton "feared that any misstep in the wilds
of Afghanistan by a CIA-backed team would redound against
him in the domestic political battle."[143]

These same concerns with factional political interests and
the fear of potential public relations damage continued to hamper attempts to neutralize bin Laden. Even after the attacks
on the training camps made bin Laden increase his security,
there was another opportunity to kill him. In December 1998,
intelligence indicated that bin Laden would be at a house in
the governor's compound in Kandahar. However, a cruise missile attack on the compound was vetoed out of concerns with
killing civilians and damaging a mosque, sending enraged Muslims around the world on a rampage against Americans. Once
more, fear of attacks by offended Muslims, most of whom already
hated the United States in any case, was more important than

killing the adversary. Other options, such as attacks by AC-130 gunships or Special Operations forces, were discarded for the same "unwillingness to take risks and lack of vision and understanding," according to Lieutenant General William Boykin.[144] The memory of Carter's failed attempt to rescue the embassy hostages in 1980 was another powerful deterrent to such operations. Given that direct U.S. action was off the table, tribal proxies remained the politically safest option. The proxies were given the legal authority to kill bin Laden in a Memorandum of Notification drafted by the CIA, but Clinton inexplicably made the language more ambiguous when he returned the Memorandum to the Agency giving the CIA the same authority in February 1999.[145] In December 1999, Ahmed Shah Massoud, the leader of the Afghan Northern Alliance fighting the Taliban, offered to attack bin Laden's Derunta training complex, but the CIA was uncertain whether it had the authority to authorize the attack, thus putting the organization at risk of violating the ban against assassination.[146] In the event, the proxies never got (or took) the chance to capture bin Laden, perhaps deterred (and no doubt mystified) by the provision that they could not kill him.

The other politically safer alternative was a cruise-missile attack, which as Scheuer points out, "is always ineffective and indecisive but allows us to preempt most international criticism of a disproportionate and indiscriminate response and . . . reduces the domestic political problems that would be caused by American battlefield casualties."[147] However, American risk aversion was so intense that even these "ineffective and indecisive" attacks never got off the ground. In February 1999, the CIA learned that bin Laden and some princes from the United Arab Emirates were hunting birds in the desert near Kandahar. Despite some reliable intelligence, the attack was vetoed by White House coordinator for counterterrorism Richard Clarke, who had just returned from the UAE after negotiating the sale of fighter aircraft worth $8 billion: "No doubt,"

Lawrence Wright speculates, "the image of dead princes scattered in the sand played in his mind, along with the failures" of previous cruise-missile attacks.[148] After Clarke contacted a UAE official about such fraternization with an international terrorist, the camp was dismantled. One CIA official believed that this action eliminated future opportunities for killing bin Laden, who never returned to the camp.[149] The last chance to kill bin Laden came in May 1999, when CIA assets in Afghanistan had located him near Kandahar. According to the 9/11 Commission Report, "the reporting was very detailed and came from several sources. If this intelligence was not 'actionable,' working-level officials said at the time and today, it was hard for them to imagine how any intelligence on Bin Ladin in Afghanistan would meet the standard."[150] The reasons the attack was not approved remain murky and disputed, but clearly the intelligence community's ingrained risk aversion—intensified by the recent accidental bombing of the Chinese embassy in Belgrade—and the administration's fear of political punishment should anything go wrong cost us another chance to take out the architect of 9/11.

With the military option off the table and attacks with cruise missiles subjected to unrealistic standards of intelligence reliability and success, there was not even a pretense made of retaliation for the Cole bombing in 2000. Despite strong evidence from the CIA that bin Laden and al Qaeda were involved, the administration seemingly was not inclined even to deliver an ultimatum to the Taliban to hand over bin Laden or bomb the al Qaeda training camps, let alone take more serious military action. After any retaliation was deferred until "proof" emerged of al Qaeda's guilt, one State Department official wondered prophetically, "Does al Qaeda have to attack the Pentagon to get their attention?"[151] Whether the CIA feared to state more definitively al Qaeda's involvement, or the administration was loath in its last months to launch an attack that could compromise its attempts at an Israeli-Palestinian peace agreement, the murders of 17 U.S. sailors were left unavenged.[152] Even action based on confirmed fact established by reliable intelligence was avoided. Despite detailed knowledge of the location of al Qaeda and other Islamist training camps, through which tens of thousands of jihadists passed and received training in weapons and explosives, before 9/11 "neither the United States nor any of its allies made a serious, systematic, and sustained effort to destroy the camps in even one of the countries in which they were located," Scheuer writes, including the Bekaa Valley Hezbollah camps that for 20 years had been a font of Iranian-sponsored assaults on America.[153] Even after the attack on the *Cole,* the camps weren't attacked. Clinton's only response to the *Cole* attack was yet another American retreat: he ordered all U.S. Navy vessels to head for the safety of open waters and to avoid using the Suez Canal.

Rationalizations for inaction caused by political fear and interest often centered on the presumed delicacy of diplomatic negotiations of various sorts, illustrating once more the eternal bad habit of democracies to use the words of diplomacy as a substitute for unpleasant and risky action. Equally useless were the U.N. Security Council Resolutions, which included economic and travel sanctions and an embargo on weapons shipments to the Taliban.[154] Indeed, the diplomatic efforts during this period, particularly attempts to reach out to the Taliban regime in Afghanistan, were no more successful than had been the previous efforts to engage the Iranian regime dating back to the Carter administration. Attempts by the Clinton administration to engage the Taliban began in 1995. After the fall of Kabul to the Taliban, Secretary of State Warren Christopher told diplomats in Pakistan to convey to the Taliban that "we wish to engage the new 'interim government' at an early stage."[155] For the next few years, a series of State Department suitors courted the Taliban, trying to cajole its leaders to kick bin Laden out of Afghanistan and shut down the terrorist training camps. But the Taliban, like Philip II and Hitler, brilliantly alternated pleasing promises with evasion and delay as they consolidated their brutal rule over Afghanistan and strengthened their ties to al Qaeda. Even after the East Africa embassy bombings engineered by bin Laden, Secretary of State Madeleine Albright, who had succeeded Christopher in 1997, agreed "to engage in a serious and confidential dialogue with the Taliban."[156] These naïve diplomatic efforts to lure the Taliban away from bin Laden failed miserably, based as they were on a complete misreading of the Taliban's and bin Laden's similar roots in Islamist jihadist doctrine. As Michael Rubin summarizes, "Over the course of its five-year engagement ... the Clinton State Department gained nothing. The Taliban had, like many rogue regimes, acted in bad faith. They engaged not to compromise but to buy time. They made many promises but did not keep a single one."[157]

In the end, after two decades of feeble responses to the jihadist murder of Americans abroad, bin Laden was left free to plan the most devastating assault on American soil in history, convinced by our appeasing behavior that the United States was indeed tottering on "foundations of straw," and thus ripe for destruction.

The Vietnam Syndrome Returns

After the destruction of the World Trade Center towers and the murder of 2,973 Americans on 9/11, the United States under President George Bush seemingly had cast off the appeasing delusions of the previous 30 years. The President's address to Congress on September 20 was a vigorous repudiation of the appeasing policies that had allowed al Qaeda and bin Laden to confirm their estimation of American weakness and fear: "Tonight, we are a country awakened to danger and called to defend freedom. Our grief has turned to anger and anger to resolution. Whether we bring our enemies to justice or bring justice to our enemies, justice will be done." The President also put on notice the nations, most obviously Afghanistan, that had harbored the terrorists: "And we will pursue nations that provide aid or safe haven to terrorism. Every nation in every region now has a decision to make: Either you are with us or you are with the terrorists." And passive or half-hearted responses were now discarded for preemptive action: "We will take defensive measures against terrorism to protect Americans."[158] In this same speech, Bush put the ultimatum to the Taliban that Clinton should have after the *Cole* bombing. And when the Taliban refused to hand over bin Laden, in October the war began. By December, the Taliban and al Qaeda were routed, though not definitively destroyed.

This American recovery of nerve, however, would prove to be as transient as the displays of flags after the attacks of 9/11. Soon all the old bad ideas, particularly the post-Vietnam narrative of American guilt over its alleged sins of global oppression, were circulating among the intellectual elite, who began attacking the war in Afghanistan as Vietnam-like neo-colonialist aggression. Anti-war protests were organized in major cities and on university campuses, most conjuring old anti-corporate, pacifist, and internationalist leftist ghosts from the Vietnam era. Most of the protests were put together by International ANSWER, a coalition of radical leftist groups, such as the Workers World Party and the Party for Socialism and Liberation, supporting communist remnant regimes like Cuba and North Korea and terrorist organizations like Hamas.[159] The tenor of these protests can be seen in the comments made by America's most famous, well remunerated, and anti-American radical, MIT professor Noam Chomsky, who announced a few weeks after the war started that America is "the greatest terrorist state" and was planning a "silent genocide" in Afghanistan by deliberately starving Afghans.[160] Radical historian Howard Zinn compared the bombing of Afghanistan to the attacks on 9/11, "a crime which cannot be justified."[161] But even presumably less

extreme leftists could not resist assailing the war in Afghanistan
as another misguided neo-imperialist adventure. A mere three
weeks into the war, *New York Times* columnist R. W. Apple,
Jr., for example, raised the specter of Vietnam in a column published October 31. "Could Afghanistan become another Vietnam?" Apple fretted, dredging up the "ominous word
'quagmire.'"[162]

Trapped in the Vietnam narrative like a fly in amber, the
left assaulted every attempt to undo the bad laws and policies
that had facilitated the massive national security failure of 9/11.
In October 2001, Congress passed the Patriot Act, which eliminated many of the impediments to intelligence gathering that
had accrued since the Church hearings. Many of the provisions gave our intelligence agencies the same surveillance powers long available to criminal investigations. More important
was the clarification in Section 218 eliminating the "wall"
between the FBI and CIA discussed above. This change was
necessary, given the opportunities to preempt the 9/11 plot that
were missed because of the reluctance of the FBI and CIA to
communicate with each other over the "wall." The worst failure that resulted from the "wall" happened in August 2001,
when FBI headquarters denied field agents permission to search
the computer of Zacarias Moussaoui, who was probably training to be part of a second wave of attacks after 9/11.[163] However, despite this glaring example of the flaws in the FISA laws,
critics, led by the American Civil Liberties Union, demonized
the Patriot Act for vastly expanding "the government's authority to spy on its own citizens, while simultaneously reducing
checks and balances on those powers like judicial oversight,
public accountability, and the ability to challenge government
searches in court." Rather than an attempt to keep Americans
from suffering another devastating attack like 9/11, to the civil-
liberties fundamentalists at the ACLU, the Patriot Act "Puts
[the] CIA back in the business of spying on Americans."[164] The
old CIA bogey conjured up in the Church hearings was bran-

dished again by those convinced that the United States was
the font of all global oppression and ruled by crypto-fascists
eager to destroy Americans' civil liberties.

All these attacks on the efforts to end the 20-year-long failures and dysfunction that led to 9/11 were nothing compared
to the firestorm of criticism that met President Bush's war
against Saddam Hussein and al Qaeda. The wisdom of heed-
ing Demosthenes's advice to the Athenians not to wait for blows
like a bad boxer but to anticipate and preempt them became
all too clear in the aftermath of 9/11 and the failure of those
entrusted with our safety to "connect the dots" and take action
against the terrorists. In the case of Iraq, there were many
"dots" to connect: Hussein's past record of aggression against
his neighbors and brutal oppression of his own people, as many
as 300,000 of whom were executed and buried in mass graves;
his violation of 16 U.N. resolutions and the terms of the cease-
fire ending the first Gulf War; his continuing evasion of his
responsibility to reveal his weapons of mass destruction programs, culminating in the ejection of U.N. weapons inspec-
tors from Iraq in 1998; his past record of using chemical
weapons against the Iranians and Kurds; the public relations
nightmare of the U.N. sanctions, which even bin Laden mentioned as evidence of American hostility to Muslims, claiming
"one million innocent children have been killed";[165] the corruption of the U.N. food-for-oil program, which provided billions for Hussein to finance the reconstitution of his weapons
programs; the weakening resolve of U.N. Security Council
members France and Russia for maintaining the sanctions;
the cost and dangers to U.S. Air Force personnel of enforcing
the northern and southern "no fly" zones created to protect
the Kurds and Shiites, Hussein's political enemies and victims;
and Hussein's record of giving aid and succor to numerous terrorists, including the vicious Palestinian terrorist Abu Nidal
and future bin Laden lieutenant abu Musab al-Zarqawi.

For all these reasons, removing Hussein had been official

U.S. foreign policy since 1998, when Congress passed the Iraq Liberation Law, which stated "that it should be the policy of the United States to seek to remove the Saddam Hussein regime from power in Iraq and to replace it with a democratic government."[166] And the necessity of eliminating the threat of Hussein was sharpened to urgency in the aftermath of the most devastating assault in U.S. history, one that could have been prevented with more vigorous and timely responses to the storm of intelligence pointing to an attack. Thus the picture of Hussein that emerged by connecting these "dots" was not one of the Iraqi dictator contained "in the box" by over a decade of ineffective sanctions and U.N. inspections but of a murderous autocrat possessing the potential means and the already demonstrated will to strike once more at the United States and its interests at the first opportunity.[167] This was the conclusion of President Bill Clinton five years earlier, in a speech delivered in February 1998: "What if he fails to comply [with the U.N. resolutions], and we fail to act, or we take some ambiguous third route which gives him yet more opportunities to develop this program of weapons of mass destruction and continue to press for the release of the sanctions and continue to ignore the solemn commitments that he made? Well, he will conclude that the international community has lost its will. He will then conclude that he can go right on and do more to rebuild an arsenal of devastating destruction. And some day, some way, I guarantee you, he'll use the arsenal."[168]

In line with Clinton's scenario, Hussein indeed failed to comply yet again with U.N. resolutions, and so on October 16, 2002, Congress passed the Authorization for Use of Military Force Against Iraq Resolution. The U.N. followed a month later with Security Council Resolution 1441—the *seventeenth* regarding Iraq—giving Hussein one month to disclose his WMD programs and stockpiles or face "serious consequences."[169] The Iraq war was thus consistent with the bipartisan consensus that had developed for almost a decade, a policy made urgent and obvious by the 9/11 attacks and its graphic display of the costs of delay and inaction.

However, to a left mired in its ancient narratives of American global oppression, the war was like Vietnam, just another episode in a fascist power's imperialist adventurism in the service of capitalist profits and exploitation of Third World resources. Even before the war started, the left had added the coming conflict in Iraq to its roster of anti-globalization and anti-Israel protests. In October 2002, hundreds of thousands of demonstrators had appeared at rallies across the country. At them, David Horowitz writes, "Spokesmen denounced America as a 'rogue state' and a 'terrorist state,' likened the president to Adolf Hitler, equated the CIA with al Qaeda, described America's purpose as 'blood for oil,' and called for 'revolution.'"[170] In March 2003, the same month the war began, Vermont governor Howard Dean tapped into this anti-war sentiment and galvanized his long-shot campaign for the Democratic nomination for president by attacking the war in Iraq and asking, "What I want to know is what in the world so many Democrats are doing supporting the President's unilateral intervention in Iraq?"[171] Dean's campaign was given further traction by the numerous anti-war protests, "sit-ins," rallies, and "teach-ins" across America and the world, many of them organized by ANSWER, that had taken place in 2002 and reached a crescendo in March 2003 with the beginning of hostilities. The rallies and protests displayed the reflexive anti-Americanism of the international left, with its Marxist clichés about "imperialism" and "colonialism" and the evils of capitalism. Worse yet were the expressions of support for the enemy and disregard for the lives of the protesters' fellow citizens who would soon be fighting in Iraq. At a teach-in at Columbia University in March, an anthropology professor hoped for America's defeat and "a million Mogadishus," evoking the 1993 killing of 18 American servicemen in Somalia.[172] Bin Laden could not have said it better.

The Democrats Politicize the War

Buoyed by this noisy, telegenic opposition to the war, in June 2003 Dean announced his candidacy for the nomination with another repudiation of the Iraq War: "But there is a fundamental difference between the defense of our nation and the doctrine of preemptive war espoused by this administration. The President's group of narrow-minded ideological advisors are undermining our nation's greatness in the world. They have embraced a form of unilateralism that is even more dangerous than isolationism."[173] Dean's rapid rise from obscurity to front-runner with a $45 million war chest and a cadre of Internet activists soon caught the attention of the other candidates, particularly Senators John Kerry and John Edwards, both of whom had voted to authorize the war and soon were decrying the very conflict they had publicly supported. As the *Wall Street Journal* editorialized, "As Mr. Dean climbed the polls by denouncing the war, he made opposition to it a party litmus test."[174]

Democrats justified this politically convenient shift usually by indulging the magical thinking that "diplomacy," no matter how often it had failed in the past, could have definitively neutralized the threat from Hussein: "I'm saddened," Senate Minority Leader Tom Daschle had said days before the war began, "saddened that this president failed so miserably at diplomacy that we're now forced to war."[175] The Democratic candidates, in the words of the *New York Times,* now "offered a near-unified assault ... on President Bush's credibility in his handling of the Iraq war," alleging "unsubstantiated evidence" in the President's argument for going to war, lamenting the casualties in Iraq, and predictably complaining about his "failure to enlist the help of the United Nations in conducting the war," even though Bush had spent several months attempting to get the U.N. to lend a hand in restoring its own tarnished credibility as a force for global order.[176]

This was the beginning, Horowitz writes, of "a Democratic offensive against the war's commander in chief, which would be pursued relentlessly and without letup for the next year, becoming the focus of the presidential campaign."[177] The media colluded in this assault, emphasizing casualties, civilian dead, military mistakes, and all the other unfortunately typical byproducts of modern warfare. When the war started, CNN reporter Peter Arnett let the media bias cat out of the bag when he was caught telling Iraqi television that "our reports of civilian casualties here are going back to the United States. It helps those who oppose the war."[178] Perhaps the most conspicuous example of the Democrats' relapse into the pre-9/11 posture of American self-loathing and retreat was the enthusiastic presence of Democratic leaders such as Al Gore, Barbara Boxer, Tom Harkin, and Tom Daschle at the premier of Michael Moore's anti-American cinematic libel *Fahrenheit 9–11* in June 2004. Moore's myopic, far-left ideology is obvious in a comment he made that same month about the terrorists who were murdering Americans and their fellow Iraqis: "The Iraqis who have risen up against the occupation are not 'insurgents' or 'terrorists' or 'The Enemy.' They are the REVOLUTION, the Minutemen, and their numbers will grow—and they will win."[179] Such rooting for the enemy killing American soldiers did not hinder former President Jimmy Carter, who along with former Vice-President Al Gore was leading the partisan attack on Bush, from inviting Moore to sit next to him at the Democratic National Convention in 2004. Factional political interest abetted by the liberal media thus facilitated a return to the Vietnam-era Democratic Party's aversion to military force and hostility to its own country, along with its naïve faith, evidenced by Democrats' complaints about Bush's "unilateralism" and "failed diplomacy," in the same diplomatic agreements and transnational organizations that had failed to contain Saddam Hussein for 12 years, let alone keep America safe from terrorists.

The attack on George Bush failed to put a Democrat in the White House in 2004. The American electorate was not yet ready for a return to the discredited idealism of Jimmy Carter embodied in the Democratic candidate John Kerry, one of the most left-wing members of the Senate. During the decade of al Qaeda's assaults on America's interests, Kerry had supported massive cuts in the intelligence budget and pledged to "almost eliminate CIA activity." As a candidate, he asserted that terrorism was a manageable criminal problem, a "nuisance" like prostitution, and despite his vote in support of the Iraq war and his numerous public statements approving Hussein's ouster, he turned against the war as the fruits of "the most inept, reckless, arrogant and ideological foreign policy in modern history."[180] Kerry was an incompetent candidate devoid of charisma and full of liberal hauteur, but in four years the same foreign policy idealism that had contributed to the appeasement of Islamist jihadism would return in a more politically attractive package.

Meanwhile, for the remainder of Bush's second term, Thomas Sowell writes, "As in the case of the Vietnam war, much of the media and the intelligentsia in general declared what was happening in Iraq to be a 'civil war' and 'unwinnable,' and many urged the immediate withdrawal of American troops."[181] The Democrats and their media subsidiaries kept up a continuous public assault against every dimension of the war, employing the mythic Vietnam template. When no WMD were found in Iraq—something critics now knew for sure only because of the war—the "Bush lied" mantra appeared as a means of discrediting a war that was in fact started not just to discover the WMD, which the U.N. and American and European intelligence agencies had all agreed that Hussein possessed. Rather, the Congressional Authorization cited a number of reasons, including Iraq's "brutal repression of its civilian population," its "continuing hostility toward, and willingness to attack, the United States," its willingness "to aid and harbor other international terrorist organizations, including organizations that threaten the lives and safety of United States citizens," and its breach of international law and numerous United Nations resolutions.[182]

Moreover, the emphasis in the authorization legislation was on WMD "capability," not just the possession of existing stockpiles. Although no WMD stockpiles turned up, the report of the Iraq Survey Group, made public in October 2003, indeed established the existence of WMD-related programs and equipment, laboratories and safe houses that concealed equipment from U.N. monitors, research on biological weapons, documents and equipment related to uranium enrichment, plans for long-range missiles, and evidence of attempts to acquire long-range missile technologies from North Korea. All these programs could be quickly rebooted for Hussein's own purposes, or for sale to terrorists. These facts were set aside, however, in order to provide political cover to those Democrats who had voted for an increasingly difficult and unpopular war, and for the partisan advantage gained by casting the Iraq war as another case of right-wing adventurism predicated on fabricated intelligence and outright lies, just as in 1964 the Vietnam war was escalated based on the allegedly false intelligence that led to the Gulf of Tonkin resolution.

Also redolent of the Vietnam formula of "escalation" leading inevitably to a "quagmire" was the near-universal Democratic opposition in early 2007 to the "surge" of troops to Iraq as part of a counterinsurgency strategy to reduce the violence against U.S. forces and Iraqi civilians. The *New York Times* and Congress both railed against this change in strategy. *Times* columnist Paul Krugman wrote, "The only real question about the planned 'surge' in Iraq—which is better described as a Vietnam-style escalation—is whether its proponents are cynical or delusional," an estimation seconded in a *Times* editorial. Congressional Democrats agreed with Krugman. Senator Barack Obama called the surge "a mistake" and a "reckless escalation," and introduced legislation to remove all U.S. combat forces from Iraq by March 31, 2008. Senate Majority Leader Harry Reid and House Speaker Nancy Pelosi sent a letter to President Bush calling the surge "a serious mistake," while Democrats in both houses introduced non-binding resolutions rejecting the surge.[183] Worst of all was Senator Reid's announcement in April 2007 that "this war is lost and the surge is not accomplishing anything."[184] A few months later Joseph Biden concurred: "We need to stop the surge and start to get our troops out." Even after the decline in violence in Iraq was evident by the fall of 2007, the media and the Democrats continued to call the surge a failure. Senator Durbin accused the President and General David Petraeus of manipulating statistics, and Senator Hillary Clinton said the General's report required "the willing suspension of disbelief."[185] And when the evidence of the decline in violence became impossible to ignore, liberals offered fantastic rationalizations to camouflage their partisan attack on a successful strategy—Nancy Pelosi even attributed the decline in violence to the "goodwill of the Iranians."[186]

Thus the political self-interest of the liberal media and many Democratic Congressmen—along with their ideological commitment to the Vietnam narrative of an unjust American military intervention abroad—took precedence over the larger national security interests of the United States in stabilizing Iraq and showing our enemies that, contrary to the estimation of the jihadists, America was not mired in "cowardice and feebleness" and would not run from setbacks and casualties, but fight back with devastating effect. This relentless second-guessing of the war even as our troops were under fire appeased an enemy waging a terroristic war against our morale.

Terrorists' "Rights" Trump National Security

More dangerous to the efforts to forestall another attack on the homeland was the incessant assault on the interrogation methods used to gather information from captured terrorists. After the intelligence failure that led to 9/11, the Bush administration carefully crafted interrogation techniques that could extract information without violating laws against torture. These techniques were all vetted for legality in 2002 and again in 2005 by the Justice Department's Office of Legal Counsel, documents to this day luridly mischaracterized as the "torture memos." The techniques approved, such as waterboarding, were precisely and meticulously calibrated to avoid being torture, which in legal terms requires the *intent* to cause "severe mental and physical pain and suffering."[187] Thus a physician and psychologist were present at the interrogations to monitor the detainee's condition and stop the procedure if necessary. Moreover, almost 27,000 Air Force personnel had been waterboarded between 1992 and 2001 as part of their Survival, Evasion, Resistance, and Escape (SERE) training, without resulting in serious or prolonged physical or mental harm.[188] If waterboarding were torture, then subjecting U.S. citizens to this training, which includes other interrogation techniques approved for use against captured terrorists, would be illegal. As Marc Thiessen concludes, "The fact is, *none* of the techniques used by the CIA meet the standard of torture in U.S. law. This is for two reasons: first, because the CIA's interrogators did not *specifically intend* to inflict severe pain and suffering; second, because they did not *in fact* inflict severe pain and suffering."[189]

More important, the techniques used by the CIA on just a few high-value detainees worked, generating more than 6,000 intelligence reports. Most significant was the information gleaned from Khalid Sheikh Mohammed, the mastermind of the 9/11 attacks who kidnapped and claims to have personally decapitated *Wall Street Journal* reporter Daniel Pearl. Numerous planned terrorist operations against the U.S. were disrupted with the help of this information, including the August 2006 Heathrow plot to blow up seven trans-Atlantic flights using liquid explosives, and other plans to crash planes into buildings in America and blow up embassies and military camps abroad.[190] "From our interrogation of KSM and other senior al-Qa'ida members," former CIA director George Tenet writes, "and our examination of documents found on them, we learned many things—not just tactical information leading to the next capture. For example, more than twenty plots had been put in motion by al-Qa'ida against U.S. infrastructure targets, including communication nodes, nuclear power plants, dams, bridges, and tunnels. All these plots were in various stages of planning when we captured or killed the pre-9/11 al-Qa'ida leaders behind them."[191]

Despite the success of the interrogation program in keeping America free from terrorist attacks for the last nine years, Thiessen writes, "irresponsible government officials have shared secrets they swore to protect with the news media, and left-wing journalists have twisted this information to paint our intelligence community as a band of rogue operators who abandoned our ideals in the fight against terror"[192] The media and other critics were recycling the hoary, liberal fable of a quasi-fascistic U.S. government employing the CIA to violate human rights, an evil only the brave and righteous media—visions of the Pentagon Papers, Watergate, and subsequent Pulitzer Prizes dancing in their heads—could prevent. Along the way, the false charges originating with captured terrorists trained to lie about their treatment, the selective quotations from leaked government documents, and the sheer sloppy thinking of many pundits and reporters were woven by the media into a distorted narrative that slandered and disheartened the brave men and women charged with keeping us secure from attack. Particularly egregious were the many false analogies, ubiquitous in the press and echoed by Democratic Senators Christopher Dodd and Dick Durbin, between waterboarding and the torture techniques used by the Spanish Inquisition, the Khmer Rouge in Cambodia, and Nazi Germany.[193] None of those sadistic torturers were trying to obtain information vital for protecting lives, none had physicians and psychologists present to monitor their victims' health and safety, and none left them without permanent physical damage. In fact, most of those victims died after hours of excruciating agony; not a single detainee in CIA custody has died as the result of supervised interrogation, or suffered permanent injury. However, this sort of irresponsible reporting, exploiting the lurid connotations and imprecision of the word "torture" in everyday use, convinced many in America and elsewhere that the United States was the peer of some of the most brutal and murderous regimes in history.

This assault was, of course, partly in service of partisan political self-interest on the part of Democrats afflicted with "Bush derangement syndrome," an irrational hatred of the man they regarded as the dunce who had "stolen" the 2000 election and then had had the effrontery to get reelected in 2004 by ginning up the oafish masses' inordinate fear of terrorism after 9/11. The controversy about the detainment camp at Guantánamo Bay in Cuba was another point of partisan attack against the administration's efforts to keep American safe and destroy the terrorist networks. Only a fraction of the approximately 80,000 fighters captured in the war on terror, fewer than 800, were sent to Guantánamo, and with a few exceptions they were the worst of the worst, the committed jihadists whose self-confessed mission is to kill Americans. By 2004, 200 detainees had been released and repatriated, some of them to go on to kill Americans again. After tribunals examined the remaining 269, only 38 were deemed not to be enemy combatants.[194] Of these hundreds, only two had special interrogation plans approved for their questioning, and as Thiessen writes, "the techniques used by military interrogators were far less coercive than the techniques used by the CIA."[195] Waterboarding, for example, was explicitly forbidden. For the last four years, detainees have been interrogated only if they volunteer, which they do in order to get special privileges.

Conditions at Guantánamo, moreover, are vastly better than those in most prisons in Europe and the United States, and light years ahead of the jails in the Middle East, where torture is used regularly. Journalist Thomas Joscelyn describes the amenities available to detainees in "Club Gitmo," as Rush Limbaugh calls it: "They can play soccer, basketball, or foosball; exercise on elliptical equipment; and consort with their fellow detainees for up to 20 hours per day in the outdoor recreation area. They can take art classes or learn English," and have access to a library of over 14,000 books, Arabic-language periodicals, and several satellite television channels, including al Jazeera.[196] They receive first-class health care and eat better than American soldiers, all their food prepared according to *halal* standards of ritual purity. Other considerations for the detainees' religious sensibility are shown as well, with holidays like Ramadan respected, periodicals censored to remove offensive images of women, Korans provided and handled by guards only while wearing gloves, and arrows pointing to Mecca painted on floors to guide the faithful in their daily prayers. Contrary to the charges of critics, more than a dozen investigations and reviews of conditions have established that Guantánamo is a model facility, much more humane than many prisons in the European countries whose criticisms have made Guantánamo an international symbol of torture and abuse.

Despite these easily available facts about Guantánamo, critics have called the facility a "gulag," "the Bermuda Triangle of human rights," and a "shocking affront to democracy."[197] Domestic critics like historian Arthur Schlesinger Jr. called the camp "a national disgrace," and the *New York Times*'s Thomas Friedman alleged that "the abuse at Guantánamo and within the whole U.S. military prison system dealing with terrorism is out of control," a charge based primarily on claims made by detainees.[198] A month later the *Times*'s historically challenged editorial page decried what "Guantánamo exemplifies—harsh, indefinite detention without formal charges or legal recourse,"

which "may or may not bring to mind the Soviet Union's sprawl-
ing network of Stalinist penal colonies."[199] Guantánamo's bad
image partly resulted from its careless conflation in the media
with the abu Ghraib detention center in Iraq, where in 2004
an army investigation—not journalists—uncovered and eventually punished abuses by guards that had nothing to do with
interrogation or detention policy but everything to do with poor
training, inadequate supervision, and crowded conditions.
However, having transformed the killers detained at Guantánamo into the victims of Bush's "torture" and brutal "gulag,"
the left has felt no compunction about providing legal aid to
the detainees. Some of the lawyers have exploited lawyer-client
privileges to pass along information detrimental to security,
like the three who showed photographs of CIA interrogators
to clients charged with planning the 9/11 attacks. According to
the CIA, these actions compromised ongoing operations and
endangered the CIA officers and their families, as well as possibly violating the 1982 federal law prohibiting exposing covert
intelligence agents.[200]

These distorted views of Guantánamo are driven by politics, not facts, for they came *after* the 2004 report by Albert T.
Church III, a cousin of CIA critic Senator Frank Church, which
concluded, "We can confidentially state that based upon our
investigation, we found nothing that would in any way sub-
stantiate detainees' allegations of torture or violent physical
abuse at GTMO." Church's conclusion was confirmed by a
bipartisan Independent Panel that investigated treatment of
detainees in Iraq, Afghanistan, and Guantánamo, and determined that abuse took place in only .123 percent of detentions,
and .066 percent of interrogations—hardly a rate to warrant
Friedman's phrase "out of control," or justify the implication
that it was systemic policy.[201] Moreover, Church reported, the
perfectly legal interrogations—almost all conducted with techniques like those in the Army Field Manual that President
Obama has approved for interrogating terrorist suspects—saved

lives by generating intelligence about terrorist activities.[202] The truth, however, served neither the partisan political interests of the Democrats and the liberal media nor their utopian idealism that believes America can be protected against fanatic murderers with the Geneva Conventions, the International Court of Justice, and the alleged power of fidelity to principles that the enemy contemptuously dismisses as evidence of our weakness and doubt.

The Fetish of Diplomacy

Another theme of the liberal assault on George Bush was his abandonment of diplomacy, internationalism, and multilateralism to gratify an itchy trigger-finger, resulting in a decline in American prestige, along with increased difficulties in achieving our foreign policy aims. This liberal consensus was expressed in a *Los Angeles Times* editorial: "The Bush administration's hubris and relentless disregard for our allies abroad shredded the fabric of multilateralism. . . . The Bush years, defined by ultimatums and unilateral actions around the world, must be brought to a swift close with a renewed emphasis on diplomacy, consultation and the forging of broad international coalitions."[203] This was published in January 2009, after years of the mainstream media's depictions of George Bush as a unilateralist "cowboy" eager to torture detainees and spy on U.S. citizens had contributed to the election of Illinois Senator Barack Obama as President in 2008. Senator for a scant two years before running for President, Obama had been a vocal critic of the Iraq war and an opponent of the "surge." He had explicitly campaigned on a foreign policy predicated on moralizing internationalism, a preference for diplomacy and transnational institutions, a focus on human rights and foreign development, and the assumption that the United States was flawed and in need of some humility after the reckless aggression and oppressive practices of the Bush administration.

In a 2007 *Foreign Affairs* article, Obama had sounded all these themes from the old Vietnam narrative of America's "arrogance of power," as foreign policy dove Senator J. William Fulbright called it in his 1966 book of that name. To Obama, the war in Iraq is a "civil war" like the Vietnam conflict, a quagmire-like "morass" requiring withdrawal of U.S. forces as quickly as possible before the slide into disastrous "escalation." In addition, "we must launch a comprehensive regional and international diplomatic initiative to help broker an end to the civil war in Iraq." A distrust of force and a preference for diplomatic engagement emerges from Obama's essay as the keys to pursuing America's interests and security. He writes of the need "to reinvigorate American diplomacy," since "tough-minded diplomacy, backed by the whole range of instruments of American power—political, economic, and military—could bring success even when dealing with long-standing adversaries such as Iran and Syria." This renewal of diplomacy will accompany a restoration of multilateralism and participation in international institutions: "To renew American leadership in the world, I intend to rebuild the alliances, partnerships, and institutions necessary to confront common threats and enhance common security." At the same time, Obama sounds the note of American guilt for its recent sins and the power of principled example to affect the behavior of other states: "To build a better, freer world, we must first behave in ways that reflect the decency and aspirations of the American people. This means ending the practices of shipping away prisoners in the dead of night to be tortured in far-off countries, of detaining thousands without charge or trial, of maintaining a network of secret prisons to jail people beyond the reach of the law." No word on whether any of those policies have generated intelligence or kept Americans safe. Finally, American exceptionalism is out, as the United States is just one imperfect nation among many, and it needs to use its power and wealth to help less fortunate countries "not in the spirit of a patron but in the spirit of a partner—a partner mindful of his own imperfections."[204]

In short, Obama's foreign policy represented a return to the Carter philosophy that had helped put in power an Islamist regime in Iran and ignited a Soviet global expansion in Afghanistan, Latin America, and central Africa.[205] As Arthur Herman wrote in January 2009, Obama came into office "trailing clouds of Carterite rhetoric and Carteresque ideas about the inutility of military force, the sovereign worth of 'aggressive diplomacy' (an incoherent and meaningless phrase), and the need to accommodate ourselves to a world in which we are no longer even an *economic* superpower, let alone an example to mankind."[206] As such, like Carter's, Obama's foreign policy philosophy downplays the dangers to America's interests and security, touts the value of American patience and deference, seeks arms reductions, privileges international law and transnational institutions like the International Criminal Court, and rejects American exceptionalism, which is merely a native prejudice, given that every country believes it is exceptional, as Obama told a *Financial Times* reporter.[207] In September 2009, Obama said in the accents of British moralizing internationalism during the 1930s, "In an era when our destiny is shared, power is no longer a zero-sum game. No one nation can or should try to dominate another nation. No world order that elevates one nation or group or people over another will succeed. No balance of power among nations will hold."[208] Obama is unclear, however, about what to do when a people or nation *does* elevate itself over others and tries to dominate them through force.

Obama Follows the Chamberlain Playbook

In Obama's first year in office, his appeasing foreign policy actions resembled those of the Carter years and threatened the same malign consequences for our efforts to destroy the jihadist enemy. In the attempt to "embrace a new era of engagement based on mutual interests and mutual respect," as he told the U.N., Obama has indeed attempted to engage repressive regimes that do not share our "interests" and do not "respect" us. He has shaken hands with Venezuelan strongman Hugo Chávez, backed Chávez's disciple in Honduras against that country's legal removal of him from power, hounded Israel over the construction of apartment buildings in East Jerusalem in order to curry favor with the Palestinians, canceled the missile defense agreement with Poland and the Czech Republic as part of his attempt to push the "reset button" with Russia, made several overtures to Cuba, and sent diplomatic officials on six trips to Syria, a country that hosts, supports, and arms terrorist organizations like Hezbollah, assassinated Lebanon's former prime minister Rafiq Hariri, and facilitates the transit of insurgents into Iraq—during one period, over 90 percent of jihadists traveling to Iraq, according to the U.S. military.[209] Syrian autocrat Bashar al Assad has reciprocated Obama's outreach by hosting a confab in February 2010 with Hezbollah's leader Hassan Nasrallah and Iranian president Mahmoud Ahmadinejad. And, of course, Obama has, as he himself put it, "bent over backwards" in his attempts to reach out to Iran.[210] Unfortunately, such efforts at outreach have generated little in return other than contemptuous responses and actions contrary to our interests.

As for the war against jihad, Obama has particularly targeted the detainee and interrogation programs that have kept America safe for nine years, but that our enemies and allies alike have demonized out of national self-interest or utopian idealism. On January 22, Obama signed Executive Order 13491, ending the CIA's interrogation program and prohibiting the enhanced interrogation techniques, and Order 13492, shutting down the Guantánamo detention facility, a goal still unmet as of January 2011.[211] The reasons for closing Gitmo were feeble at best, having nothing to do with its success at neutralizing committed terrorists eager to attack America and everything to do with the public relations problems caused by distorted, exaggerated, and false allegations about detainee abuse. Obama spokesman Dennis Blair, for example, called Guantánamo a "damaging symbol to the world," in effect giving veto power over U.S. national security to the self-interested, ignorant, or mendacious opinions of our enemies and allies.[212]

Much more damaging to national security were Obama's actions ending the CIA interrogation program and proscribing the enhanced interrogation techniques that had yielded so much valuable information and forestalled several terrorist attacks. Compounding this error, on April 16, 2009, Obama ordered the release of the Justice Department memos that in the process of vetting the techniques for legality described them in detail. The President made this decision despite the strong objections of six CIA directors, including Obama's own appointee, Leon Panetta, and eight covert field operatives who visited the White House to warn the President that he was putting agency operatives at risk.[213] Revealing these techniques to the world meant that reserving the option to use them in the future, as Obama had done in his executive order, was meaningless: "Releasing the details of how, and why, these enhanced techniques are applied," Thiessen writes, "give the enemy a roadmap for how to overcome them."[214]

To compound even further the folly of the President's actions, the same month that Obama ordered the memos to be released, Attorney General Eric Holder appointed a special prosecutor to determine if the CIA officers involved in the interrogation program were guilty of breaking the law—despite the fact that five years earlier, the Justice Department had already determined, based on the CIA's Inspector General's report, that only one person, a CIA contractor later prosecuted, had violated the law. Apart from the legal expense and damage to the reputations and careers of the CIA officers targeted by Holder's investigation, the "morale of the CIA has been shaken to its foundation," in the words of former CIA director Porter Goss. "Instead of taking risks, our intelligence officers will soon resort to wordsmithing cables to headquarters while opportunities to neutralize brutal radicals are lost."[215] In just a few months, Obama had sent the CIA back to the September 10 culture of risk aversion and timidity that had contributed to the disaster of 9/11.

Obama's decisions partly reflected, of course, partisan political interests. He had campaigned on the liberal theme of how the Bush administration's "illegal war" and "gulags" and "torture" flouted the Constitution and international law and in the process damaged America's moral authority. Thus he had to take actions that placated liberal Democrats and proved that he was the "un-Bush," even if America's security was compromised along the way. Carter-era idealism about foreign relations was also at work in Obama's decisions. The charge that Bush's "hubris and relentless disregard for our allies" had damaged America's interests, and so "a renewed emphasis on diplomacy, consultation and the forging of broad international coalitions" was needed, as the *Los Angeles Times* editorial put it, was another constant during the campaign. The executive orders ending the enhanced interrogation techniques and shutting down Guantánamo were partly in deference to international opinion, a signal that the U.S. was eager once more to be a good international citizen, which in effect means subordinating our interests to those of the imagined "global community." The problem is that the foreign opinions about the actions taken to keep Americans safe—many from countries with horrific human rights records— reflect adherence not to some universal moral principle, but rather to the national interests and political needs of the individual countries, interests that more often than not conflict with our own.

Flattering the Jihadists

Obama's "renewal of diplomacy" has been another much touted and praised dimension of his presidency so far, meeting with approval from our European allies and a Nobel Peace Prize bestowed not for the President's deeds but for his rhetoric. Europeans and American liberals are pleased with this shift from Bush's alleged unilateral arrogance back to Jimmy Carter's multilateral humility, just as Obama had pledged to do when he accepted the Democratic Party's nomination: "But I will also renew the tough, direct diplomacy that can prevent Iran from obtaining nuclear weapons and curb Russian aggression. I will build new partnerships to defeat the threats of the 21st century: terrorism and nuclear proliferation; poverty and genocide; climate change and disease."[216] In Obama's inaugural address, this outreach was specifically directed at Muslim nations, many of which provide the foot soldiers of jihad: "To the Muslim world, we seek a new way forward, based on mutual interest and mutual respect," and he pledged that "we will extend a hand if you are willing to unclench your fist."[217] Obama has delivered on this promise, predicating his outreach, as did Jimmy Carter, on the recognition of our own "culpabilities and shortcomings" as the *Boston Globe* wrote in October 2009.[218]

Obama inadvertently signaled his new appeasing attitudes toward the Muslim world when he bowed low to Saudi King Abdullah, the premier financer of Islamist global proselytizing, right after sending back to England a bust of Winston Churchill. This apologetic outreach to Muslims, spiced with remarkable historical ignorance, was most visibly on display in the speech he gave in Cairo on June 4, 2009. The President identified Western sins, not Islamist terrorism supported by states in the Middle East, as the source of the "tension" between the West and Islam: "colonialism that denied rights and opportunities to many Muslims, and a Cold War in which Muslim-majority countries were too often treated as proxies without regard to their own aspirations." Complementing this confession of guilt was the historically dubious claim that Islam had "carried the light of learning through so many centuries, paving the way for Europe's Renaissance and Enlightenment," including a whole host of inventions such as printing, the compass, and the arch, that in fact had originated elsewhere. Most egregious was the assertion that "Islam has demonstrated through words and deeds the possibilities of religious tolerance and racial equality," a "proud tradition of tolerance" evident "in the history of Andalusia and Cordoba during the Inquisition."[219]

This last assertion was particularly laughable, given that, as historian Victor Davis Hanson points out, "Córdoba had few Muslims when the Inquisition began in 1478, having been reconquered by the Christians well over two centuries earlier."[220] And the claim of Andalusian "religious tolerance" would no doubt have surprised the several thousand Jews massacred in Grenada in 1066, or the 300 Christians crucified in 818 during a three-day rampage of killing and pillaging in Córdoba, or the 700 Christians slaughtered in Toledo in 806.[221] This oft-repeated assertion of Islamic tolerance of other religions is possible only by dint of profound ignorance about the humiliating and precarious second-class status of Christians and Jews living under Islamic hegemony, a political and social status akin to that of black Americans in the Jim Crow south. All this appeasing flattery and protestations of guilt accompanied yet another outreach to Iran, with which, the President said, "We are willing to move forward without preconditions on the basis of mutual respect." In his eagerness to engage Iran, Obama seemingly is willing to wink at that country's continuing involvement in attacks against Americans in Afghanistan and Iraq, which includes supplying terrorists with training and funds, as well as plastic explosives, armor-piercing roadside bombs, rocket-propelled grenades, 240mm rockets, and surface-to-air missiles—graphic testimony that Iran has little "respect" for the United States or its principles.[222]

In this speech Obama reprised 30 years of American

ignorance about the true nature of Islam and the Iranian revolution, reducing both to Western guilty liberal obsessions such
as colonialism and our alleged crimes during the Cold War,
which Obama seems to have forgotten the U.S. won against
one of the most murderous regimes in history. Worse yet was
the Western therapeutic assumption that Islam's problems arise
not just from the West's historical sins, but also from a lack of
self-esteem because its mythical achievements have not been
adequately acknowledged. Obama's choice to head up NASA,
Charles Bolden, continued this dubious tack, announcing in
July 2010 that part of his job would be "to find a way to reach
out to the Muslim world and engage much more with domi-
nantly Muslim nations to help them feel good about their his-
toric contribution to science ... and math and engineering."[223]
This psychological assessment is difficult to square with Islam's
traditional chauvinism, evident in Koranic verses such as 3.110,
which calls Muslims "the best of nations raised for (the benefit) of men." No ancient anachronism, this sentiment reap-
pears in the preamble of the Cairo Declaration of Human
Rights in Islam (1990), which reaffirms "the civilizing and historical role of the Islamic Ummah [community of Muslims]
which God made the best nation that has given mankind a universal and well-balanced civilization."[224]

Also missing in Obama's panegyric was any mention of the
Islamist revival of the fourteen centuries-long tradition of jihad,
likewise justified by, as Qutb put it, "a sense of superiority
based on the permanent truth centered in the very nature of
existence," a truth "above the logic of force, the concept of
environment, the terminology of society, and the customs of
people, as indeed it is joined with the Living God Who does
not die."[225] Nor did Obama grasp the nature of the Islamic
regime in Iran, which, as we saw above, is part of a movement
to wage global jihad in order to restore Islam's preeminence,
a goal that the nuclear weapons program, begun in 1984, will
go a long way toward achieving. Given the religious foundations

of the Iranian regime and its hostility to the "Great Satan," and the geo-strategic clout nuclear weapons would bestow on Iran, Obama's solicitous plea for "mutual respect" is no more likely to change its behavior than have the numerous previous American "outreaches" dating back to the administration of Jimmy Carter.[226] Now, however, the stakes are much higher: the possibility that Iran will become a nuclear power and radically reconfigure the balance of power in the Middle East, or provide nuclear weapons to terrorists eager to acquire them: "It would be a sin," bin Laden has said, "for Muslims not to try to possess the weapons that would prevent the infidels from inflicting harm on Muslims."[227]

Munich Redux: Obama and Iran

Obama's belief that the power of his personality and his repeated flattering "outreach" to Muslims would change their perceptions of America, let alone their behavior, has not been validated by reality. The August 2010 Arab Public Opinion Poll revealed that in contrast to 2009, when 51 percent of Arabs were "hopeful" regarding Obama's Middle East policy, a year later only 16 percent were. Moreover, while 15 percent were "discouraged" in 2009, in 2010 63 percent are.[228] No more successful has been Obama's extended hand to the mullahs in Iran "without preconditions," as can be seen from the regime's contemptuous and dismissive responses to his efforts. A videotaped greeting on the occasion of the Persian new year in March 2009 was dismissed by the "supreme leader" Ayatollah Khamenei, who announced a few weeks later that "the path of Iran's nuclear progress could not be blocked."[229] Sometime in May 2009, Obama sent a personal letter to Khamenei calling for "co-operation in regional and bilateral relations," a missive no more successful than Jimmy Carter's letter to Khomeini during the hostage crisis.[230] In response, the regime initiated a brutal crackdown on the protests against the rigged

June 12 presidential election, protests Khamenei attributed to American "agents" and their provocations. Not even Obama's delay in speaking out against the attacks on protesters mollified the ayatollah. Indeed, during the height of the mullahs' crackdown on the protesters, the State Department welcomed Iranian diplomats to Fourth of July celebrations in honor of the freedoms the Iranians were denying to their people. In October 2009, after Iran failed to disclose a uranium-enrichment facility in Qom, Obama responded, "We remain committed to serious, meaningful engagement with Iran," and promised that the "offer stands" of "greater international integration if [Iran] lives up to its obligations," the same obligations the regime has serially ignored and gamed for over a decade.[231] And Iran's support of al Qaeda continues, according to General Petraeus, who in March 2010 said that al Qaeda "continues to use Iran as a key facilitation hub, where facilitators connect al Qaeda's senior leadership to regional affiliates."[232]

Given the solicitous timidity of Obama's appeasing responses to Iran's serial hostile behavior—arming and training the killers of American troops, pursuing weapons of mass destruction, nurturing terrorist organizations, threatening to destroy our ally Israel, and imprisoning three U.S. citizens on the pretext they are "spies"—it is no wonder that the two deadlines (in September and December 2009) Obama set for Iran to come clean on its nuclear program, and the accompanying empty threats that have attended these deadlines, have been contemptuously ignored. For all of Obama's solicitous outreach and diplomatic wheedling of our allies, "the United States does not have an effective long-range policy for dealing with Iran's steady progress toward nuclear capability," as Defense Secretary Robert M. Gates wrote in a January 2010 memo leaked to the *New York Times*.[233]

In his naïve idealism about the ability of diplomacy to neutralize an aggressor, and his misplaced vanity over the persuasive powers of his mere personality, Obama recalls Neville Chamberlain and the Munich debacle. Indeed, Obama's failure so far to inhibit Iran's nuclear ambitions with diplomatic engagement reflects the long record of diplomacy's failure when one side manipulates the process and participates in bad faith, while the other has made it clear that force has been taken off the table.[234] The only weapon the U.S. has wielded so far against Iran is economic sanctions, that old device—remember the toothless sanctions the League of Nations imposed on Mussolini after his invasion of Ethiopia in 1935— for camouflaging an unwillingness to act by doing just enough to create the illusion that something is being done but not enough to compel the enemy to change his behavior. The Iran Sanctions Act of 1996 has been largely ineffective, not the least because companies continue to do business with Iran, some of them receiving federal contracts and grants despite breaking the law. Indeed, in 14 years not one company has been punished for violating the sanctions act.[235]

The three U.N. Security Council Resolutions have not done any better, nor have offers of economic incentives convinced Iran to give up its pursuit of nuclear weapons. Sanctions that do have at least a chance to be truly effective—such as blocking the import of gasoline and the export of oil—are eschewed for various reasons, such as the fear that they would hurt the average Iranian and increase support for the regime. Of course, equally possible is that Iranian rage would be directed *against* an unpopular regime, hastening its demise. More pertinent is the economic pain such sanctions would cause to the countries that trade with Iran, buy its oil, and sell it gasoline. As if to underline the futility of economic sanctions, in April 2010, just as the Obama administration was crowing over China's vague promises to support "tough" sanctions, two Chinese state companies were selling gasoline to Iran, dropping the intermediaries they had been using for such transactions.[236]

On June 8, 2010, the U.N. Security Council passed yet another round of sanctions on Iran, yet these omitted any energy embargo, and the other prohibitions on arms imports and the financial sector do not promise to be any more effective than previous ones. About a month later, President Obama signed into law further restrictions on international banks that do business with Iran. However, such piecemeal sanctions are unlikely to deter a regime that has frequently demonstrated its disregard for its own citizens' comfort and that is motivated in part by spiritual imperatives indifferent to material goods. Moreover, this latest U.N. resolution will fail if its goal, as has been that of the three previous ones, is merely to compel Iran to accept monitoring from the International Atomic Energy Agency to enforce its provisions. Such a settlement could allow Iran eventually to possess "nuclear latency," the ability to create a bomb when it needs to, while the West can assert that it has kept the bomb out of Iran's hands.[237] As John Bolton points out, "Any resolution that leaves Iran's current regime with control over the entire nuclear fuel cycle is simply a face-saving way of accepting" that Iran will successfully develop nuclear weapons. "Given Iran's fulsome 20-year history of denial and deception, there is simply no doubt that its efforts toward building nuclear weapons would continue."[238] As North Korea did successfully, Iran can cheat, lie, delay, and otherwise manipulate the diplomatic and inspections process to buy enough time to develop the weapons. And given this administration's aversion to force—and the reality that the only credible threat of force, an Israeli attack, would involve huge material and diplomatic costs to that nation for at best a short delay in Iran's progress toward the bomb—continuing diplomatic efforts will amount to little more than an act of appeasement that in as few as two years, according to the CIA, will leave Iran a nuclear power, with serious consequences for our interests abroad and our security at home.[239]

The jihadists we have been battling for 30 years know they cannot defeat the U.S. in a conventional war. Unlike Hitler's Germany, there is no Islamic nation with a war machine that represents an immediate existential threat to the U.S., nor is a world war likely to erupt, given the overwhelming supremacy and unrivaled lethality of the U.S. military. The jihadists instead are fighting a long, grinding war against our morale, a cosmic spiritual struggle between, as bin Laden puts it, "two separate camps—one of faith, where there is no hypocrisy, and one of infidelity."[240] The "believers" have absolute confidence in the righteousness of their fight and its sanction by the divine, so that they will kill and die for what they believe. The "infidels" are full of doubt, fear, and self-loathing, and so are unwilling not just to die and kill for their beliefs, but even to discomfort the enemy or endure the mendacious, self-interested calumny of other nations. In this fight, the material and economic superiority of the infidel is great, but the spiritual power of the believer is greater: "Do not let your strength and modern arms fool you," bin Laden has warned Americans, "for they but win a few battles yet lose the war. Patience and steadfastness are greater, and the end result is the most important thing."[241] Whether this Islamist estimation of America is accurate or a fatal misjudgment—as it briefly appeared to be in the aftermath of 9/11—will become clear in the coming years.

America's Response

Just as England and France had failed to take advantage of several opportunities to challenge Germany's violations of the Versailles Treaty and Hitler's aggressive probes of the Allies' resolve, so too, starting in 1979, the United States failed to act with mind-concentrating force against the jihadist assaults on its people and interests. And just as the failure to counter Germany's assaults on the Versailles settlement damaged England's prestige, thus inviting the escalation of aggression that led to World War II, America's similar serial failures, equally damaging to its international prestige, emboldened the escalation of violence that culminated in 9/11.

The reasons America failed to act in 1979 had nothing to

do with a lack of the military capability to defeat the Iranians in a war. In the first few months after the Iranian embassy takeover, Carter's advisers proposed various options for responding to the kidnapping, including destroying Iran's oil industry or imposing a naval blockade in order to shut down all imports and exports. They all were rejected because they were considered too risky.[242] Such measures, if part of a calculated escalation of force, could have been effective, given that the political situation in Iran was fluid and divided, as the Islamists had not yet consolidated their power and marginalized the secular nationalists, whose conflicting interests now resurfaced after the brief harmony forged to overthrow the Shah. Of course, such proposals carried substantial risks and costs, particularly the deaths of the hostages and the possible intervention of the Soviet Union. The former contingency was politically toxic, although leaders are supposed to make such hard calculations of what Lincoln called the "awful arithmetic," the tragic reality that some people die today so that more don't die tomorrow. As for the Soviet Union, it was no more likely to start a war, let alone a suicidal nuclear war, over Iran than it was over Cuba or Vietnam. The Soviets certainly did not fear *our* military response when they invaded Afghanistan a month after the seizure of the embassy, one of a series of Third World expansions in the 1970s equally dismissive of our displeasure.

The next lost opportunity came after the Marine barracks bombing in 1983, which followed the lack of retaliation for the April embassy bombing. The failure to punish the killing of our soldiers in Beirut was much worse than letting the Iranians get away with kidnapping our citizens, for it more starkly illustrated just how far America would go to avoid a hard fight, even when our own troops had been killed and our country humiliated by a terrorist gang. Moreover, not retaliating sent our enemies the message that terrorism could force the U.S. to change its policies, establishing a precedent we are still living with. Several options for a punishing response were feasible. Selected targets in Iran and Syria, sponsors of the attacks, could have been bombed, sending those states a message, which they still have not received 27 years later, that they would be held accountable for attacks by their proxies. Bombing the Bekaa Valley camps, followed by an invasion in force to expel the Iranians and the Islamists, would have degraded the jihadist networks and disabused the Islamists of their estimations of our weakness and cowardice. So too with Mogadishu in 1993, so too with Afghanistan after the 1998 east Africa embassy bombings. There is no reason to think the overthrow of the Taliban in 1998 would not have been as swift as it was in 2001.

All these decisions would have been hard, for they were replete with unforeseen consequences and unknown contingencies, incalculable risks and potentially exorbitant costs. But so too have been the consequences and contingencies, the risks and costs of *not* acting.

These opportunities were lost and the enemy appeased rather than punished, not so much because the material obstacles to them could not be surmounted or the material resources to prevail were lacking. Those obstacles and risks were nowhere near what the U.S. faced in December 1941 when, still mired in the Great Depression, it declared war on the world's two mightiest military machines. America did not punish the Islamists for reasons similar to those that kept England from confronting Hitler—the post-Vietnam collapse of confidence and faith in the goodness of American power and the ideals it served, a failure of nerve caused by short-sighted political interest, fear, and various ideological nostrums both old and new.

Democracy and the Dangers of Factional Interests

By now it is obvious that political factionalism has been the bane of democratic governments from ancient Athens to

America, particularly when a democracy confronts external threats. Short-term partisan interests, made urgent in the U.S. by the two-year election cycle, can frequently trump long-term security needs. Decisions that involve putting American troops in danger are particularly risky when electronic images of war's horrors can be immediately broadcast to the citizenry in living color. Such brutal images, often presented without context, evoke powerful emotions easily exploited by political enemies, as exemplified by the controversy over Bush's ban on publishing photographs of soldiers' coffins returning from Iraq and Afghanistan, a policy that his political enemies claimed was intended to sanitize the wars and obscure their costs. This problem has been worsened these days by the permanent reelection campaign, 24/7 cable news and talk industry, daily opinion polls, and the instantaneously metastasizing opinions and commentary of the blogosphere, all of which have intensified the power of accountability to the citizenry that has always compromised action in democracies. After Vietnam, the first war in which live footage of soldiers fighting and dying was beamed into the intimacy of American living rooms, the political danger of being responsible for such images has become an inhibiting factor for those weighing the use of force to achieve security and foreign policy aims, even if appeasing an aggressor results.

From Carter to Obama, America's appeasement of Islamic jihad cannot be fully understood without taking into account the electoral pressure put on American leaders as they struggled to calculate how quickly the images of casualties and the destruction typical of war would drain their political support, at the same time they weighed as well the need to do something to placate an angry electorate. It is a testimony to George Bush's political leadership that he did not give in to such pressure even as the war in Iraq was beset with setbacks and difficulties and the Democrats and the media incessantly and at times brutally attacked his policies and person. Other politicians have not been as stalwart. As we have seen, during the Clinton era this political calculus made the use of diplomacy and cruise missiles, no matter how ineffective and indecisive, the safest and cheapest option when the need to do something was politically pressing. And the political traction that the little-known Howard Dean gained from opposing the war in Iraq encouraged the Democratic front-runners in the 2004 presidential campaign to forget their previous loud support for the war and to use it as a weapon against George Bush. Similarly, Barack Obama predicated his campaign against John McCain on opposition to a war that Senate Majority Leader Harry Reid pronounced was "lost" even as our troops were battling an enemy whose aim was precisely to create the defeatism that makes appeasement much easier.

In international relations as well, conflicting national interests frequently compromise the alliances and collective strategies necessary for defeating global jihadist terrorism, self-interests usually dressed up in some lofty ideal or other. In 2002, France and Germany fought against a U.N. resolution to remove Hussein from power, not because of the principle of internationalism or the ideal of the diplomatic resolution of crises, but because it was not in those countries' economic and political interests. The current war in Afghanistan is being waged under the auspices of NATO, but the European members have provided relatively few combat troops, leaving the bulk of the fighting, killing, and dying to the American military. And what soldiers they do send are subject to restrictions on their use, and to the vagaries of domestic political pressures to withdraw them, demands that recur with every European election. As for the multilateral attempts to reign in Iran's nuclear ambitions, the failure of the U.N. Security Council to impose serious sanctions is the result of Russia and China's reluctance to risk their extensive political and economic ties to the mullahs' regime. In a pointed rejection of U.S. efforts to impose sanctions, Russia announced during Secretary of State Clinton's March 2010 visit to Moscow that it would complete a nuclear power plant for the Iranians. Meanwhile China has invested heavily in developing oil fields and building oil refineries in Iran, as well as selling weapons to the mullahs, as have the Russians.

Fear, Terror, and the "Rushdie Rules"

As for the second of the Thucydidean causes of appeasement, fear obviously is the whole point of jihadist terror, which aims not at military defeat but at the moral paralysis that leads to appeasing the enemy. This fear is more insidious and effective than that afflicting Englishmen during the 1920s and 1930s as they contemplated the effects of aerial bombardment sure to take place in the next conflict. As terrifying as that prospect was, it was something that would attend the outbreak of hostilities and so to some extent could be prepared for, as the British did by developing radar stations and the Hurricane and Spitfighter fighter planes, or during the Munich crisis by issuing gas masks, filling sand bags, and conducting evacuation drills. Modern terror attacks derive their power precisely from being unexpected and seemingly random, occurring not during war but in peace—in the case of 9/11, literally coming out of a clear blue sky. Such attacks intrude into our daily lives and the spaces in which we travel and work, puncturing the cocoon of security from violence that we think our wealth and technology and progress have provided. Hence terrorist violence creates a chronic anxiety that, unlike attacks during war, has no imaginable end brought by the victory or surrender that ends conventional wars, and so is even more demoralizing and conducive to appeasing policies. Suicide bombing compounds this effect, for now the perpetrators are seemingly irrational fanatics in the service of a strange god, caring nothing for all the goods—life, liberty, and the pursuit of happiness—that define our lives and so cannot be deterred by threats of punishment or death. Thus by a cold actuarial calculus the numbers of dead from terrorist attacks have been minuscule, but the impact on the perceptions of the terrorists' enemies has been enormous, leading to appeasing behavior and policies.

The Islamists, however, do not have to stage terrorist attacks to rouse this fear. Less spectacular forms of violence have also been potent weapons in the jihad against the West, so much so that the pervasive threat of violent retaliation is enough to make Westerners change their behavior. The ready recourse to violence against those seen as enemies of Islam not just by jihadists but also by ordinary Muslims has appeared over and over for the last 20 years. So has the usually cringing and appeasing response of the societies attacked.

The first major instance of this technique of modern jihadist intimidation was the fatwa Khomeini issued in February 1989 against Indian novelist Salman Rushdie, whose novel *The Satanic Verses* was deemed "against Islam, the Prophet, and the Koran."[43] Inspired by Khomeini, Muslims worldwide marched, rioted, and bombed bookstores, with over 20 people dying. The Italian translator of the novel was severely beaten, the Norwegian publisher shot, and the Japanese translator murdered. The phenomenon of a religious and political leader of a nation inviting the murder of a foreign writer living in another country whose laws he had not violated was extraordinary. So too was the frightened reaction of many in the West to this assault against the critical political goods of free speech and the rule of law. Bookstores refused to stock the novel, publishers delayed or canceled editions of it, and Muslims in Western countries publicly burned copies and called for Rushdie's murder with impunity. Some in the West seemingly agreed with this attack on intellectual freedom. Preeminent British historian Hugh Trevor-Roper declared that he "would not shed a tear if some British Muslims, deploring Mr. Rushdie's manners, were to waylay him in a dark street and seek to improve them."[244] A professor at UCLA said Khomeini was "completely within his rights" to demand Rushdie's death. Western governments, with the exception of French President François Mitterrand, were slow in responding, and timorous when they did. After riots in Islamabad, the U.S. embassy assured Muslims that the "U.S. government in no way supports or associates itself with any activity that is [in] any sense offensive or insulting to Islam." As Daniel Pipes concludes of these appeasing reactions, the West "ran scared of Tehran."[245]

Particularly after the 9/11 attacks provoked some pushback against Muslim aggression, violence or the threat of violence has been frequently directed against those in the West who "insult" Allah, Islam, or the Prophet—a phenomenon that Pipes calls the "Rushdie Rules." The 2004 brutal murder of Dutch filmmaker Theo van Gogh on the streets of Amsterdam by a second-generation Moroccan immigrant angered over the film *Submission,* which criticizes Islam's subordination of women; the riots, death threats, and at least 139 dead following a Danish newspaper's publication in 2005 of innocuous cartoons that used depictions of Mohammed not to insult Islam but to defend free speech; the violence that followed Pope Benedict's 2006 Regensburg address, in which he quoted a Byzantine emperor criticizing Mohammed for theologizing violence, an estimation confirmed by the subsequent riots, vandalizing of Christian churches, murder of a nun in Somalia, and kidnapping and beheading of a priest in Iraq—these are the more famous recent instances of Muslim violence striking directly at the heart of Western freedom. Critics of Islam who manage to escape death are compelled to live incognito, as does Ibn Warraq, author of *Why I Am Not A Muslim,* and Bat Ye'or, the scholar of dhimmitude. Others live in hiding, like Ayaan Hirsi Ali, condemned for collaborating with Theo van Gogh on *Submission* and penning *Infidel,* her attack on Muslim misogyny and intolerance. And some face prosecution by their own craven governments, like the late Oriana Fallaci, author of two books defending Western values against Islamic intolerance, or Dutch member of parliament Geert Wilders, indicted for his outspoken defense of Western values and his criticisms of Islam's theologically justified violence in his short film *Fitna*.

The West Still Runs Scared

More significant are the responses to this assault on Western freedom, most of which have been desperate attempts to appease Muslim sensibilities in order to avoid more violence. After van Gogh's murder, the producer canceled a screening of *Submission* at a festival devoted to censored movies, and many Dutch intellectuals opined that van Gogh's "vulgarity" and "insensitivity" had led to his death. In England, one writer for *Index on Censorship*, an organization created to defend freedom of speech, called van Gogh a "free-speech fundamentalist" who deserved to die because he "roared his Muslim critics into silence with obscenities."[246] The Dutch justice minister proposed strengthening blasphemy laws to promote "integration" and to limit "possible explosive material in society to avoid reactions" like van Gogh's murder.[247]

Although many European newspapers reprinted the Mohammed cartoons, and Danish Prime Minister Fogh Rasmussen refused to apologize, no British newspapers reprinted them, and only one major American paper did. Not a single major television news outlet, including Fox News, showed the cartoons. The *New York Times* called its decision to not reprint them "a reasonable choice for news organizations that usually refrain from gratuitous assaults on religious symbols," a claim that would astonish Christians who remember the *Times*'s reproduction of artworks showing a crucifix dipped in urine and the Virgin Mary covered in elephant dung.[248] Arch-"Crusaders" George W. Bush and Tony Blair both condemned the cartoons, and the European Union proposed a "media code" to regulate speech about religion. EU Justice Minister Franco Frattini assured the Muslim world, "We are aware of the consequences of exercising the right of free expression, we can and we are ready to self-regulate that right," frankly admitting that fear of violent "consequences" would lead to restrictions on free speech.[249]

In America, Yale University Press in 2009 decided not to reprint the cartoons and other images of Mohammed in a book about the controversy, citing "an appreciable chance of violence occurring if either the cartoons or other depictions of the Prophet Muhammad were printed," although hopes for Saudi money for the university may have played some role.[250] Perhaps inspired by Yale's Falstaffian valor, a few months later the New York Metropolitan Museum of Art pulled from public view its artworks depicting Mohammed. After the Pope's Regensburg speech, the *New York Times* opined, "It is tragic and dangerous when one sows pain," and advised the Pope "to offer a deep and persuasive apology, demonstrating that words can also heal."[251] Whether what the Pope quoted was *true* or not didn't matter to the *Times*. Rather than defend a central right of Western political freedom against those who would use force to limit it, many in the West instead capitulated to Muslim violence, masking their fear with the therapeutic "sensitivity" and "respect" seldom granted to any other faith.

This fear of Muslim violence has created a culture of appeasement evident everywhere in America. Even before 9/11 demonstrated graphically the enormity of Islamist violence, people observed the "Rushdie Rules" and trod warily around Muslim sensibilities. Jay Leno apologized for a comedy sketch about an amusement park in Iran; an NPR host offered "sincere apologies" for relating a story about Mohammed's using a special coffee to sexually service forty women in one night; publisher Simon & Schuster recalled a children's book that mentioned Mohammed's historically factual beheading of his enemies; another publisher recalled a book that depicted Mohammed, contrary to Islamic strictures about visually representing the Prophet; Internet service providers removed sites that "defame" the Prophet; advertizing agencies and newspapers pulled ads "offensive" to Muslims—these are just a few examples of how anything, no matter how trivial, deemed offensive to Muslims is apologized for and quickly removed from the public square.[252] As for movies and television, Muslim and Arab terrorists, such as those featured in the blockbuster *True Lies* (1994), have disappeared from the screen. Indeed, filmmaker Roland Emmerich, whose 2009 film *2012* depicts the destruction of St. Peter's, the Sistine Chapel, and Rio de Janeiro's monumental statue Christ the Redeemer, frankly admitted omitting Muslim holy sites out of fear of a "fatwa." These days, the most dangerous cinematic global threat is a CIA agent, a corporate CEO, an American soldier, or a fundamentalist Christian, the clichéd villains columnist Ross Douthat calls the "White Male enemy at home."[253]

From Running Scared to Groveling

More reprehensible is the timidity of news media presumably dedicated to publicizing the truth and entertaining a wide variety of opinions no matter whose ox is gored. Indeed, telling the truth about Islamic violence is considered evidence of bias or racism. In 2007, a fear of offense led the Society of Professional Journalists to promulgate guidelines for covering Arabs and Muslims, which included strictures such as "when writing about terrorism, remember to include white supremacist, radical anti-abortionists and other groups with a history of such activity," even though the number of attacks and people killed by those groups is minuscule compared to the victims of Muslim terrorism. Indeed, a phrase like "Muslim terrorism," "Islamic terrorist," or "Muslim extremist" is forbidden according to the supposed caretakers of public truth.[254] *Washington Post* managing editor Phillip Bennett in a March 2008 speech at a university in California followed his profession's party line, decrying

"the easy assumptions, gross generalizations or untested rhetoric that shape perceptions of Muslims." Such protestations
of sensitivity ignore the question of whether these "generalizations" or "perceptions" are based on reality and hence are
valid.[255]

In fact, far from unfairly stereotyping Muslims, over the
past several years mainstream media have bent over backwards
to document and decry every offense against Muslims, no matter how trivial, and to publish stories and profiles whitewashing Islam's more unsavory doctrines. Islamic religious leaders
are described in laudatory, respectful terms never used in stories about rabbis or Christian leaders. As Bruce Bawer writes
of one such story, a Pulitzer prize-winning *New York Times* puff
piece about a Brooklyn imam, the "article was a prime example of the way the mainstream media cover Islam today: empha-
size personal and superficial details that are likely to generate
sympathy while sidestepping or whitewashing core beliefs,
domestic arrangements, cultural practices, social rules, and
long-term political goals that might actually inform, enlighten—
and therefore alarm—readers."[256] The purpose of such cover-
age is to present Islamist jihad as a fringe deformation of the
"true" Islam, which is depicted as inclusive, tolerant, and peace-
loving. If there are violent Muslims, they are a minority no different from violent people in other religions. This was the
duplicitous message of a CNN six-hour documentary called
God's Warriors, broadcast in 2007. This report equated the tiny
number of Jewish or Christian extremists with the tens of thousands of Muslim jihadists active all across the globe. Worse
yet, the latter were rationalized as reactors to the Jewish settlements in the West Bank: "The impact of God's Jewish warriors goes far beyond these rocky hills. The Jewish settlements
have inflamed much of the Muslim world," host Christine
Amanpour explained.[257] Of course, the 14 centuries-long doctrine of jihad found in the Koran, in the Hadith, a collection
of the sayings and doings of Mohammed recorded as the guide

for pious Muslim behavior, and all four schools of Islamic jurisprudence—a theology of violence absent in Judaism and Christianity—is downplayed by Amanpour during her exercise in specious moral equivalence.

This anxious solicitude about Muslim sensibilities, not extended to any other faith, permeates many in the federal government as well. Spokesmen ignore the specific doctrines of Islam upon which the Islamists base their actions, and present instead a sanitized version compatible with American values. An assistant to the Secretary of State in the Clinton administration claimed that there was no conflict between Islam and "such Western ideals as personal freedom or individual choice." A "fact sheet" from the Department of State said that "most Americans and most Muslims share fundamental values such as peace, justice, economic security, and good governance."[258] Someone at State apparently never read Koran 5:51: "O you who believe! do not take the Jews and the Christians for friends; they are friends of each other; and whoever amongst you takes them for a friend, then surely he is one of them; surely Allah does not guide the unjust people."[259] Clinton's Secretary of State Madeleine Albright called Islam "a faith that honors consultation, cherishes peace, and has as one of its fundamental principles the inherent equality of all who embrace it." Ask a Muslim woman murdered in an "honor killing" what she thinks of Albright's "inherent equality." Hillary Clinton also praised Islam's "deepest yearning of all—to live in peace," a claim hard to support from Islam's historical record of invasion, conquest, occupation, pillage, and enslavement, not to mention the current global violence perpetrated by Muslims.[260] The Bush administration continued this apologetic vein. Islam's "teachings are good and peaceful, and those who commit evil in the name of Allah blaspheme the name of Allah," the President said in his address to the nation after 9/11.[261] Secretary of State Condoleezza Rice called Islam the religion "of love and peace." And two Bush administration officials

wrote in 2005 about the need "to support the courageous Muslims who are speaking the truth about their proud religion and
history, and seizing it back from those who would hijack it for
evil ends."[262] The authors don't mention that these few "courageous Muslims" are vastly outnumbered by those who support
the jihadists and cheer their attacks.

Of course, the corollary to all this solicitous puffery is the
constant chastising of Americans who "mischaracterize Islam"
or indulge in "unfortunate stereotypes" and "prejudices." Advo-
cacy organizations like the Council on American-Islamic Relations (CAIR), a creation of Hamas that has raised money for,
and received money from, terrorist organizations, exist to
threaten and harass those who criticize Islam, even if their
criticisms are true. However, despite these ties to Islamists, its
incessant hounding of critics, and its thinly veiled apologetics
on behalf of terrorists, CAIR is a respected resource for government, universities, and law enforcement agencies eager to
avoid the taint of "Islamophobia" and demonstrate their commitment to "diversity."[263] As Daniel Pipes points out, however,
"In adopting a determinedly apologetic stance, they [federal
officials] have made themselves an adjunct of the country's
Islamic organizations. By dismissing any connection between
Islam and terrorism, complaining about media distortions, and
claiming that America needs Islam, they have turned the U.S.
government into a discreet missionary for the faith."[264] And
they are appeasing the enemy by gratifying his chauvinistic
belief that Muslims are the "best of nations" whose destiny is
to rule the world, and that the West, for all its military and
economic power, is weak, lacks resolve, and so deserves to be
subordinated to Muslims. Why else would Westerners continually extol the wondrous goodness of Islam?

Lurking behind all these distortions of Islamic doctrine,
sensitivity to Muslim sensibilities, and appeasing retreat in the
face of threats and intimidation is fear, as Bruce Bawer points
out: "The exceptional effort to erect a protective wall around

Islam is the result not of a wave of hatred directed *at* Muslims but of fear inspired by a flood of violence *by* Muslims."[265] Yet fear alone does not explain this appeasement of the jihadists. Questionable ideas are at work as well, either as a genuine motivating force or as a rationalization for behavior ultimately attributable to fear.

Internationalism Fails Again

The Kantian notion that super-national organizations and international laws and covenants can create peace and maintain global order through reasoned deliberation rather than force, which contributed to the British policies of appeasement in the interwar years, has continued its hold over many in the West. This faith in transnational institutions like the United Nations has not diminished over the last several decades since the League of Nations failed spectacularly to prevent the two decades of aggression that led to World War II. No more effective has been the United Nations in meeting the challenge of jihad to global order. Indeed, the U.N. has often legitimized terrorism, most notoriously when it invited Yasser Arafat, sporting a holster on his hip, to address the General Assembly in November 1974. "Only six months after Palestinian terrorists killed these school-children [at schools in Ma'alot and Qiryat Shemona], and a year and a half after he ordered the murder of three Western diplomats," Alan Dershowitz writes, Arafat was greeted "like a hero and statesman, not as a cold-blooded murderer with the blood of American diplomats, Israeli Olympians, and Jewish children on his hands."[266] A few weeks later the U.N. passed resolutions 3236 and 3237, which recognized the terrorist Palestinian Liberation Organization as the legitimate representative of the Palestinian people, and subtly justified terrorism in the Palestinians' pursuit to "regain their rights."[267]

The next year, the U.N. approved the notorious resolution 3379—passed on the 37th anniversary of *Kristallnacht*, the

November 1938 Nazi pogrom against German Jews— defining Zionism as a form of racism, which was not repealed until 16 years later. And in 1979, a U.N. General Assembly resolution approved an exception to the international ban against taking hostages, allowing it if the hostage-takers were fighting "against colonial occupation and alien occupation and against racist regimes in the exercise of their right of self-determination," an indulgence obviously intended for the PLO and directed at Israel.[268] Subsequent U.N. actions have focused not on Islamic terrorism and the states that support it, but on protecting Muslims from "a rising trend of Islamaphobia [sic]," as the U.N. "investigator on racism" put it in September 2007, claiming that Islamophobia is "the most serious form of religious defamation," and decrying those "equating Islam with violence and terrorism." Two months later, the General Assembly passed a "Resolution of Combating Defamation of Religions," in which the only faith singled out for protection was Islam.[269] Nothing was said about the continuing persecution of Christians living in Islamic nations or the rampant anti-Semitism portrayed by government-controlled media in countries like Egypt.

The legitimacy given to the PLO by the U.N. was quite simply a reward for terrorism, and thus an incitement to further violence, as Dershowitz documents.[270] Equally enabling of jihadism has been the complete silence of the U.N. Human Rights Council on the numerous acts of jihadist violence, much of it sponsored and supported by U.N. member-states like Syria and Iran, even as Israel is subjected to serial condemnation. In April 2005, the Islamic members of the U.N. Human Rights Commission, precursor to the Human Rights Council, refused to condemn killing in the name of religion, and countered that criticizing Muslim terrorists was "defamation of religion."[271] The supposedly improved successor to the UNHRC, the Human Rights Council, has been no better. In March 2007, its response to the Mohammed cartoon controversy was *not* to take a stand for the "human right" of free speech and against the violence that threatens this right, but to pass a resolution calling for a ban on the defamation of religion. Nor is the HRC interested in denouncing the jihadist charter of Hamas, which calls for the destruction of Israel, despite the tireless efforts of human rights activist David Littman since 1989 in goading the Council to condemn the genocidal violence of that document, most recently in March 2010.[272] Indeed, in 2009 Littman was banned for a month from the U.N. for upsetting representatives from Muslim states.[273] Meanwhile, 27 Council resolutions have been directed against Israel, the only country that is a permanent item on the Council's agenda; no other country has been directly criticized for human rights violations.[274]

The reason for the U.N.'s failure is the same as the reason for the failure of the League of Nations: it comprises sovereign nations that do not all share universal values or aims but instead use the institution to pursue their own national interests, which more often than not conflict with our own. Thus the attempts by both George Bush and now Barack Obama to get the Security Council to impose meaningful sanctions on Iran are thwarted by members like Russia and China, since it is not in their geopolitical or economic interests to punish Iran for failing to comply with another ineffective institution of internationalism, the International Atomic Energy Agency. Nor are all peoples as pragmatic and rational as Westerners imagine them to be, and thus amenable to transnational negotiation via institutions like the U.N. The notion, for example, that a nuclear-armed Iran can be dealt with by a Cold War-like policy of "containment" assumes that the mullahs are pragmatists rationally calculating chances in order to remain in power. This view discounts the role of Shiism's cult of martyrdom and the force of the Islamist goal of increasing Muslim power in order to fulfill Allah's will, an aim much more important than the survival of any one nation. "I say let this land [Iran] burn," Khomeini said in 1980. "I say let this land go up in smoke, provided Islam remains triumphant in the rest of the world."[275]

Another venerable expression of moralizing internationalism, the Geneva Conventions, has also failed at its primary purpose of defending civilians from armed violence. On the contrary, in 1977 Protocol I was added to the Conventions, a change pushed by the Soviet Union and the Palestinian Liberation Organization that in effect extended legal combatant status and POW protection to anyone fighting in a conflict, including terrorists.[276] Even though the U.S. never ratified the Protocol, Obama's Executive Order 13491 in January 2009 extended the Geneva Convention's Article 3 protections for captured lawful combatants to members of al Qaeda, thus legitimizing terrorists' efforts "to promote the legitimacy of their aims and practices," as Ronald Reagan said when he rejected Protocol I.[277] "What the USSR and the PLO," Thiessen writes, "failed to achieve two decades ago, President Obama has granted with the stroke of his pen."[278] Once again, agreements born of delusional faith in some "global community" of shared values codified in international law fail at their utopian goal to eliminate the tragic realities of human conflict, since aggressors and terrorists will simply ignore or violate such agreements. Instead, these international treaties become the tools of political interests, whether domestic, as in the Democrats' use of the Geneva Conventions as a stick to beat the Bush administration, or international, as in the attacks on America's treatment and interrogation of detainees on the part of both our enemies and our allies.

The Fool's Gold of Diplomacy

The corollary to the moralizing internationalism that has bred transnational institutions and agreements is the primacy put on diplomatic discussion and negotiation for resolving disputes between states. As we saw in the previous two chapters, historically this ideal has been compromised by the bad faith that one side frequently brings to the negotiation, which often is used to camouflage aggression or buy time in order to achieve an aim without having to sacrifice anything in return. And such negotiation can become an end in itself, allowing those unwilling to act to substitute procedural words for deeds. Too often, as historian Robert Conquest wrote about Cold War diplomacy with the Soviets, "since diplomats' forte is negotiation, they believe negotiation to be good in itself.... But the Soviets did what their interests required when the alternative seemed less acceptable, and negotiation was merely a technical adjunct." Thus diplomatic negotiation is not necessarily a sincere desire to reach a peaceful accommodation acceptable to both sides, but rather a means to a self-interested end. Seeing clearly the adversary's interests and ends, rather than projecting our own on to the enemy, thus becomes the most important factor in diplomacy. "It is easy enough," Conquest reminds us, "to fall into the trap of thinking that others think, within reason, like ourselves. But this trap is precisely the error that must be avoided in foreign affairs."[279]

Diplomacy is an important part of any state's foreign policy, but in dealing with adversaries, diplomacy must be backed by a credible threat to use force if agreement is not reached or if the terms of an agreement are violated. Ronald Reagan's engagement of the Soviet Union in the 1980s worked because it was accompanied by a determined military buildup and vigorous pushback against Soviet global aggression in places like Granada, Afghanistan, and Nicaragua. This threat of force is necessary because states have interests that conflict with ours, and often will give up those interests only in the face of losing an even greater interest—to survive intact. As Thomas Hobbes wrote in *Leviathan,* "For the laws of nature, as justice, equity, modesty, mercy, and, in sum, doing to others as we would be done to, of themselves, without the terror of some power to cause them to be observed, are contrary to our natural passions, that carry us to partiality, pride, revenge, and the like. And covenants, without the sword, are but words and of no strength to secure a man at all."[280] Thirty years of diplomatic outreach to Iran has been fruitless for the simple reason that starting in 1979 Iran has not believed that the U.S. has the will to use force in order to compel the regime to change its behavior, or to destroy it, no matter how much American blood is on its hands. Indeed, in these circumstance, the continuing efforts to deal with Iran on the grounds of what Carter and Obama both call "mutual respect," and on the assumption that Iran desires integration into the international community and the good diplomatic and economic relations with other countries that we desire, have only intensified Iranian contempt for us and encouraged the mullahs to believe that they can pursue with impunity their aim of acquiring nuclear weapons.

Avatars of Leftist Ideology

This faith in transnational institutions and international law and agreements arose from the dubious Enlightenment notion that an increasingly rational humanity is progressing away from war and violence and toward global peace and order predicated on a "harmony of interests." Other ideals, also the offspring of Enlightenment materialist and rationalist assumptions, have contributed to the reflex of appeasement in dealing with the jihadists. Varieties of Marxist ideology still extant have skewed our response to the Islamists, particularly the old notion that capitalism has created a peculiarly alienating and oppressive society, one that it has imposed on the world through imperialism and colonialism.

The standard left-wing clichés about the dehumanizing and alienating horrors of industrial capitalism and its privileging of profit over people, by now over 150 years old, have been taken up by jihadists and integrated into their indictment of the West as an idolatrous sink of godless iniquity.[281] Sayyid Qutb excoriated the modern West and America in particular, where he had

spent three years in the late 1940s, in terms frequently redolent of leftist complaints about modern life under capitalism
and what Marx called the "alienation" it creates in human relations and between people and their labor. "Look at this capitalism with its monopolies, its usury," Qutb wrote, "at this
individual freedom, devoid of human sympathy and responsibility for relatives except under force of law; at this materialis-
tic attitude which deadens the spirit."[282] Just as Marx predicted
capitalism's demise brought about by class warfare, Qutb noted
that the affluence of the West was doomed because of the "mald-
istribution within those nations, which allows hatred, grudges,
misery and fear of the unexpected to take root." And just as generations of Marxists have blamed chronic warfare on capitalism in its imperialist phase, so too Qutb noted that these
inequitable economic and social conditions create "worry" and
"fear" over "the total ruin which threatens the whole world at
any moment, as risks of all-out war continue to be in the air."[283]
The Islamists even developed an idea similar to Marxism's "false
consciousness," the way capitalism dupes the proletariat into
ignoring their authentic interests and obscures the true nature
of institutions and relations. The Iranian Ali Shari'ati, the "intellectual pioneer of revolutionary Islam" who translated Fanon's
Wretched of the Earth into Persian, spoke of *gharbzadegi,* the
"intoxication with the west/darkness," or Al-e Ahmed's "Westoxification," that seduces Muslims from the true faith.[284]

Like Khomeini, who also exploited left-wing liberationist
rhetoric in his attack on the West, today's jihadists in their
pronouncements also shrewdly manipulate anti-globalization
and other anti-Western leftist themes in order to cultivate
support from those who despise their own countries. After
9/11, Hamas, the terrorist offshoot of the Muslim Brotherhood, in its "Open Letter to America" interpreted the attacks
as a way for Americans "to see exactly how much you
oppressed, how corrupt you are, how you have sinned," including in their indictment favorite leftist charges like slavery, even

though America abolished slavery 145 years ago while it still exists today in some Muslim lands.[285] In his 2002 address "To the Muslims of Iraq," bin Laden exhorted the Iraqis not to fight for "capitalists, the lords of usury, and arms and oil dealers." Especially when addressing Americans, bin Laden returns to these anti-capitalist themes likely to find approval among many liberals and leftists. In his important 2002 address, "Why We Are Fighting You," he even chastised the U.S. for refusing to sign the Kyoto agreement "so that you can secure the profit of your greedy companies and industries," stated that "your law is the law of the rich and wealthy people," and accused Americans of using "your power to destroy more people than any other nation in history—not to defend principles and values, but to hasten to secure your interests and profits." After the invasion of Iraq in 2003, bin Laden told American soldiers that they were "spilling [their] blood to swell the bank accounts of the White House gang and their fellow arms dealers and the proprietors of great companies." Before the 2004 elections, he spoke to the American voters, warning them not to support a war "in order to give business to their [the Bush administration's] various corporations—whether in the field of armaments, oil, or construction." And sounding like the ACLU, Michael Moore, or the Democratic Congressional leadership, bin Laden claimed that Bush brought "tyranny and the suppression of freedoms to his own country—and this they called the 'Patriot Act,' implemented under the pretext of combating terrorism."[286]

Any of these statements would not be out of place in the speeches given at anti-war and anti-globalization rallies, or in the writings of Noam Chomsky, Howard Zinn, Robert Fisk, William Blum (whose anti-American screed *Rogue State* bin Laden recommended in 2006), or any of the legions of fundamentalist leftists who, like bin Laden, believe America is "the worst civilization in the history of mankind" because it doesn't match up to their utopian ideal.[287] Indeed, many of these ideas are not that different from what can be read in the *New York Times* or *Newsweek,* or heard on NPR, CNN, or CNBC, or viewed in many movies and television shows, or found on the syllabuses of college courses across America.

Supping with the Jihadist Devils

This jihadist indictment of America, indistinguishable from old left-wing and liberal clichés, has helped to forge what David Horowitz calls the "unholy alliance," despite the homophobia, misogyny, intolerance, and religious obscurantism that should make the jihadists the mortal enemies of liberals and leftists. This alliance, first created in the 1960s by the left's tactical embrace of the terrorist PLO, quickly manifested itself in the aftermath of 9/11, when leftist commentators engaged in irrational, unfounded, ignorant, irrelevant, and at times bizarre criticisms of the United States that in effect rationalized and confirmed al Qaeda's own justifications for murder.[288] The dean of the prestigious Woodrow Wilson School advised us to "think about our own history, what we did in World War II to Japanese citizens by interning them"—a non-sequitur and a false analogy. A Brown English professor equated the attacks to the first Gulf War, which was "also terrorism"—a sophistry. A journalist at a University of North Carolina teach-in wanted the President to apologize to "all the millions of victims of American imperialism"—ignorance of the term in history. Another professor of English, this one from Rutgers, opined that the "ultimate cause [of 9/11] is the fascism of U.S. foreign policy over the past many decades"—sheer confusion about the meaning of "fascism." And a University of Texas journalism professor asserted that 9/11 "was no more despicable than the massive acts of terrorism . . . that the U.S. government has committed during my lifetime"—a despicable lie.[289] The premier practitioner of this species of fantastic complaint is MIT professor Noam Chomsky, who when the war in Afghanistan started accused the U.S. of intentionally starving three to four million Afghans in a "silent genocide"; like Hamas, interpreted the 9/11 attacks as justified payback for American "depredations" against the Third World and American Indians; and while on tour in Islamabad, echoed the Islamist charge that the U.S. is the "world's biggest terrorist state" and the war in Afghanistan the "worse kind of terrorism."[290]

Statements such as these reflect the post-Vietnam narrative of American evil and culpability, a self-loathing brew of historical ignorance, juvenile utopianism, specious moral equivalence, and reflexive anti-American condemnation that for over three decades has constituted the received wisdom of liberal intellectuals in the universities and the media. As such, it has been a powerful political and cultural force for appeasement by eroding our will to fight and by undermining our confidence that the fight is just and so worth the cost in blood and treasure. And it has confirmed the jihadists' estimation that we are weak and corrupt, our civilization resting on "foundations of straw," as bin Laden said. And why wouldn't he believe in our corruption and weakness, when many of our own intellectuals, some of our politicians, and much of our popular culture have been telling him so for decades?

Multicultural Delusions

This antique leftist narrative of American crimes against humanity has been rendered even more toxic by its marriage to another dominant ideology, multiculturalism, with which it shares many features. Multiculturalism is not about respecting other cultures or celebrating diversity. Rather, in essence it comprises old-fashioned noble-savage and Romantic mythic idealizations of non-Western, dark-skinned "others." To the multiculturalist, these peoples live more authentic, humane, harmonious, and fulfilling lives because they are free from the depredations of industrial capitalism with its alienating labor, dehumanizing technological complexity, and endemic racism and sexism. These ancient myths were integrated into Marxism via the anti-imperialism and anti-colonialism that anointed the Third World victims of capitalist exploitation as the revolutionary vanguard: "Natives of the underdeveloped countries unite!" communist philosopher Jean-Paul Sartre wrote in his introduction to Franz Fanon's *The Wretched of the Earth,* substituting the Third World for the old communist "workers of the world."[291] This strange theoretical hybrid used to be called Third Worldism, the notion that "every Westerner is presumed guilty until proven innocent," as French social critic Pascal Bruckner puts it. As a result, Bruckner continues, "We Europeans have been raised to detest ourselves, certain that within our world, there is a certain essential evil that must be relentlessly atoned for. This evil is known by two terms—colonialism and imperialism."[292] The same melodramatic narrative defines multiculturalism. The Third World "other," denizen of a more exotic and authentic culture, is now also the privileged victim of Western historical crimes, his dysfunction and aggression explained away as understandable reactions to Western imperialist and colonialist oppression.

This last charge spices multiculturalism's fantasy idealizations with tired Marxist categories like "imperialism" and "colonialism." Rather than denoting historical phenomena with the complex mix of good and evil that defines everything flawed humans do, these terms refer to "a malign force with no program but the subjugation and exploitation of innocent people," as Robert Conquest defines their use these days, with the further implications, both historically false, that neither one ever benefited colonized peoples and that both account for the difficulties of the Third World today, decades after the departure of the colonial powers. These verbal "mind-blockers and thought-extinguishers," Conquest continues, serve "mainly to confuse, and of course to replace, the complex and needed process of understanding with the simple and unneeded process

of inflammation."[293] As such, these terms are as politically useful for the domestic left as they have been for the Islamists,
making a specious anti-imperialism a constant in attacks on
America's war against jihadism. Princeton professor Cornel
West claimed that George Bush exploited 9/11 "to launch an
imperial vision of the United States dominating the world."
Rashid Khalidi, professor of Modern Arab studies at Columbia, accused the U.S. of "stepping into the boots of the former
colonial rulers." And newspaper columnist Maureen Dowd
charged Bush with taking the "opportunity . . . to reduce the
rest of the world to subservience."[294]

The result of this fashionable self-flagellation is to excul-
pate the Islamists and justify appeasing policies for dealing
with them. Given that they are the victims of an exploitative
Europe and America, these denizens of superior Third World
cultures are always innocent, always beyond criticism, and
always owed reparations in the form of foreign aid and other
support from the West. Indeed, criticizing non-Western cultures is itself another manifestation of the racist, xenophobic,
intolerant Western arrogance that has been the handmaid of
colonial and imperial exploitation.

Edward Said's "Malignant Charlatanry"

This hybrid of multicultural ideology and leftist politics has
directly compromised our understanding of Islam and the Middle East, particularly through the work of the late Edward Said
and his book *Orientalism* (1978), "a work of malignant charla-
tanry," Robert Irwin writes, "in which it is hard to distinguish
honest mistakes from willful misrepresentations."[295] According to Martin Kramer in his analysis of the politicizing of Middle Eastern studies, Said's work has "crippled" the discipline,
which "came under a take-no-prisoners assault, which rejected
the idea of objective standards, disguised the vice of politiciza-
tion as the virtue of commitment, and replaced proficiency

with ideology."[296] As the numerous errors of fact and the presentist judgments in *Orientalism* show, Said, a professor of comparative literature at Columbia who had grown up a child of privilege in Egypt before attending Princeton and Harvard, was not an expert on Middle Eastern history, religion, or culture but a critic of Western literature and a connoisseur of dubious French theories about the relativism of truth and its dependence on power. At the moment the cultural left was discovering the Palestinians as the perfect vehicle for indulging sentimental Third Worldism, anti-Western clichés, post-Holocaust anti-Semitism, and the Marxist romance with revolutionary violence, Said reinvented himself as a Palestinian who had been displaced and dispossessed by the Zionists, those stooges of the postwar neo-colonial West.[297] Thus Said was perfectly placed to exploit the academic left's obsessions with imperialism and colonialism, as well as its multicultural exaltation of the West's exotic victims, "the ravaged colonial peoples," Said writes in *Culture and Imperialism,* "who for centuries endured summary injustice, unending economic oppression, distortion of their social and intimate lives, and a recourseless submission."[298]

The essence of *Orientalism* is the post-modern notion that historical truth is merely an interpretive construct, a "discursive formation" that serves and justifies political power. To Said, the four centuries of Western study of Islam and the Middle East, the field once called "orientalism," are not a record of the scholarly pursuit of truth and understanding but, in fact, "a Western style for dominating, restructuring, and having authority over the Orient."[299] This domination is predicated on a belief in the superiority of Europeans to Middle Eastern peoples, who are characterized as the alien and frightening "Other," the fiction necessary for creating and validating Western identity. And this dehumanization in turn has justified the domination of the "Other" by Western colonial powers. Thus, Said alleges, "every European, in what he could say about the

Orient, was consequently a racist, an imperialist, and almost totally ethnocentric," and Orientalism is a "political doctrine willed over the Orient because the Orient was weaker than the West, which elided the Orient's difference with its weakness."[300]

In a subsequent 1981 book, *Covering Islam,* Said applied this thesis to American academic work on Islam, which he chastised for displaying "both a peculiarly immediate sense of hostility and a coarse, on the whole unnuanced, attitude toward Islam." These scholars, Said alleges, respond to "national and corporate needs," with the result that "anything said about Islam by a professional scholar is within the sphere of influence of corporations and governments."[301] One of these "national and corporate needs" is to create the bogeyman of international terrorism in order to justify supporting Israel's neo-colonialist oppression, as well as dominating and exploiting the oil-rich Middle East. Thus Said sneered at "speculations about the latest conspiracy to blow up buildings, sabotage commercial airliners," speculations that reflect not actual events but "highly exaggerated stereotypes," an assertion quickly disproved by the terrorist attacks of the 1980s and 1990s.[302] This ad hominem attack on the scholars with whom Said disagreed may have been juvenile, but it was perfectly suited to the politicized Middle Eastern studies departments that elevated fidelity to left-wing ideology and dubious French theory over linguistic and methodological skills, both of which had begun to decline in the 1960s.[303] Moreover, as Lee Smith points out, by attacking his critics "Said helped set the terms by which Western intellectuals and reporters could write about the Arabs and Islam."[304] And by those terms, even the Muslim terrorist was never at fault, for he was at some level the victim of vicious Western stereotypes manufactured to justify colonial and imperial oppression.

This apologetic narrative of Muslim innocence and Western guilt has come to dominate the Middle East studies programs and scholarship in most major American universities, and from there gone on to distort our broader understanding of Islam and the region it dominates. As a result, before 9/11, the professors "failed to ask the right questions, at the right times, about Islamism," Kramer writes. "They underestimated its impact in the 1980s; they misrepresented its role in the early 1990s; and they glossed over its growing potential for terrorism against America in the late 1990s. Twenty years of denial had produced mostly banalities about American bias and ignorance, and fantasies about Islamists as democratizers and reformers."[305] Despite the 9/11 attacks and the constant stream of communiqués in which the Islamists explain their actions in terms of traditional Islamic doctrine and scripture, most Middle Eastern scholars have continued to promote and popularize beyond the academy Said's narrative of Western distortions and oppression as ultimately responsible for Islamist terrorism, all the while ignoring or misrepresenting the traditional Islamic theology that the jihadists themselves cite as the justifications for their actions.

Whitewashing Jihad

Particularly egregious has been the pervasive mischaracterizations of Islam as the "religion of peace," and jihad as a form of spiritual self-improvement rather than violence against the enemies of Islam. Typical of the "jihad deniers," as Lee Harris calls them, is UCLA law professor Khaled Abou El Fadl, who in 2002 stated, "Islamic tradition does not have a notion of holy war. *Jihad* simply means to strive hard or struggle in the pursuit of a just cause."[306] Georgetown professor John Esposito, writing in the *Washington Post,* likewise claims, "In the Koran, Islam's sacred text, jihad means 'to strive or struggle' to realize God's will, to lead a virtuous life, to create a just society and to defend Islam and the Muslim community."[307] Even the National Counterterrorism Center has endorsed the apologists' take on jihad, advising its employees in March 2008,

"Never use the terms 'jihadist' or 'mujahideen' in conversation to describe terrorists," since "In Arabic, jihad means 'striving in the path of God' and is used in many contexts beyond warfare."[308] An op-ed in the *New York Times* in June 2008 continued this deception, arguing that jihad is "a quest to find one's faith or an external fight for justice," begging the question of what sort of "justice" Muslims have in mind.[309] After all, many Muslims consider subjecting the whole world to Islamic shari'a law "justice." And in August 2009, John Brennan, Obama's assistant for Homeland Security and Counterterrorism, chanted once again this false mantra, averring, "Nor does President Obama see this challenge as a fight against 'jihadists.' Describing terrorists in this way—using a legitimate term, 'jihad,' meaning to purify oneself or to wage a holy struggle for a moral goal—risks giving these murderers the religious legitimacy they desperately seek but in no way deserve."[310]

More recently, historian of religion Philip Jenkins told National Public Radio that "the Islamic scriptures in the Quran [regarding war] were actually far less bloody and less violent than those in the Bible," and the Muslim understanding of the Koran verses had "matured" so that now jihad means an "internal struggle."[311] What Jenkins misses is that the violence in the Old Testament involves historically specific wars conducted according to the brutal practices typical of the times, not a general, timeless theological doctrine embodied in scripture. This moral equivalence of Muslim violence and that of other religions has become a cliché in Islamic apologetics, as we saw earlier with CNN's documentary *God's Warriors*. Retired Princeton professor Richard Falk wrote in 2003, "The Great Terror War has so far been conducted as a collision of absolutes, a meeting ground of opposed fundamentalisms."[312] In his book *Unholy War*, John Esposito, despite presenting the extensive evidence for the tradition of Islamic violent jihad, manages to write with a straight face, "Terrorists can attempt to hijack Islam and the doctrine of jihad, but that is no more legitimate than Christian and Jewish extremists committing their acts of terrorism in their own unholy wars in the name of Christianity and Judaism."[313] But Jewish or Christian extremists, the number of whose attacks is minuscule compared to those of the jihadists, cannot find anywhere in Jewish or Christian theology or scripture divine authority for such violence similar to the sanction for jihad in the Koran and Hadith. The bloody battles recorded in the Old Testament are "descriptive, not prescriptive," as Raymond Ibrahim writes, and they reflect history, not theology.[314] As for Christian scripture, there is not a single verse or commandment endorsing violence. This specious equivalence of jihadists and Christians is a favorite of secular liberals, for their greatest villain is the "fundamentalist" Christians who "fuel their tanks at the same holy gas station" as the jihadists, according to atheism apologist Richard Dawkins.[315]

Unlike Christianity and Judaism, however, there is in Islam a long, continuous tradition of theologized violence, legitimized by prescriptive Koranic verses whose import is the general obligation to fight against unbelievers and other enemies of Islam: "So when the sacred months have passed away, then slay the idolaters wherever you find them, and take them captives and besiege them and lie in wait for them in every ambush"; "Fight those who do not believe in Allah, nor in the latter day, nor do they prohibit what Allah and His Messenger have prohibited, nor follow the religion of truth, out of those who have been given the Book [Jews and Christians], until they pay the tax in acknowledgment of superiority and they are in a state of subjection"; "O you who believe! fight those of the unbelievers who are near to you and let them find in you hardness; and know that Allah is with those who guard (against evil)"; "And kill them wherever you find them, and drive them out from whence they drove you out, and persecution is severer than slaughter ... such is the recompense of the unbelievers"; "I will cast terror into the hearts of those who disbelieve. There-

fore strike off their heads and strike off every fingertip of them."
In these verses and others, the uncreated, timeless, immutable
words of Allah, the theological injunction to fight the unbelievers and subject them to Muslim hegemony is obvious.[316]
And contrary to the "inner struggle" interpretation of jihad,
Danish linguist Tina Magaard's study of the Arabic root *ja-ha-
da* in the Koran concludes: "Only a single ja-ha-da reference
(29:6) explicitly presents the struggle as an inner, spiritual phenomenon, not as an outward (usually military) phenomenon.
But this sole reference does not carry much weight against the
more than 50 references to actual armed struggle in the Koran,
and even more in the Hadith."[317] The latter text confirms the
notion of jihad as violent struggle, as does the 14-centuries-
long tradition of Koranic commentators, jurisprudents, and
Muslim historians.[318]

Certainly the Ayatollah Khomeini, a revered scholar of
Islamic doctrine, understood jihad as meaning armed struggle: "Islam says: Kill all the unbelievers just as they would kill
you all!! . . . Islam says: Kill in the service of Allah those who
want to kill you! . . . Whatever good there is exists thanks to
the sword and the shadow of the sword!" he preached in 1942.[319]
So did Hassan al-Banna, founder of the Muslim Brothers, who
wrote, "Fighting the unbelievers involves all possible efforts
that are necessary to dismantle the power of the enemies of
Islam including beating them, plundering their wealth, destroying their places of worship, and smashing their idols."[320] And
millions of Muslims worldwide also understand this meaning
of jihad found in the Koran and the Hadith: violent struggle
against the enemies of Islam, even if only a fraction of them
will personally take up arms and fight. Once we accept this
obvious truth, the recourse to violence by Muslims—15,000
violent attacks just since 9/11— makes sense.[321]

And who should we believe has a better understanding of
Islam, Western apologists like Karen Armstrong, who claims

that Islamist "ideology is deliberately and defiantly unortho-
dox," and "until the 1950s, no major Muslim thinker had made
holy war a central pillar of Islam"?[322] This last claim is a remarkable omission of earlier traditional theorists of jihad, such as
Ibn Taymiyyah and Ibn al-Qayyim, both active during the 13th
century. Nor does it square with the lecture delivered by 'Abd
al-Rahman al-Ajar, the representative of the pasha of Tripoli
sent in 1785 to negotiate with John Adams and Thomas Jefferson over the ransom for Americans kidnapped by Barbary
pirates: It was ". . . written in the Koran," al-Rahman explained,
"that all Nations who should not have acknowledged their
[Muslims'] authority were sinners, that it was their right and
duty to make war upon whoever they could find."[323] Are we to
believe Armstrong has a better understanding of Islam than
these Muslims, or Qutb, or al-Banna, or bin Laden? He wrote,
"And the West's notions that Islam is a religion of Jihad and
enmity toward the religions of the infidels and the infidels
themselves is an accurate and true depiction."[324]

Nor is bin Laden "distorting" the true understanding of
jihad. He is simply confirming the continuous chain of the
jihadist imperative, starting with Mohammed's farewell address
in 642, "I was ordered to fight all men until they say 'There is
no god but Allah.'" This command was echoed by Khomeini
in 1979, "Until the cry 'There is no God but God' resounds over
the whole world, there will be struggle"; repeated by bin Laden
himself in 2001, "I was ordered to fight the people until they
say there is no god but Allah, and his prophet Muhammad";
and quoted in a power-point slide delivered at Walter Reed
Hospital by Nidal Malik Hassan, the Fort Hood jihadist who
murdered 13 soldiers and wounded 38 as he shouted the traditional jihadist war cry, *"Allahu Akbar."*[325] Shouldn't we rather
heed these plain words of the Koran, Mohammed, the Ayatollah Khomeini, and the millions of Muslims worldwide who celebrated the attacks on 9/11 as jihad in defense of the faith and

who continue to support jihadist terror? If bin Laden and the Islamists have "hijacked" and "distorted" Islam, where is the mainstream Muslim protest against such a desecration of their faith? "Nowhere in [the Islamic world]," Robert Spencer writes, "is there a significant anti-jihad, anti-al Qaeda, or anti-bin Laden movement; while Muslims worldwide rioted over cartoons in a Danish newspaper and remarks by Pope Benedict XVI, they have never rioted over Osama bin Laden's supposed hijacking of their faith."[326]

This refusal to acknowledge the role of violence in Islam, or to accept, as Lee Smith argues, "that force is at the core of the way most Arabs understand politics," reflects the failure of imagination that Robert Conquest warned about in our conduct of foreign relations. Because we in the West developed a political culture, starting with the ancient Greeks, that has subordinated force to deliberation, consensus, and law, we assume that those political principles are universal, rather than making us "a privileged exception, the beneficiaries of a historical anomaly," as Smith points out.[327] However, if we listen carefully to what the Islamists tell us, and observe how what they do reflects what they say, then we will have to recognize that violence is an acceptable and respected tool both of politics and religion in the Muslim Middle East, and so the failure to respond with force against our enemies does not create admiration for our superior values, but contempt for our status as a "weak horse."

The Arrogant Blindness of Secularism

The larger cultural pathology that inhibits our accurate understanding of the jihadist enemy and his motives is our failure to take seriously religion and spiritual aims. The two-centuries-long secularization of the West, while not yet as advanced in the U.S. as it is in Europe, has removed the Christian understanding of human nature and purpose from our public political conversation about our national aims, goods, and the collective decisions that reflect both. For us, religion has lost its once central role as the provider of ultimate meaning and purpose in our lives, and so we believe that all faiths are essentially the same, a collection of comforting holiday rituals and a source of private therapeutic solace. In the American public square, Christianity is now merely an individual lifestyle choice, no more privileged or important than other choices, such as Wicca, Scientology, Buddhism, or Islam, like them deserving of public space but not of any superior authority over our collective political actions, from which religion has now been explicitly excluded. On the other hand, as Bernard Lewis points out, "in most Islamic countries, religion remains a major political factor," for "most Muslim countries are still profoundly Muslim, in a way and in a sense that most Christian countries are no longer Christian . . . in no Christian country at the present time can religious leaders count on the degree of belief and participation that remains normal in the Muslim lands . . . Christian clergy do not exercise or even claim the kind of public authority that is still normal and accepted in most Muslim countries."[328] Having banished spiritual causes and aims from our explanations for action, we look instead to material causes or psychological ones, the origins of which lie in the material world or the individual's immediate environment. In this way we distort and obscure the motives of the jihadists, whose frame of reference is a spiritual narrative unfolding over centuries and concerned with the obedience of the believers to Allah's will and intentions as revealed to Mohammed in the Koran and embodied in the Prophet's words and deeds.

We have met this materialist fallacy already, in the failure of our leaders to understand accurately and take seriously the self-professed religious motives of the jihadists, starting with the Ayatollah Khomeini and continuing to the present. Since the Iranian Revolution, explanations of jihadist terror have run the gamut of causes reflecting the materialist determinism characteristic of our secularized culture. Thus poverty and lack of education frequently are posited as the causes of jihadist violence. Echoing one of the West's favorite determinists, Karl Marx, the *New York Times* in the aftermath of 9/11 opined that "the disappointed youth of Egypt and Saudi Arabia turn to religion for comfort," an estimation seconded by Bill Clinton: "These forces of reaction feed on disillusionment, poverty and despair."[329] The economic determinism beloved of the left has also provided a ready explanation in the injustices of globalization: Barbara Ehrenreich fingered "the vast global inequalities in which terrorism is rooted."[330] In reality, the Islamist movement has been driven by the educated middle and upper classes of Muslim societies, like the teachers Hassan al Banna and Sayyid Qutb, the civil engineer bin Laden, the mechanical engineer Khaled Sheikh Mohammed, the medical doctors Zawahiri and Abdel Azziz al-Rantisi, a founder of Hamas, or the electronics engineer Ramzi Yousef, mastermind of the 1993 World Trade Center bombing. And such an analysis based on economic deprivation raises the question of why billions of other impoverished, badly educated, and disillusioned people across the globe have not turned to terrorist violence to anywhere near the extent Muslims have.

Blaming Ourselves For Jihadist Violence

Equally reflective of this materialist bias is our habit of explaining jihadist violence as reactions to our own foreign policy sins against Muslims, from propping up dictators to supporting Israel. We discussed above the charges that our imperialist or colonialist or globalization sins account for the Muslim rage against us. However, this claim does not stand up to the historical record, nor can it be defended on the basis of any realistic standard of judgment applied equally to all peoples and nations. The U.S. never has had colonies in the Middle East, and its interventions after World War II—which took place in the context of the Cold War containment of Soviet aggression— on balance more often than not benefited Muslims rather than harmed them, starting in 1956, when the U.S. forced England, France, and Israel to back off their armed attempt to undo Egyptian strongman Gamal Nasser's nationalization of the Suez Canal. Since then, America supported the Afghan *mujahidin* against the Soviet invaders, rescued Kuwait from Hussein, bombed Christian Serbs to keep them from massacring Muslim Bosnians and Kosovars, and liberated Kurds and Shiite Iraqis from Hussein. The American overthrow of Hussein also puts the lie to the notion that support of Middle East dictators stokes jihadist rage, for eliminating that brutal dictator didn't help improve America's standing with the jihadists. Yes, Muslims have died during the Afghan and Iraq wars, but other Muslims have killed most of them in brutal terrorist attacks. In fact, the number of Muslims killed by the U.S. is tiny compared to the number of Muslims killed by other Muslims in the Iraq-Iran war of the 1980s, in which half a million Muslims died, including a whole generation of Iranian children marched into battle with nothing other than plastic keys to paradise. Nor has the U.S. perpetrated anything like Syrian dictator Hafez al-Assad's brutal 1982 crushing of the Muslim Brotherhood in Hama, in which the city was bombarded for weeks with heavy artillery, killing from 10,000 to 25,000 people, mostly civilians.

And if we take the longer historical view, over the centuries Muslims have conquered, killed, ravaged, plundered, and enslaved Christians and occupied their lands in vastly greater numbers than all the dead resulting from European colonial incursions or America's recent wars in Muslim lands put together. And why do we take seriously complaints about Western imperialism coming from adherents to Islam, one of history's most successful conquerors and empire-builders, which, as Ephraim Karsh writes, "acted in a typically imperialist fashion from the start, subjugating indigenous populations, colonizing their lands, and expropriating their wealth, resources, and labor"?[331] Why do we agonize over the so-called "occupation" of Judaea and Samaria, the heart of ancient Israel now called the West Bank, and say nothing over the continued Turkish Muslim illegal occupation of northern Cyprus and the looting and vandalizing of 500 Christian churches there?[332]

This argument that jihadist violence is payback for American offenses against Muslims is nothing but a specious pretext for assaults driven by religious convictions, particularly the chauvinistic notion that Muslims comprise the "best of nations" whose divine destiny is to rule others. If crimes against Muslims by non-Muslims were the real issue, then Russia would be the focus of jihadist rage, for that nation, whether under czars, communists, or the current regime, historically has more Muslim blood on its hands than any country in the West, from the siege of Izmail in 1790, when 40,000 Muslim men, women, and children were slaughtered, to the invasion of Afghanistan, which killed a million; to the brutal war against Muslim separatists in Chechnya, which killed over 100,000 and left the capital Grozny looking like Berlin in 1945. However, despite this slaughter and the 80-year Soviet occupation of Muslim Central Asia, Russia is not the Islamists' "Great Satan," for since the collapse of the Soviet Union it does not represent the primary challenge to the Islamist dream of recovering Islam's global hegemony. And the Russians, unlike self-loathing Westerners eager to atone for their colonial and imperial sins, are contemptuous of such blackmail and will not alter their foreign policy behavior in response to foreign displeasure.

Scapegoating Israel

The most popular Islamist pretext, one attractive to both the left and the right in the West, is the so-called "occupation" by "Zionists" of lands supposedly the homeland of the Palestinian people. "The creation and continuation of Israel," bin Laden told Americans in October 2002, "is one of the greatest crimes, and you are the leaders of its criminals."[333] Commander of U.S. Central Command General David Petraeus, in his March 2010 testimony before the Senate Armed Services committee, recycled this received wisdom: "The conflict foments anti-American sentiment, due to a perception of U.S. favoritism for Israel. Arab anger over the Palestinian question limits the strength and depth of U.S. partnerships with governments and peoples in the AOR [area of responsibility] and weakens the legitimacy of moderate regimes in the Arab world. Meanwhile, al-Qaeda and other militant groups exploit that anger to mobilize support."[334] This sentiment has also been expressed by Obama's National Security Adviser James L. Jones, Defense Secretary Robert Gates, and Obama himself, who said in April 2010 that the conflict is "costing us significantly in terms of both blood and treasure."[335] Hence the diplomatic furor ginned up by the Obama administration in March 2010 over the building of apartment houses in East Jerusalem, despite Israel's publicly repeated position that Jerusalem will remain undivided in any ultimate peace agreement.[336] Meanwhile, the administration says nothing when the same month as Obama's publicly expressed displeasure with Israel, the allegedly moderate Palestinian Authority names a public square in Ramallah, the de facto capital of the PA, after a woman who in 1978 killed 38 Israelis, including 13 children; names a street there after a bomb-making engineer responsible for the murder of hundreds of Israelis and one American; and PA leader Mahmoud Abbas eulogizes Abdallah Daoud, the terrorist who in 2002 occupied and befouled the Church of the Nativity in Bethlehem, saying "We must maintain the way of the Shahid [Martyr] Daoud."[337]

The demonizing of Israel has been a masterstroke of Muslim and Islamist propaganda. For the left, the Palestinians became the darlings of revolutionary violence, even more attractive because they were fighting against Jews, who for over a

century have been the leftist's emblem of capitalist depredations, and against Israel's sponsor America, the greatest global
challenge to the leftist utopia. For the realist right, supporting
tiny, resource-poor Israel was simply not worth alienating our
Arab allies, whose oil fuels the global economy. And for anti-
Semites on both the left and the right, the Jew-hatred driven
underground by the Holocaust could now be safely indulged
in by dressing it up as anti-Zionism and a professed concern
for the dispossessed Palestinians. This pretext, however, is
based on an Orwellian rewrite of history that erases the 3,000-
year presence of Jews in the Holy Land and makes the descendents of conquerors, occupiers, and immigrants the rightful
possessors.

Accepting this historical myth in effect sacrifices our foreign policy needs and aims to the self-serving and specious
arguments of peoples for whom Israel's very existence is the
most visible and painful embodiment of Islamic failure, dishonor, and retreat. As Lee Smith writes, "Leaving aside the
dubious wisdom, never mind the moral clarity, of choosing
allies and making policy based on the emotions of other countries' citizens, for whom by definition U.S interests are not
paramount, the reality is that Israel is the United States' greatest strategic asset in the region."[338] Alienating Israel, as Obama
is doing in order to appease the Palestinians and the Islamists,
will not stop the jihadists from wanting to kill us. They are
angry not about Israel's apartment buildings but about its existence. But marginalizing Israel will send a message to our other
Middle Eastern allies, whose biggest concern is a nuclear-
armed Iran, that the U.S. is a "weak horse" and an unreliable
partner.

Sniggering at Patriotism

Finally, like that of England in the 1920s and 1930s, American
appeasement reflects the decline of patriotism, the loyalty to

and affection for one's country and its beliefs, and the willingness to fight, kill, and die to protect the homeland that has
made us what we are. Yet for many Americans who no longer
believe in their country's goodness, such "patriotic pride is
morally dangerous," as philosopher Martha Nussbaum claims,
for we should give allegiance to "the moral community made
up of all human beings."[339] Believing in this non-existent "world
community," such people are quick to attribute all the world's
ills to the freest and most benign global power in all of history.
Thus, ever since the Vietnam War we have witnessed American citizens who benefit from the freedom and prosperity of
their homeland actively supporting and encouraging an enemy
who is killing their fellow citizens, an enemy who despises all
the freedoms and human rights America's critics enjoy and
claim to cherish. Such corrosive attitudes are dangerous, as
Thomas Sowell reminds us:

> One may of course live in a country parasitically, accepting all
> the benefits for which others have sacrificed—both in the past
> and in the present—while rejecting any notion of being obliged
> to do the same. But once that attitude becomes general, the
> country becomes defenseless against forces of either internal
> disintegration or external aggression. In short, patriotism and
> national honor cannot be reduced to simply psychological
> quirks, to which intellectuals can consider themselves supe-
> rior, without risking dire consequences.[340]

Indeed, this disdain of patriotism, which Orwell in the
1940s thought was limited to many English intellectuals, has
become received wisdom in the United States and is considered a sign of cosmopolitan sophistication even by many outside the intellectual class.

This willingness to give aid and comfort to the enemy, as
we have seen, has been evident throughout the war against the
jihadists. Americans who support the terrorists, whether intentionally or not, either don't know or don't care that our enemies,

as the statements of bin Laden repeatedly tell us, are explicitly fighting a war of morale, exploiting the self-loathing and willingness to work against our country's interests and security that are displayed by such actions. Those aiding the enemy no doubt rationalize their behavior as legitimate "dissent," but the ever escalating, utopian standards behind most of this criticism recalls George Orwell's description of leftist journals in the 1930s: "The immediately striking thing about all these papers is their generally negative, querulous attitude, their complete lack at all times of any constructive suggestion. There is little in them except the irresponsible carping of people who have never been and never expect to be in a position of power. Another marked characteristic is the emotional shallowness of people who live in a world of ideas and have little contact with physical reality."[341] The jihadists aren't fooled by specious appeals to legitimate "dissent" to rationalize words and deeds that compromise our country's interests and security. They understand that such dissent arises from the collapse of passionate belief in the political ideals and goods that have created the freedom enjoyed by those who hate their own country and have lost the political virtues of self-sacrifice, loyalty, and duty. And if so many of America's most privileged and affluent citizens believe in their own country's guilt and corruption so much that they will aid the enemy, why shouldn't the jihadists take them at their word and try to destroy such a global villain?

Volunteer Dhimmi

All these appeasing behaviors—born of fear, self-flagellating guilt over presumed historical crimes, multicultural fantasies about the non-Western "other," deprecation of religion and spiritual motives, disdain for America, and delusional ideals about some international "harmony of interests" and the transnational institutions that through diplomatic negotiation can resolve disputes better than force—such behaviors conform to the traditional Islamic notion of the *dhimmi,* the "subjugated, non-Muslim individuals or people that accept the restrictive and humiliating subordination to an ascendant Islamic power to avoid enslavement or death," as scholar Bat Ye'or defines them.[342] Responses and actions that we in the West believe reflect superior values, such as tolerance, compromise, and respect for others and their differences, to jihadists as well as to many traditional Muslims are signs of fear born of spiritual weakness and a lack of confidence in our beliefs as something worth killing and dying for. Rather than signs of our superiority, they are instead interpreted as acknowledgments of *Islam's* superiority and as concrete displays of the demeanor suitable for the *dhimmi,* particularly when this tolerance and respect is not reciprocated by Muslims, since acceptance of a double standard is always an admission of inferiority.

The appeasement of jihad, then, ultimately reflects a failure of imagination akin to that of many English writers and leaders in the 1930s, who could not imagine a leader possessing the murderous fanaticism of an Adolf Hitler. This strange sort of ethnocentrism assumes that the whole world believes as we do and desires the same goods and ends. For secular materialists, as increasingly most people in the West are becoming, life is the supreme good for which little is worth sacrificing. But for those acting and living in the context of what they see as spiritual reality, even life itself, both their own and the lives of others, is the lesser good, to be sacrificed if doing so serves God. "So whoever has realized," bin Laden told Al Jazeera, "that the rewards of this world are few and that the next world is better and more permanent, he is the one who responds to the commands of God almighty" to wage jihad, thereby "showing that this life, this world, is an illusory pleasure."[343] This certainty and confidence in the righteousness of their cause gives the jihadists the strength that offsets our military and economic power, which is not backed up by confidence in the rightness of the beliefs this power should serve and protect.

In short, as bin Laden and other Islamists continually remind us, because they have this conviction, they love death more than we love life, echoing the words of Khalid ibn al-Walid in 636 before the battle of Qadisiyya against the Persians: "I have come to you with an army of men that love death, as you love life."[344] For men such as these, negotiation, compromise, tolerance, protestations of respect, promises of democratic freedom, and materialist bribes will have little effect. Only a demonstrated, relentless willingness to take them at their word and give them what they love will end their aggression.

Conclusion

The Hamlet of Nations

———————— ◆ ————————

*As a result [of affluence], the toughness of desert life is lost.
Group feeling and courage weaken. Members of the tribe
revel in the well-being that God has given them. Their
children and offspring grow up too proud to look after
themselves or to attend to their own needs. They have disdain
also for all the other things that are necessary in connection
with group feeling. This finally becomes a character trait and
natural characteristic of theirs. Their group feeling is
altogether destroyed. They thus invite their own
destruction.... When group feeling is destroyed, the tribe is
no longer able to protect itself, let alone press any claims. It
will be swallowed up by other nations.*

IBN KHALDÛN[1]

*We cannot allow ourselves to become the Hamlet of Nations,
worrying endlessly over whether and how to respond. A great
nation with global responsibilities cannot afford to be
hamstrung by confusion and indecisiveness.*

GEORGE P. SHULTZ[2]

Appeasement has its roots in the eternal verities of human nature. Fear, passion, and the lust for power, prestige, and pelf can drive people to pursue short-sighted and selfish aims at the expense of long-term security. For all their strengths, democracies are plagued by the pressure of factional or other self-interests on the political decisions made in response to a threat. Democratic accountability

271

likewise can be dangerous to national defense. From the "denunciation" and subsequent trials in ancient Athens to the electoral pressures, partisan criticism, and impatient second-guessing of policy typical of modern democracies incessantly bombarded by 24/7 mass media, the public mechanisms of political oversight and accountability can become impediments to the unified, coherent, long-term strategies usually required when the state faces a determined aggressor. So too the deliberation, discussion, and verbal persuasion that undergird political freedom can in some circumstances retard timely action and give leaders unwilling to act the cover of verbal processes, thus substituting words for deeds.

Democracy, then, by allowing broad participation in government, gives greater scope to the people's shortsighted passions and interests at the expense of long-term calculation, and allows impatience with sacrifice and suffering to affect policy. Even the champions of democracy have long noted these tendencies. "Democracy appears to me better adapted for the conduct of society in times of peace," Alexis de Tocqueville wrote in 1835, "or for a sudden effort of remarkable vigor, than for the prolonged endurance of the great storms that beset the political existence of nations. . . . But it is this clear perception of the future, founded upon judgment and experience, that is frequently wanting in democracies. The people are more apt to feel than to reason; and if their present sufferings are great, it is to be feared that the still greater sufferings attendant upon defeat will be forgotten." These disadvantages, de Tocqueville continues, also extend to the conduct of foreign affairs in general, for "a democracy can only with great difficulty regulate the details of an important undertaking, persevere in a fixed design, and work out its execution in spite of serious obstacles. It cannot combine its measures with secrecy or await their consequences with patience."[3] Athens in the fourth century B.C., England in the 1920s and 1930s, and today the United States, each in its own way illustrate the truth of de Tocqueville's observation.

The democratic flaw that arises from the privileging of discussion and persuasion also compromises the relations of democracies to other states. Foreign affairs are impossible without diplomacy, but absent clear and realistic aims, and without the credible willingness to use force if necessary to deter and persuade adversaries to come to an agreement and abide by it, diplomatic negotiation becomes an end in itself and another method for creating the illusion of action when the will or ability to act is lacking. And as Philip II, Hitler, and Iran all illustrate, an adversary can manipulate such negotiation to disguise his true aims, buy time, and misdirect his foe, making policies of appeasement more palatable by providing diplomatic camouflage. Effective diplomacy requires, then, the imagination to see beyond the pretexts and professed aims of the adversary and recognize his true goals, no matter how bizarre or alien to our own way of thinking.

As Robert Conquest writes, the greatest danger of diplomatic engagement arises from this failure of imagination:

> We are still faced with the absolutely crucial problem of making the intellectual and imaginative effort *not* to project our ideas of common sense or natural motivation onto the products of totally different cultures. The central point is less that people misunderstand other people, or that cultures misunderstand other cultures, than that they have no notion that this may be the case. They assume that the light of their own parochial common sense is enough. And they frame policies based on illusions. Yet how profound is this difference between political psychologies and between the motivations of different political traditions, and how deep-set and how persistent these attitudes are![4]

The Athenians, dismissive of a people they long looked down on as semi-barbarians, could not imagine at the beginning of Philip's march to dominance that, as Demosthenes put it, "a man raised in Pella, a small, obscure place at the time, would become so bold as to desire rule over the Greeks and to make that his purpose."[5] The British could not take seriously Hitler's novel fanatic ideology, seeing instead another "man on horseback" pursuing long-familiar aims of continental dominance, or a leader restoring his country's honor besmirched by an unfair peace settlement, or merely a "screaming little defective in Berlin," as H. G. Wells put it.[6] Worse yet, despite the evidence of *Mein Kampf,* Hitler's public rants, and Nazism's racialist lunacy and totalitarian brutality evident within months of Hitler's coming to power, many in England continued to believe that the Führer could be reasoned with and appeased with concessions. And as it has for 30 years, America continues to miss the significance of Islam's theology of violence, traditional chauvinism, and imperial ambitions that lie behind the Iranian regime's pursuit of nuclear weapons. Instead, Obama continues to believe that trade and economic sanctions can "change the calculus of a country like Iran so that they see that there are more costs and fewer benefits to pursuing a nuclear weapons program," as the President said after his Nuclear Security Summit in April 2010.[7] Only a complete misunderstanding of the mullahs in Tehran could make Obama think that the West has any material "benefits" in exchange for which Iran will give up the pursuit of weapons that would make it the most dominant Muslim state in the Middle East and bring closer to realization the dream of recovering Islam's rightful global dominance.

More broadly, this failure of imagination lies behind an ideal peculiar to modernity, the "moralizing internationalism" predicated on an imagined "harmony of interests," such that, as John Stuart Mill wrote, "the good of no country can be obtained by any means but such as tend to that of all countries, nor ought to be sought otherwise, even if obtainable."[8] This view is based on the assumption that all men are for the most part rational and that global civilization is progressing away from violence and irrational aims toward the goods

Westerners prize and desire. As such, it rejects the existence of differing and conflicting goods, which are dismissed as mere illusions born of ignorance, superstition, poverty, or historical injustices. Thus multinational institutions and international laws and covenants can be created to express this harmony of interests and goods, and defuse any conflicts that may arise among those states not yet sufficiently enlightened about their true interests. These assumptions lay behind the creation of first the League of Nations and then the United Nations, still the premier global exemplar of these views, despite its serial failures over the last 60 years. And it still informs much of our own foreign policy, which assumes that all peoples are "just like us," and so they desire the political freedom and material prosperity we prize, and prefer peace to war, deliberation to violence, material goods to spiritual, and getting along with other states to dominating them.

But the peoples of the world do not all share similar goods, aims, and ideals. As George Orwell recognized, "the divisions between nation and nation are founded on real differences of outlook. Till recently it was thought proper to pretend that all human beings are very much alike, but in fact anyone able to use his eyes knows that the average of human behaviour differs enormously from country to country."[9] For some peoples, freedom and prosperity may not be as important as religious purity, national honor, revanchist passions, or domination of their neighbors. And because all peoples in fact don't desire the same goods, the multinational institutions that have proliferated over the last two centuries have always primarily been instruments for sovereign states to pursue their particular national interests, particularly those states that because of weakness cannot achieve their aims through force. Among the ancient Greeks, the multistate leagues were such instruments of each city-state's interests, a tool Philip wielded effectively and shrewdly to extend his influence beyond Macedon. The League of Nations failed spectacularly at preventing the growing state violence of

the Thirties, mainly because it was not in the national interests of most countries to pass or enforce resolutions that could
be effective at achieving the League's lofty aims. Nor did the
Geneva Conventions or Hague Conventions prevent some of
the most gruesome and sadistic cruelty in history, since some
states, like the Soviet Union, simply didn't sign them, and others that did, like Nazi Germany, ignored them when it suited
their interests, or just to indulge their ideological brutality. And
the United Nations has become what Churchill feared, a "cockpit in the Tower of Babel," in which those states without the
courage of their convictions substitute talk for action and those
pursuing their own malignant aims, like the jihadist regime in
Iran and its supporters, find the procedural camouflage and
global respectability that further their designs. Meanwhile,
they contemptuously ignore the various international conventions and covenants created to protect people from such
violence.

These weaknesses of democracy, however, are an acceptable trade-off for the many benefits of democratic government.
For all its risks of selfish or shortsighted policies, the political
freedom that extends participation in government to all the citizens makes the state their "common thing," as the Greeks put
it, their own possession, hence giving them a powerful interest
in the state's flourishing and survival. Moreover, from the plains
of Marathon and the waters of Salamis, to the beaches of Nor-
mandy and the alleys of Fallujah, this sense of ownership in
turn has made the citizen-soldiers of democracies lethal fighters once they have been roused to "a sudden effort of remarkable vigor." This vital strength of democracy, however, is in turn
dependent upon the continuing commitment of the people to
the way of life, political ideals, and shared beliefs that bind
them into a nation. And it is nourished by their confidence that
freedom and autonomy, no matter their dangerous side effects,
are ultimately better than, not just different from, any possible
alternative, and so are worth fighting, suffering, dying, and

killing for. Perhaps Pericles, leader of the world's first democracy, put it best in his funeral oration:

> Any one can discourse to you forever about the advantages of a brave defence, which you know already. But instead of listening to him I would have you day by day fix your eyes upon the greatness of Athens, until you become filled with the love of her; and when you are impressed by the spectacle of her glory, reflect that this empire has been acquired by men who knew their duty and had the courage to do it, who in the hour of conflict had the fear of dishonour always present to them, and who, if ever they failed in an enterprise, would not allow their virtues to be lost to their country, but freely gave their lives to her as the fairest offering which they could present at her feast.[10]

As our three examples of appeasement show, when that passionate attachment to the state as the citizens' own possession and expression of their identity is eroded, when the political virtues expressing that attachment—courage, self-sacrifice, duty—are weakened, when the state is viewed as a mere dispenser of entitlements and the umpire of conflicting centrifugal interests, then democracies are vulnerable to the temptations of appeasement and its sacrifice of long-term security for short-term comfort.

For us moderns, questionable ideas and ideologies have also contributed to the erosion of patriotism that makes appeasement an attractive policy. Transnational institutions, along with international laws and covenants, promise to create global peace and prosperity based on the premise that by reducing the malign influence of mutually exclusive national interests and their zero-sum conflicts, the xenophobic swamps that foment wars can be drained. This demonization of national feeling is indulged in by many in the West who consider some mythic "global community" and its international laws and institutions as the proper object of their loyalty and source of their identity. But it is dangerous for a people's ability to ward off aggression. As historian Michael Burleigh asks:

> Can any nation survive without a consensus on values that transcend special interests, and which are non-negotiable in the sense of 'Here we stand'? Can a nation state survive that is only a legal and political shell, or a 'market state' for discrete ethnic or religious communities that share little by way of common values other than the use of the same currency? Can a society survive that is not the object of commitments to its core values or a focus for the fundamental identities of all its members?[11]

A culture without that consensus and collective commitments will find it difficult to maintain what the 14th-century Arab historian Ibn Khaldûn called "group feeling," the solidarity that gives a people its cohesive strength. For Khaldûn, luxury renders a people incapable of enduring hardship and suffering, and encourages a self-centered obsession with personal comforts and pleasures that loosen the ties that bind them into a people and leave them vulnerable to a tougher, more determined adversary. George Orwell agreed: "However little we may like it, toughness is the price of survival. A nation trained to think hedonistically cannot survive amid peoples who work like slaves and breed like rabbits, and whose chief national industry is war."[12] Certainly in America, our unprecedented affluence and leisure render many of us loath to make the sacrifices, perform the public service, and endure the harsh, sometimes brutal actions required by a global hegemon faced with numerous rivals and an impassioned enemy who *will* endure those sacrifices and can justify through faith a terroristic violence.

Abetting this erosion of national loyalty for us today has been the Marxist-inspired demonization of imperialism and colonialism, the twin historical sins for which all Westerners must proclaim their guilt in word and deed for, in the words of French anthropologist Claude Lévi-Strauss, "the monstrous and incomprehensible cataclysm represented, for such a broad and innocent part of humanity, by the development of Western civilization."[13] Convinced by the false charge that the United States has committed crimes against the world and continues to be driven by greed and the lust to dominate other peoples, we find it harder to act with the confidence born of the knowledge that our aims are just, our motives good, and the outcome worth the tragic costs of action. Multiculturalism has worsened this tendency to self-flagellation, positing the cultural and moral superiority of the Third World victims of colonialism over their greedy, repressed, and power-hungry Western brutalizers. For those who believe in this melodramatic history, how can they give their love and loyalty and service to such a global villain? Worse yet, why then *shouldn't* we appease rather than resist the peoples whose attacks are justified payback for our own aggression?

The "sniggering of the intellectuals at patriotism and physical courage," as Orwell put it of prewar English anti-patriotism, "the persistent effort to chip away English morale and spread a hedonistic, what-do-I-get-out-of-it attitude to life, has done nothing but harm. It would have been harmful even if we had been living in the squashy League of Nations universe that these people imagined. In the age of Fuehrers [sic] and bombing planes it was a disaster."[14] Since Orwell's day, these attitudes have spread beyond the intellectual class to large swaths of Americans through the movies, television shows, and school curricula that make sniggering at one's country the height of cosmopolitan sophistication, and apologizing for its alleged sins, as President Obama is fond of doing, the sign of a superior morality. Such attitudes are deadly, however, when we are faced with a foe that believes so passionately in his beliefs and their superiority that he is willing to destroy not just us and our families, but also himself and his own family in support of them.

Finally, the secularization dominating the West today has weakened the transcendent beliefs that once underwrote patriotism with the assurance that political freedom and human rights, the goods that define our country and make it worthy of our affection and loyalty, are created not by fallible men or the accidents of history but by "the laws of nature and of nature's God," as Thomas Jefferson put it in the Declaration of Independence. Moreover, the various materialist determinisms that have filled the vacuum left by religion's retreat from the public square have rendered us incapable of recognizing and acknowledging spiritual motives, particularly those of a faith so radically different in its goods and aims as Islam is from our own etiolated Christianity and Judaism. In 1947, T. S. Eliot recognized the dangers of modernity's mistaken assumption about religion's irrelevance: "The Liberal still thinks in terms of political differences which can be settled by negotiation, and of religious differences which have ceased to matter; he assumes further that the cultural conflict is one which can, like political conflict, be adjusted by compromise, or, like religious conflict, be resolved by tolerance. But the culture conflict is the religious conflict on its deepest level: it is one whole pattern of life against another."[15] In contrast, convinced that religion is a Marxian "opiate" or a Freudian "illusion," or at best a lifestyle choice and source of private therapeutic solace, we dismiss it as an effect of some more significant material cause. Thus we rationalize away the jihadists' careful justifications for their violence in the theology of Islam and seek to ameliorate what we think are the true causes—poverty, lack of political participation, or historical injustices— rather than realizing that those who believe they are divinely sanctioned to kill others will not be talked or bribed out of their beliefs, but can only be destroyed.

Appeasement has its roots in human nature, but it grows and flourishes in the lack of confidence in the Western way as history's best social and political order, a doubt nourished by accepting the lie that it is the civilization most culpable for all of humanity's ills. "A culture in which the habit," Catholic theologian George Weigel writes, "the virtue, of self-critique and self-correction has deteriorated into self-contempt is a culture that is unlikely to be able to meet the challenge of a self-confident culture in the war of ideas—including moral ideas.... A West that sees in its past nothing but pathology—racism, colonialism, religious wars and persecutions, sexism, and all the rest—is a West that cannot, and almost certainly will not, defend its present."[16] For the United States, the stakes of failure are high not just for us but for the whole world. Like it or not, intended or not, America has assumed the mantle of the keeper of global order once possessed by the British empire. If prosperity, freedom, and peace are to have a chance of becoming a possibility for the rest of the world rather than remaining the increasingly beleaguered privilege of the West, then the world needs what Niall Ferguson calls a "liberal empire," for there are "parts of the world where legal and political institutions are in a condition of such collapse or corruption that their inhabitants are effectively cut off from any hope of prosperity. And there are states that, through weakness or malice, encourage terrorist organizations committed to wrecking a liberal world order."[17] In a globally interconnected economy, to borrow Robert Kagan's metaphor, the "saloonkeepers" need a "sheriff" to "enforce some peace and justice in what Americans see as a lawless world where outlaws need to be deterred or destroyed, often through the muzzle of a gun."[18] The United States is the only country that can perform the task of maintaining global order, if only because it is the only state with the military power and reach to do so. But it won't if America's traditional fear of "entangling alliances" and what Ferguson calls "imperial denial" are worsened by a collapse in the confidence that the U.S. is indeed worthy of that role and is better than any alternative.[19]

More important, that lack of confidence erodes our national prestige by projecting weakness that invites challengers to our interests and security. A global hegemon, whether ancient Rome

or Victorian England, derives its power and security not just
from its military or economic resources but from its prestige,
the certainty on the part of both allies and adversaries that it
will use those resources to further its aims, support its friends,
and punish its challengers. And these actions that maintain a
nation's prestige are in turn made possible by the confidence
in the goodness and rightness of the ideals that justify power
and its use, and that give people the moral fortitude to face
Lincoln's "awful arithmetic" and the tragic consequences,
unforeseen contingencies, and deadly mistakes that always
accompany the use of force. But once that prestige is tarnished,
as it is by the appeasement of an enemy or the failure to punish aggression, new enemies will arise. Like the jihadists who
look with contempt on what bin Laden calls the "weak horse,"
they will be encouraged by the weakness such appeasement
displays and the failure of nerve that follows the collapse of
belief in the ideals justifying the use of power. Both the Roman
and British empires declined for many reasons, but one they
both share is the loss of pride and faith in what it meant to be
a Roman or a Briton, and the breakdown in the passionate
belief in their own unique national excellence, inspiring them
with the confidence that they deserved their empires and justifying the sacrifices of blood and treasure necessary to defend
them.

An America lacking that confidence and riddled with doubt
and self-loathing risks becoming what ex-Secretary of State
George Shultz feared—the "Hamlet of Nations," afraid to act
because it is no longer sure of what it believes or whether what
it believes is worth killing and dying for. That doubt and fear
make appeasement an attractive alternative and erode national
prestige, provoking more aggression and more appeasement.
The 30–year history of America's war with jihad has followed
this pattern, pointing us to the grim possibility that an Islamist
regime will possess nuclear weapons it can use against our
allies or hand off to like-minded jihadists. If that happens, the

wages of such appeasement are unlikely to be as final as the Greek city-states' loss of political freedom or as devastating as the global war needed to destroy Nazism and Japanese militarism. But another attack on the homeland with a nuclear device or even a "dirty bomb," or an attack on Israel and the retaliation sure to follow, will lead to more disruptive and expensive wars abroad, more restrictions of our freedoms at home, more erosion of our morale and will, and more appeasing policies, with dire consequences for our national character and way of life. Then indeed American exceptionalism, as President Obama already believes, will have passed from history.

Notes

[1] *Iliad* 22.132–37, 146–56. Trans. Robert Fagles (New York, 1990).

[2] Text available at http://online.wsj.com/article/ SB121083798995894943.html.

[3] For the liberal criticism of Bush's speech see Evan Thomas, "The Mythology of Munich," *Newsweek* (23 June 2008).

[4] Telford Taylor, *Munich. The Price of Peace* (New York, 1979), pp. xiii, 250–51.

[5] In Martin Gilbert, *The Roots of Appeasement* (New York: 1966), p. ix. See also Keith Robbins, *Appeasement*, 2nd ed. (Oxford and Malden, Mass, 1997), p. 7.

[6] For more on "good" appeasement see Paul Kennedy, "A Time To Appease," *National Interest* (22 June 2010), available at www.nationalinterest.org/Article.aspx?id=23542.

[7] *The Decline and Fall of the Roman Empire*, chap. 26.

[8] *Ab urbe condita* 1.1. Trans. Aubrey de Sélincourt (Hammondsworth, Eng., 1960).

[9] Thucydides 1.76.2.

[10] Fragment 110 (Bergk).

[11] Thucydides 2.44.4. Trans. Richard Crawley, in *The Landmark Thucydides,* ed. Robert B. Strassler (New York, 1996).

[12] In *The Origins of War* (New York, 1995), p. 407; see also p. 569.

[13] *New York Times* (27 June 1954).

[14] *Iliad* 22.309–312, trans. Robert Fagles.

[15] Thucydides 2.43.4.

[16] Justin, *Epitome of the Philippic History of Pompeius Trogus* 9.3, trans. J. S. Watson (London, 1853), at http://www. forumromanum.org/literature/justin/english/trans9.html.

[17] Thucydides 3.82.2. For Lincoln's phrase see Mark E. Neely Jr., *The Last Best Hope on Earth* (Cambridge, Mass., 1993), p. 74.

[18] At 3.82.2.

Chapter One

[1] Demosthenes 18.67–68, trans. Harvey Yunis, *Demosthenes, Speeches 18 and 19* (Austin, TX, 2005). All dates in this chapter are B.C. unless noted otherwise. For the ancient sources for this period, see Ian Worthington, *Philip II of Macedonia* (New Haven, 2008), pp. 210–15.

[2] Xenophon 7.5.27. Trans. G. T. Griffith, in G. T. Griffith and N.G.L. Hammond, *A History of Macedonia,* vol. 2 (Oxford, 1979), p. 217.

[3] George Cawkwell, *Philip of Macedon* (London, 1978), p. 22.

[4] In *Alexander of Macedonia, 356–323 B.C.* (1974; Berkeley and Los Angeles, 1991), p. 6.

[5] Fr. 225, in Gordon S. Shrimpton, *Theopompus the Historian* (Montreal and Kingston, 1991), p. 119.

[6] Demosthenes 9.31, in *Demosthenes. Orations.* vol. 1, trans. J. H. Vince (Cambridge, Mass. and London, 1930).

[7] Arrian 7.9.2. Trans. Aubrey de Sélincourt (Harmondsworth, Eng., 1958).

[8] Diodorus, 16.1.3. In *Diodorus Siculus: The Reign of Philip II,* trans. E. I. McQueen (London, 1995), p.19.

[9] Diodorus 16.3.4.

[10] Alfonso Moreno, *Feeding the Democracy* (Oxford, 2007), p. 10. See also Peter Hunt, *War, Peace, and Alliance in Demosthenes' Athens* (Cambridge, 2010), pp. 35–39; see also Demosthenes 18.301.

[11] D. M. Lewis et al., *The Cambridge Ancient History,* vol. 6, *The Fourth Century B.C.,* 2nd ed. (Cambridge, 1994), pp. 558–60. For the Athenian Assembly in the 4th century, see Mogens Herman Hansen, *The Athenian Democracy in the Age of Demosthenes,* trans. J. A. Crook (Norman, OK, 1991), pp. 156–57.

[12] Aristotle, *Rhetoric* 1411a, in Cawkwell, p. 72.

[13] Worthington, *Philip II of Macedonia,* p. 24.

[14] Cawkwell, pp. 70–71.

[15] G. T. Griffith, *A History of Macedonia II,* p. 231.

[16] Worthington, p. 41.

[17] *A History of Greece XI,* new ed. (London, 1869), p. 37.

[18] Diodorus Siculus 16.8.6. A talent comprised 6,000 drachmae. In the second half of the fourth century, a day's pay ranged from 1½ to 2½ drachmae.

19 Worthington, p. 44.

20 In *A History of Macedonia II*, p. 258.

21 Demosthenes 2.23. Trans. R. D. Milns, in *The Spectre of Philip. A Study of Historical Evidence* (Sydney, 1970), pp. 51–52.

22 *A History of Greece*, p. 45.

23 Worthington, p. 58.

24 *Philip II of Macedonia*, p. 59.

25 Polyaenus 2.38.2. In Cawkwell, *Philip of Macedon*, p. 61.

26 Diodorus 16.35.6. Griffith doubts that the 3,000 prisoners were drowned, arguing that Diodorus is referring to the corpses of the 6,000 dead. *A History of Macedonia II*, pp. 276–77.

27 Justin 9.2, trans. J. S. Watson.

28 Worthington, pp. 64–65.

29 Cawkwell, pp. 62, 67.

30 Grote, p. 100.

31 Demosthenes 3.5, trans. J. H. Vince.

32 Demosthenes 4.34.

33 Demosthenes 23.109, 3.7; Cawkwell, p. 84.

34 Griffith, *A History of Macedon II*, p. 315.

35 Diodorus 16.53.2

36 Worthington, p. 78.

37 *Olynthiacs I, II, III*.

38 Worthington, p. 76; Cawkwell, p. 86, gives a total of 38.

39 Worthington, pp. 80–82, Cawkwell pp. 86–90; T.T.B. Ryder, "Demosthenes and Philip II," in *Demosthenes. Statesman and Orator*, ed. Ian Worthington (London, 2000), p. 57.

40 *On the Embassy*, Aeschines 2.13. Trans. Chris Carey, in *Aeschines* (Austin, TX, 2000).

41 Cawkwell, p. 97; see also Isocrates 5.73–75.

42 The speeches are both called *On the Dishonest Embassy*. The issue is revisited in 330 in another prosecution, this one instigated by Aeschines (*Against Ctesiphon*), over a crown the Assembly voted to bestow on Demosthenes in recognition of his efforts against Philip; Demosthenes's speech is called *On the Crown*.

43 Diodorus 16.95.2, trans. McQueen.

44 Demosthenes 19.305, 308, trans. Yunis. Demosthenes coins a word, *hellênikôtatos*, literally "Greekest man," translated by Yunis as "purest Greek."

[45] George Cawkwell, "The End of Greek Liberty," *Transitions to Empire: Essays in Greco-Roman History, 360–146 B.C., in Honor of E. Badian*, eds. Robert W. Wallace and Edward M. Harris (Norman and London, 1996), p. 105.

[46] Demosthenes 19.259, trans. Yunis.

[47] Theopompus Fragment 162, trans. C. B. Gulick, in Shrimpton, p. 168. See also Fragments. 224, 225; Demosthenes 2.17–19.

[48] In Cawkwell, "The End of Greek Liberty," p. 106.

[49] Cawkwell, *Philip of Macedon*, p. 100.

[50] A point made a few years later by the orator Hegesippus, in a speech attributed to Demosthenes. Demosthenes 7.37.

[51] Worthington, p. 94.

[52] *A History of Macedonia II*, p. 340.

[53] Demosthenes 19.20–21; 321, trans. Yunis.

[54] Fragment. 166, in Shrimpton, *Theopompus the Historian*, p. 84.

[55] Demosthenes19.291.

[56] Justin 8.4, trans. J. S. Watson.

[57] Worthington, in *Philip of Macedonia*, argues that the news about Philip's possession of Thermopylae had not reached Athens, which explains why Demosthenes counseled the Athenians not to abandon it (100). Cawkwell, in *Philip of Macedon*, p. 105, argues that Demosthenes was jeered in the Assembly precisely because he was arguing for trying to prevent a *fait accompli*.

[58] Demosthenes 19.35, trans. Yunis. See T.T.B. Ryder, "Demosthenes and Philip II," pp. 67–69.

[59] *History of Greece*, p. 234.

[60] See John Buckler, "Philip II's Designs on Greece, in *Transitions to Empire*, p. 85.

[61] Didorus 16.60.4, in McQueen.

[62] *A History of Macedonia II*, pp. 450–51.

[63] *History of Greece*, pp. 247, 248.

[64] Justin 8.6.

[65] 6.15, trans. J. H. Vince. For Demosthenes's reliability, see Griffith, *A History of Macedonia II*, 476–77.

[66] For Euboea's strategic significance, see Cawkwell, *Philip of Macedon*, 88–89. For Philip's possible interference there in 343, see Worthington, *Philip II of Macedonia*, 112; Cawkwell dismisses Demosthenes's claim, 127. See also T.T.B. Ryder, "Demosthenes and Philip II," p. 75.

67 [Demosthenes] 7.21, trans. J. H. Vince.

68 *Philip II of Macedonia*, p. 112. Griffith believes the proposal for a common peace came from the Athenians; see *A History of Macedonia II*, p. 490.

69 T.T.B. Ryder, "Demosthenes and Philip II," p. 74.

70 [Demosthenes] 7.22, trans. J. H. Vince.

71 Ibid. 6.6.

72 Ibid. 6.25.

73 *The Athenian Democracy in the Age of Demosthenes*, pp. 215–16.

74 These are the speeches referred to in n. 60. Demosthenes made his speech against Aeschines during the "audit" (*euthynai*) that every Athenian acting in an official capacity or overseeing state funds had to undergo at the end of his service. See Hansen, *The Athenian Democracy in the Age of Demosthenes*, pp. 222–24.

75 *Philip II of Macedonia*, p. 116.

76 *The History of Greece*, p. 249.

77 [Demosthenes] 7.2.

78 For example, Worthington, *Philip II of Macedonia*, p. 118. Aeschines 3.83.

79 *History of Greece*, p. 252.

80 Chris Carey, *Aeschines*, p. 193 n. 92.

81 *Philip II of Macedonia*, p. 119.

82 For doubts about these charges of Macedonian interference in Euboea, see Cawkwell, *Philip of Macedon*, pp. 131–33.

83 Diodorus 16.71; Worthington, *Philip II of Macedonia*, p. 123.

84 [Demosthenes] 12.23, trans. Buckler. This letter is included in the corpus of Demosthenes's speeches. See John Buckler, "Philip II's Designs on Greece," in *Transitions to Empire*, pp. 87–88.

85 The speeches are called *On the Chersonese* and the third and fourth *Philippics*. Some scholars think that the fourth *Philippic* is not Demosthenes's.

86 *On the Chersonese*, 8.39–40, trans. Vince.

87 *Third Philippic*, 9.17–18, trans. Vince.

88 As Worthington argues in *Philip II of Macedonia*, p. 132.

89 Griffith, *A History of Macedonia II*, pp. 580–81.

90 Cawkwell, *Philip of Macedon*, p. 142; Griffith, *A History of Macedonia II*, p. 589.

91 Ryder, "Demosthenes and Philip II," p. 80.

[92] Worthington, *Philip II of Macedonia*, pp. 136–37, doubts Philip's involvement; Ryder, p. 80, notes the timing of Amphissa's move—right after the Athenian declaration of war against Philip.

[93] I follow the chronology of these events given in Griffith, *A History of Macedonia II*, p. 719.

[94] Demosthenes 19.143, trans. Yunis. Demosthenes accused Aeschines of being Philip's paid agent, which is unlikely.

[95] Diodorus Siculus 16.84.3–4, trans. McQueen. See too Demosthenes's description of these events at 18.169–73.

[96] *Life of Demosthenes* 18.1, trans. Bernadotte Perrin (London and Cambridge, Mass, 1919).

[97] Diodorus Siculus 16.84.5, trans. McQueen.

[98] Demosthenes 18.175–78, trans. Yunis. Demosthenes is recalling his speech almost a decade later, in the speech *On the Crown*, see n. 60.

[99] Cawkwell, *Philip of Macedon*, p. 144.

[100] Demosthenes 18.213, trans. Yunis.

[101] *Life of Demosthenes* 18.3, trans. Perrin.

[102] *Philip of Macedon*, p. 146.

[103] For the battle see Griffith, *A History of Macedonia II*, pp. 596–603.

[104] Worthington, *Philip II of Macedonia*, p. 156.

[105] Demosthenes 18.201, trans. Yunis; Cawkell, "The End of Greek Liberty," in *Transitions to Empire*, p. 100.

[106] *Life of Phocion* 26.1, trans. Perrin.

[107] *A History of Greece XII*, p. 199.

[108] Cawkwell, "The End of Greek Liberty," pp. 108–115, quote p. 115.

[109] Thucydides 1.145, trans. Crawley.

[110] Demosthenes 18.96, trans. Yunis. At the battle of Haliartus (395), the Athenians helped the Thebans against the Spartans, and in 394 fought with the Corinthians against the Spartans.

[111] A.H.M. Jones, *Athenian Democracy* (1957; Baltimore, 1986), pp. 6–7.

[112] See David Stockton, *The Classical Athenian Democracy* (Oxford, 1990), p. 112.

[113] See Hunt, pp. 49–50.

[114] *The Athenian Democracy in the Age of Demosthenes*, p. 98.

[115] See Hansen, pp. 112–15.

[116] Justin 9.1, trans. Watson.

[117] Pausanias 3.7.11, trans. Peter Levi, *Pausanias' Guide to Greece,* vol. 2 (Harmondsworth, England, 1971).

[118] Demosthenes 2.7–8, trans. Vince.

[119] Demosthenes 14.33, trans. Vince.

[120] Demosthenes 9.28–29, trans. Vince.

[121] Isocrates 4.1, in *Isocrates II,* trans. Terry L. Papillon (Austin, TX, 2004).

[122] See Minor M. Markle, III, "Support of Athenian Intellectuals for Philip: A Study of Isocrates' Philippus and Speusippus' Letter to Philip," *The Journal of Hellenic Studies,* vol. 96 (1976), pp. 80–99.

[123] Isocrates 5.14–15, trans. Papillon. See also the two letters Isocrates wrote to Philip reprising these themes.

[124] Demosthenes 4.47, trans. Vince.

[125] Ibid. 2.25.

[126] Ibid. 14.5.

[127] Diodorus 16.53, trans. McQueen; see also 16.54.

[128] Cicero, *Letters to Atticus* 1.16.12, in Cawkwell, "The End of Greek Liberty, p. 100; Valerius Maximus 7.2.10.

[129] Demosthenes 18. 295, 296, trans. Yunis.

[130] Ibid. 19. 104, 110.

[131] Ibid. 9.37–39,41.

[132] Demosthenes 19.249, trans. Yunis; Polybius 18.14. Polybius, of course, had no first-hand experience of the city-state autonomy lost when Philip became hegemon of Greece. See Griffith, *A History of Macedonia II,* pp. 479–80.

[133] See Cawkwell's "The End of Greek Liberty," pp. 100–04, for the arguments against taking seriously Demosthenes's charges of bribery.

[134] Demosthenes 1.4, trans. Vince.

[135] Ibid.18.235. See also 19.185–86.

[136] Demosthenes 8.11, trans. Vince.

[137] Ibid. 4.40.

[138] The "accounting" (*euthunai*) involved an audit of money spent and an examination into any charges of offenses committed while the citizen was conducting public business. See Hansen, pp. 222–24,

[139] Demosthenes 4.33–34, 45, trans. Vince.

[140] Demosthenes 2.12, trans. Vince.

141 Ibid.3.14.

142 Ibid. 6.4.

143 See Cawkwell, "The End of Greek Liberty," p. 105.

144 Diodorus Siculus 16.95.3, trans. McQueen.

145 Justin 9.8, trans. Watson. See also Pausanias 8.7.4–8.

146 Demosthenes 4.50, trans. Vince; Theopompus Fragment. 262, trans. Shrimpton.

147 Thucydides 2.40.2, trans. Crawley.

148 Thucydides 1.70.6, trans. Crawley.

149 Ibid. 2.43.4.

150 Hansen, *The Athenian Democracy in the Age of Demosthenes,* pp. 268–69. See Plutarch, *Phocion* 7.3.

151 Hansen, pp. 269–70. See also W. K. Pritchett, *The Greek State at War, Part II* (Berkeley and Los Angeles, 1974), pp. 59–116.

152 Isocrates 8.53–54, trans. Papillon.

153 On arguments for and against a decline in the ideal of military service see Hunt, pp. 253–56.

154 Demosthenes 14.15, trans. Vince.

155 Demosthenes 4.7, 8, trans. A. W. Pickard-Cambridge, in *Greek Orations of the 4th Century B.C.,* ed. W. R. Connor (1966; rpt. Prospect Heights, Illinois, 1987).

156 Demosthenes 3.3, 8.46, 9.5, 1.15, 3.31, trans. Vince.

157 Demosthenes 4.19, trans. Pickard-Cambridge.

158 Demosthenes 4.24–25, trans. Pickard-Cambridge.

159 Demosthenes 8.21–22, trans. Vince.

160 Ibid. 9.70–71.

161 Hansen, pp. 263–64; for a dissenting view on these complex issues, see Edward M. Harris, "Demosthenes and the Theoric Fund," in *Transitions to Empire,* pp. 57–76.

162 Demosthenes 13.2, trans. Vince. This speech dates to 351 and advocates distributing the surplus not to the theoric fund but to citizens serving in the field.

163 Demosthenes 1.20, trans. Vince.

164 Ibid. 3.11.

165 Demosthenes 4.35.

166 Theopompus Fragments. 99, 100, 213, trans. Shrimpton.

167 Plutarch, *Demosthenes* 21.2, trans. Perrin.

168 Ibid. 30.5.

169 Demosthenes 8.42–43, trans. Vince.

170 In *Demosthenes and the Last Days of Greek Freedom* (New York and London, 1914), p. 489.

171 Diodorus 16.53.3, trans. McQueen; see Ryder, "Demosthenes and Philip II," p. 58.

Chapter Two

1 *The Second World War,* vol. 1. *The Gathering Storm* (1948; rpt. New York, 1985), p. 16.

2 Telford Taylor, *Munich. The Price of Peace* (New York, 1979), p. xiv.

3 The phrase "moralizing internationalism" from Correlli Barnett, *The Collapse of British Power* (London, 1972), p. 19 and passim.

4 For Chamberlain's remarkable reception on returning from Munich see David Faber, *Munich, 1938* (New York, 2008), pp. 1–7.

5 In *April 1919* (New York, 2001), p. 493.

6 Zara Steiner, *The Lights That Failed* (Oxford, 2005), p. 67.

7 In *A World at Arms* (Cambridge, 1994), p. 15.

8 Donald Kagan, *The Origins of War* (New York, 1995), pp. 291–92.

9 Ibid., p. 297.

10 In Andrew Roberts, *A History of the English-Speaking Peoples* (London, 2006), p. 147.

11 In Martin Gilbert, *The Roots of Appeasement* (New York, 1966), p. 36.

12 In Steiner, p. 83.

13 Sally Marks, *The Illusion of Peace* (New York, 2003), p. 25.

14 *The War of the World* (New York, 2006), p. 142.

15 In MacMillan, p. 465.

16 The Treaty of Versailles text available at http://history.sandiego.edu/gen/text/versaillestreaty.

17 In Kagan, *The Origins of War,* p. 283.

18 In Ibid., p. 288.

19 Gilbert, p. 23.

20 From *The Realities of War,* in Niall Ferguson, *The Pity of War* (New York, 1999), p. xxix.

21 In Gilbert, pp. 143–44.

[22] In Quintin Hogg, *The Left Was Never Right* (London, 1945), p. 33.

[23] Gilbert, p. 52.

[24] Michael Howard, "The Legacy of the First World War," in *Paths to War. New Essays on the Origins of the Second World War,* eds. Robert Boyce and Esmonde M. Robertson (New York, 1989), p. 47.

[25] Kagan and Kagan, p. 189.

[26] In MacMillan, p. 180.

[27] In ibid., p. 192.

[28] Steiner, p. 20.

[29] MacMillan, p. 183.

[30] Kagan, p. 299.

[31] *The Illustrated London News* (7 Aug. 1915), p. 163. In *Chesterton on War and Peace*, ed. Michael W. Perry (Seattle, WA, 2008), p. 99.

[32] In Donald Kagan and Frederick Kagan, *While America Sleeps* (New York, 2000), p. 125.

[33] In Churchill, *The Gathering Storm*, p. 6.

[34] In David Fromkin, *The Peace to End All Peace* (New York, 1989), p. 376.

[35] Steiner, p. 248.

[36] Ibid., p. 197; MacMillan, p. 480.

[37] See Steiner, pp. 197–98, for the details of repayment.

[38] Sally Marks, "The Myth of Reparations," *Central European History* 11.3 (1978), pp. 239, 245; see also Steiner, p. 202; Kagan, p. 303.

[39] In Gilbert, p. 103.

[40] Kagan, p. 306.

[41] Barnett, p. 327.

[42] Kagan, p. 312.

[43] Marks, *The Illusion of Peace*, p. 111; see Steiner, pp. 482–83.

[44] Kagan, p. 316.

[45] Marks, *The Illusion of Peace*, p. 143.

[46] MacMillan, p. 480. Other estimates give 21.5 billion. See Steiner, p. 200, n. 14.

[47] Steiner, p. 200. For the impact of reparations on the German economy, see also Ferguson, *The Pity of War*, pp. 395–432.

[48] See Barton Whaley, *Covert German Rearmament, 1919–1939* (Frederick, MD, 1984), and the summary in Kagan and Kagan, pp. 142–159.

49 Kagan and Kagan, p. 151.

50 Richard Overy, "Hitler's War Plans and the German Economy," in *Paths to War*, pp. 97–98.

51 MacMillan, p. 481.

52 Churchill, pp. 40–43.

53 Kagan and Kagan, p. 156.

54 *Paris 1919*, p. 481.

55 Marks, p. 51; Kagan and Kagan, pp. 157–58; Fromkin, p. 531.

56 Kagan, p. 308.

57 In Steiner, p. 420.

58 Kagan and Kagan, p. 169.

59 Marks, *The Illusion of Power*, p. 78.

60 Barnett, p. 332.

61 Kagan, p. 309.

62 Ibid., p. 311; Barnett, pp. 333–34; Steiner, pp. 408–10.

63 Kagan and Kagan, p. 154.

64 Barnett, p. 334.

65 Kagan and Kagan, pp. 158.

66 In Kagan and Kagan, p. 177.

67 See Kagan, p. 301; Marks, *The Illusion of Peace*, p. 37.

68 See Fromkin, pp. 536–38.

69 Steiner, p. 248.

70 Fromkin, p. 386.

71 In Kagan, pp. 312–13; see also Steiner, p. 577.

72 Kagan and Kagan, p. 159.

73 Barnett, p. 271.

74 In ibid., p. 297.

75 Kagan, p. 332.

76 Kagan and Kagan, p. 227.

77 See Steiner, pp. 577–78.

78 Churchill, *The Gathering Storm*, p. 301.

79 In Martin Gilbert and Richard Gott, *The Appeasers* (1963; rpt. London, 2000), p. xii.

80 See Barnett, p. 269.

81 Ferguson, *The War of the World*, p. 325.

82 Kagan and Kagan, p. 47.

83 Barnett, p. 285.

84 Steiner, p. 373.

85 Marks, *The Illusion of Peace*, p. 136.

86 Steiner, pp. 812–13.

[87] In Churchill, p. 66.

[88] Gordon Craig, *Germany: 1866–1945* (Oxford, 1999), p. 679.

[89] Churchill, p. 69.

[90] *The Gathering Storm*, p. 4.

[91] In Taylor, p. 214.

[92] Barnett, p. 336.

[93] In Kagan and Kagan, pp. 100–01.

[94] Steiner, pp. 357–58.

[95] Marks, *The Illusion of Peace*, p. 133.

[96] Ibid., p. 134.

[97] In the "Sinews of Peace" speech delivered Mar. 5, 1946, in Fulton, Missouri (available http://www.hpol.org/churchill/).

[98] Craig, p. 678.

[99] In Churchill, *The Gathering Storm*, pp. 102–03.

[100] Barnett, p. 419.

[101] See Churchill, *The Gathering Storm*, p. 150.

[102] Kagan, p. 341; Lansbury quote in Paul Johnson, *Modern Times* (New York, 1983), p. 348.

[103] Barnett, p. 423.

[104] *The Age of Illusion* (1963; rpt. London, 2001), p. 250.

[105] See, for example. Kagan, pp. 341–42.

[106] Steiner, p. 759.

[107] In Barnett, p. 422.

[108] *The Gathering Storm*, p. 77.

[109] Kagan, p. 344; Craig, p. 684.

[110] Craig, p. 685.

[111] Barnett, p. 406.

[112] Barnett, p. 407.

[113] Gilbert, pp. 149–50.

[114] Kagan, p. 345.

[115] Barnett, p. 408.

[116] In Gilbert, p. 171.

[117] Kagan, pp. 200–01.

[118] Churchill, *The Gathering Storm*, p. 150.

[119] Kagan and Kagan, p. 205.

[120] Kagan and Kagan, p. 207.

[121] In *The Gathering Storm*, p. 167.

[122] Taylor, *Munich*, p. 99.

[123] Kagan, p. 360.

[124] Ibid., pp. 357–58.

[125] Churchill, *The Gathering Storm*, p. 174. For examples of pro-German sentiment, see Gilbert and Gott, pp. 25–48.

[126] In Kagan, p. 359.

[127] In Taylor, p. 243.

[128] Kagan, pp. 358, 359.

[129] *The Gathering Storm*, p. 171.

[130] Barnett, p. 385.

[131] In Gilbert and Gott, p. 41.

[132] In Blythe, p. 234.

[133] In Faber, *Munich, 1938*, pp. 13, 14.

[134] Taylor, p. 347.

[135] In Sidney Aster, "Guilty Men," in *Paths to War*, p. 242.

[136] In Faber, p. 82.

[137] Barnett, p. 470.

[138] In Gilbert and Gott, p. 39.

[139] In Faber, p. 24.

[140] In Gilbert and Gott, p. 64.

[141] Kagan, p. 380.

[142] In Taylor, p. 332.

[143] Ibid., p. 347.

[144] *The Gathering Storm*, p. 237.

[145] In ibid., pp. 235–36.

[146] In Kagan, p. 386.

[147] In Faber, p. 144; Barnett, p. 473.

[148] In Gilbert, pp. 167, 169.

[149] In Sidney Aster, "'The Guilty Men,'" in *Paths to War*, p. 246.

[150] Gilbert and Gott, p.13.

[151] In Gilbert, p. 138.

[152] In Barnett, pp. 386, 387, 388.

[153] 31 May 1935, *Never Give In! The Best of Winston Churchill's Speeches*, selected by Winston S. Churchill (New York, 2003), pp. 111–12.

[154] Craig, p. 703.

[155] Kagan, p. 391; Gilbert and Gott, pp. 121, 123.

[156] In Craig, p. 703.

[157] In Taylor, p. 380.

[158] In Taylor, p. 401.

[159] In Churchill, *The Gathering Storm*, p. 277.

[160] Taylor, p. 400.

[161] In Gilbert and Gott, p. 114.

[162] In Kagan, p. 393.

[163] In Craig, p. 704.

[164] In Faber, p. 183.

[165] In Kagan, p. 393.

[166] Lord Halifax's warning in Faber, p. 183.

[167] In Faber, p. 199.

[168] In Taylor, p. 407.

[169] In Kagan, p. 395.

[170] In Faber, p. 267.

[171] *The Gathering Storm*, pp. 271, 272.

[172] Taylor, p. 806; Craig, p. 705.

[173] In Faber, pp. 332–33.

[174] In Kagan, p. 400.

[175] In Kagan, p. 402.

[176] Taylor, pp. 820–21.

[177] Barnett, p. 545.

[178] Craig, p. 706; See Faber, pp. 380 and 389–90, for a different explanation of Hitler's sudden conciliatory mood.

[179] In Kagan, p. 403.

[180] In Faber, p. 391.

[181] In Kagan, p. 405.

[182] In Faber, p. 417.

[183] In Barnett, p. 550.

[184] In Faber, p. 414.

[185] In Gilbert and Gott, p.183.

[186] In *The Gathering Storm*, p. 294.

[187] In Churchill, *The Gathering Storm*, p. 295.

[188] *The War of the World*, p. 315.

[189] In Kagan, p. 411.

[190] See Aster, "'Guilty Men,'" pp. 253–54; Gilbert and Gott, p. 243.

[191] Kagan, p. 412.

[192] *The Gathering Storm*, p. 287.

[193] In Kagan, p. 360.

[194] Kagan, p. 385; Taylor, p. 368; Faber, p. 140.

[195] *The Gathering Storm*, p. 210.

[196] See Ferguson, *The War of the World*, pp. 361–68, for the evidence that Germany could not have won a war over Czechoslovakia.

[197] Churchill, *The Gathering Storm*, pp. 278–79, 302.

[198] *The Change in the European Balance of Power, 1938–1939* (Princeton, 1984), pp. 262–63.

[199] In *The World Crisis* (New York, 1923), p. 3.

[200] Morris Eksteins, *Rites of Spring* (New York, 1989), p. 276.

[201] Barnett, p. 429.

[202] Ibid., p. 435.

[203] In Kagan, p. 321.

[204] Michael Howard, *The Continental Commitment* (London, 1989), p. 74; in Kagan, p. 321.

[205] Williamson Murray, *War in the Air: 1914–45* (London, 1999), pp. 73–74.

[206] In Kagan and Kagan, p. 192.

[207] Taylor, pp. 849, 850.

[208] In ibid., p. 211.

[209] In *The Collected Poems of W. B. Yeats* (New York, 1956).

[210] In Barnett, pp. 436–37.

[211] In ibid., p. 437.

[212] Kagan, p. 374.

[213] Martin Ceadel, *Semi-Detached Idealists* (Oxford, 2000), p. 242.

[214] Kagan, p. 341.

[215] Bertrand Russell, *Which Way to Peace* (London, 1936), pp. 30–31.

[216] In Faber, p. 357.

[217] In Uri Bialer, *The Shadow of the Bomber* (London, 1980), p. 158. Bialer's italics. Nicolson elsewhere contrasted this physical relief with the "moral anxiety" he felt over Munich; Gilbert and Gott, p. 180.

[218] In Taylor, p. 835.

[219] In ibid., p. 822.

[220] In Gilbert and Gott, p. 163.

[221] In Bialer, p. 139.

[222] Barnett, p. 494. This obsession with air power paradoxically paid dividends in the Battle of Britain, when the radar installations and the Hurricane and Spitfire fighter planes developed for defense against bombers helped turn the tide; see Kagan, pp. 374–75.

[223] Kagan, p. 373.

[224] Ibid., p. 374.

[225] Taylor, p. 648.

[226] Peter Brock, *Varieties of Pacifism* (Syracuse, N.Y., 1998), p. 90.

[227] In Ceadel, *Semi-Detached Idealists,* p. 140.

[228] Peter Brock and Nigel Young, *Pacifism in the Twentieth Century* (Syracuse, N.Y, 1999), pp. 10–14; Lansbury quote on p. 113.

[229] "My Country Right or Left" (1940), in *An Age Like This: 1920–1940,* vol. 1 of *The Collected Essays, Journalism and Letters of George Orwell,* eds. Sonia Orwell and Ian Angus (New York, 1968), p. 537.

[230] Brock and Young, p. 119.

[231] Ibid., p. 121.

[232] Ibid., p. 132.

[233] For a descriptive list, see Martin Ceadel, *Pacifism in Britain* (Oxford, 1980), pp. 317–19.

[234] Ceadel, *Semi-Detached Idealism,* p. 272.

[235] In *The War That Will End War* (New York, 1914), p. 13.

[236] David James Fisher, *Romain Rolland and the Politics of Intellectual Engagement* (Berkeley and Los Angeles, 1988), pp. 61–65.

[237] In Robert Shepherd, *A Class Divided: Appeasement and the Road to Munich* (London, 1938), p. 41. See also Hogg, pp. 43–52, for the role of pacifism and disarmament in the policy of the Labor Party.

[238] In Barnett, p. 420.

[239] In Ceadel, *Pacifism in Britain,* p. 106.

[240] Speech given to the New Commonwealth Society, Nov. 25, 1936, in *Never Give In!,* p. 155.

[241] Caedel, *Pacifism in Britain,* p. 137.

[242] Immanuel Kant, *Perpetual Peace,* trans. Nicholas Murray Butler (1932; rpt. San Diego, CA., 2009), pp. 30, 33.

[243] E.g., Antonio Franceschet, *Kant and Liberal Internationalism* (New York, 2002), pp. 71, 77–78.

[244] Kant, *Perpetual Peace,* pp. 77–78.

[245] *Perpetual Peace,* p. 9.

[246] In John Keegan, *The First World War* (New York, 1999), p. 17. The texts of The Hague Conventions are available at avalon.law.yale.edu.

[247] Text available at avalon.law.yale.edu.

[248] Barnett, p. 283.

[249] In E. H. Carr, *The Twenty Years' Crisis. 1919–1939* (1939; rpt. New York, 1966), pp. 25–26.

[250] In Carr, p. 83.

[251] 626a, trans. Benjamin Jowett.

[252] In *The Later Works*, vol. 11, 1925–1953, ed. Jo Ann Boydston (Carbondale, IL., 1990), p. 263.

[253] Kagan, p. 296.

[254] Carr, p. 118.

[255] October 24, 1935, in *Never Give In!*, p. 124.

[256] *The Gathering Storm*, p. 158.

[257] For the problems with international law in punishing an aggressor, see Robert Bork, *Coercing Virtue* (Washington, D.C., 2003), p. 17.

[258] In Carr, p. 104; see Steiner, pp. 420–21.

[259] Letter to Henry Laurens, 21 April 1778.

[260] In Barnett, pp.64–65.

[261] In Carr, p. 33.

[262] *Illustrated London News*, 21 Dec.1918; in *Chesterton on War and Peace*, pp. 323–24.

[263] Robert Paxton, *The Anatomy of Fascism* (New York, 2004), p. 46.

[264] "Wells, Hitler, and the World State," in au, *My Country Right or Left*, vol. 2 of *The Collected Essays*, p. 144.

[265] *The New Vichy Syndrome* (New York, 2010), p. 107.

[266] *Empire* (New York, 2003), p. 234.

[267] *Imperialism: A Study* (1902; rpt. London, 1938), p. 85.

[268] See Ferguson, *Empire*, pp. 268–69.

[269] In Thomas Sowell, *Intellectuals and Society* (New York, 2009), p. 225.

[270] *Modern Times*, p. 169.

[271] In Nick Cohen, *What's Left?* (London and New York, 2007), p. 235.

[272] "What I Believe," in Johnson, p. 167. Emphases in original.

[273] Address to the House of Commons, 23 Nov. 1932.

[274] In *My Country Right or Left*, p. 75.

[275] 24 Apr. 1933, in *Never Give In!*, pp. 104–05.

[276] In Roger Kimball, "The Qualities of Robert Musil," rpt. in *Experiments against Reality* (New York, 2000), p. 141.

Chapter Three

[1] "Nobel Lecture," trans. F. D. Reeve (http://www.columbia.edu/cu/augustine/arch/solzhenitsyn/nobel-lit1970.htm).

[2] Bin Laden's statement in videotape of 7 Oct. 2001. In Bernard Lewis, *The Crisis of Islam* (New York, 2003), p. xv.

[3] *The Shaping of the Modern Middle East* (New York, 1994), p. 100.

[4] Ephraim Karsh, *Islamic Imperialism* (New Haven and Yale, 2006), p. 230.

[5] Lewis Sorley, *A Better War* (New York, 1999), p. 383. Bunker quote on p. 348, Thompson on p. 356.

[6] Address to the Nation, 30 Apr. 1970. Text available at http://www.mekong.net/cambodia/nixon430.htm.

[7] Kagan, *Origins of War*, p. 369.

[8] *Years of Upheaval* (New York, 1982), p. 169.

[9] LeRoy Ashby and Rod Gramer, *Fighting the Odds* (Pullman, WA, 1994), p. 453.

[10] Ibid., p. 491.

[11] Ibid., pp. 472, 476.

[12] The extent of domestic spying was exaggerated at the time by sensationalist journalism; see Arthur Herman, "The 35–Year War on the CIA," *Commentary* (Dec. 2009), p. 13.

[13] *The Agency* (New York, 1987), p. 610.

[14] In *A Time to Heal*, in John Ranelagh, *The Agency: The Rise and Decline of the CIA* (New York, 1987), p. 616. In 1980, the law was amended to require notification only to the Intelligence Committee of each house of Congress.

[15] For the effects of the FISA act, see John Yoo, *War by Other Means* (New York, 2006), pp. 72–74.

[16] Herman, p. 16.

[17] Inaugural address available at http://www.bartleby.com/124/pres60.html.

[18] In Ranelagh, p. 643.

[19] Herman, p. 16.

[20] Ranelagh, p. 636. See also Herman, p. 15.

[21] President Reagan's Executive Order 12333 reduced some of these restrictions.

[22] Michael Ledeen and William Lewis, *Debacle* (New York, 1981), p. 67.

23 Notre Dame commencement speech available at http://teachingamericanhistory.org/library/index.asp?document= 727.

24 In Farber, p. 112.

25 See Ledeen and Lewis, pp. 124, 132–33.

26 *Debacle*, p. 142.

27 In Rubin, *Paved with Good Intentions* (Oxford, 1980), p. 236.

28 Patrick Tyler, *A World of Trouble* (New York, 2009), pp. 223–24.

29 For a detailed analysis of the intelligence failures regarding the Iranian revolution, see Robert Jervis, *Why Intelligence Fails* (Ithaca and New York, 2010), pp. 1–122.

30 In Mark Bowden, *Guests of the Ayatollah* (New York, 2006), p. 218.

31 In Bernard Lewis, *The Shaping of the Modern Middle East* (1964; New York, 1994), p. 120.

32 In Robin Wright, *In the Name of God* (New York, 1989), p. 51.

33 Rubin, p. 268. See pp. 261–72 for an analysis of the causes of the revolution.

34 Bernard Lewis, *Islam and the West* (New York, 1993), p. 141.

35 In Ian Buruma and Avishai Margalit, *Occidentalism* (New York, 2004), p. 116.

36 Ibid., p. 54.

37 *Taken Hostage,* pp.106–07.

38 Koran 3.110. M.H. Shakir translation available at www.usc.edu/schools/college/crcc/engagement/resources/texts/ muslim/quran/003.qmt.html.

39 Rubin, p. 272; see also p. 253.

40 *Debacle*, pp. 127–28.

41 In Rubin, p. 210.

42 In Daniel Pipes, *Militant Islam Reaches America* (New York, 2002), p. 62.

43 Farber, p. 2.

44 Paul Berman, *Terror and Liberalism* (New York, 2003), p.105.

45 "Man of the Year: The Mystic Who Lit the Fires of Hatred," *Time* (7 Jan. 1980).

46 Farber, pp. 101, 148. Many on the left, fooled by Khomeini's anti-colonialist and liberationist rhetoric, had a more positive view.

47 Rubin, p. 272.

48 Farber, p. 63.

[49] Bermen, p. 105. Khomeini's most famous leftist apologist was French post-modern icon Michel Foucault.

[50] Michael Ledeen, *Accomplice to Evil* (New York, 2009), p. 49; see also Ledeen and Lewis, pp. 130–31.

[51] In Barry Rubin and Judith Colp Rubin, *Anti-American Terrorism and the Middle East* (Oxford, 2002), p. 34.

[52] In Ledeen and Lewis, p.106.

[53] In ibid., pp. 106–07.

[54] In Rubin and Rubin, p. 29.

[55] In ibid., p. 33.

[56] In Farber, p. 184.

[57] Rubin, p. 234.

[58] Farber, p. 118.

[59] In Ledeen, p. 55.

[60] In Rubin, p. 322.

[61] Thirteen female and black hostages were released after a few weeks, "as a gesture to oppressed African-Americans and as a demonstration of the 'special status' accorded women under Islamic rule," Bowden, pp. 198–99. Another hostage was released in July 1980 because of illness.

[62] Rubin, p. 311.

[63] In Farber, p. 144; Rubin, p. 312.

[64] *Guests of the Ayatollah*, p. 290.

[65] 21 May 1980.

[66] Farber, pp. 129–30.

[67] In Wright, p. 82.

[68] In Farber, p. 175.

[69] *Colossus* (New York, 2004), p. 117.

[70] In Farber, p. 145.

[71] Peter W. Rodman, *Presidential Command* (New York, 2009), p. 128.

[72] Farber, p. 165.

[73] In Pipes, p. 28.

[74] Berman, p. 110.

[75] Tyler, p. 232.

[76] In Rubin and Rubin, pp. 52–53.

[77] Wright, p. 114.

[78] In Tyler, pp. 278–79.

[79] Thomas Geraghty, *Peacekeepers at War* (Washington, D.C., 2009), p. 65.

80 Ibid., pp. 70, 83.

81 In Farber, pp. 185–86.

82 Tyler, pp. 298–99.

83 In Richard Reeves, *President Reagan* (New York, 2005), p. 182.

84 Ibid., p. 196. For the cancellation of the retaliatory strike see Geraghty, pp. 172–74.

85 Tyler, p. 298.

86 *Turmoil and Triumph* (New York, 1993), pp. 230–31.

87 In Reeves, p. 202.

88 Tyler, pp. 300–01; emphasis in original.

89 Herman, p. 18.

90 Ibid., p. 19.

91 Andrew C. McCarthy, "Why Section 218 Should be Retained," at http://www.abanet.org/natsecurity/patriotdebates/ 218–2#opening. Section 218 is from the Patriot Act, which clarified the law that the misinterpretation of which had led to the "wall." Internal quotes are from the 2002 FISA Court of Review report. See also Lawrence Wright, *The Looming Tower* (New York, 2006), pp. 386–87.

92 In Herman, p.20.

93 *Intelligence Wars* (New York, 2002), p. 373.

94 Powers, p. 376.

95 *Wedge,* rev. ed. (New York, 2002), pp. 453–54.

96 In Michael Scheuer, *Through Our Enemies' Eyes*, rev. ed. (Washington, D.C., 2006), p. 19.

97 In Matthias Küntzel, "From Khomeini to Ahmadinejad" *Policy Review* (Dec. 2006–Jan. 2007).

98 Wright, *The Looming Tower,* p. 172.

99 In Scheuer, p. xxiii.

100 *The Al Qaeda Reader* (New York, 2007), p. 2.

101 "Land of Denial," *The New York Times* (5 June 2002).

102 *Through our Enemies' Eyes,* pp. 299–300.

103 Patrick Tyler's expression, in *A World of Trouble,* p. 490.

104 Lee Smith, *The Strong Horse* (New York, 2010), p. 91.

105 *Milestones* (1964; English trans, Damascus, Syria, 2007), p. 9.

106 *Milestones,* p. 84.

107 In Dinseh D'Souza, *The Enemy at Home* (New York, 2007), p. 14.

108 *Milestones,* p. 74.

109 In Buruma and Margalit, *Occidentalism,* p. 126.

[110] In Wright, *Looming Tower,* p. 29.

[111] In Wright, *Looming Tower,* p. 152.

[112] In ibid., pp.170–71.

[113] In ibid., pp. 170–71.

[114] In *Messages to the World,* ed. Bruce Lawrence (London, 2005), p. 141.

[115] Transcript available at http://www.greatdreams.com/osama_tape.htm.

[116] *The 9/11 Commission Report* (New York, 2004), p. 58.

[117] Wright, *Looming Tower,* pp. 213–14.

[118] *The 9/11 Commission Report,* p. 61.

[119] Ibid., p. 241.

[120] Ledeen, *Accomplice to Evil,* p. 186.

[121] See ibid., pp. 78–82.

[122] In Scheuer, p. 147.

[123] *Messages to the World,* pp. 54–55. From the March 1997 interview with CNN.

[124] In Scheuer, p. 148

[125] In ibid., 210.

[126] *Messages to the World,* p. 30.

[127] In Andrew C. McCarthy, *Willful Blindness* (New York, 2008), pp. 187–88.

[128] See Scheuer, pp. 150–54, for a catalogue of attacks.

[129] Wright, *Looming Tower,* pp. 308–09.

[130] In Ibrahim, p. 13.

[131] In December 1999, a sharp-eyed customs official at the U.S.-Canadian border foiled the so-called Millennium plot to attack Los Angeles International Airport.

[132] In Wright, *Looming Tower,* p. 361.

[133] In Lawrence, 195.

[134] *Clinton's Secret Wars* (New York, 2009), p. 109.

[135] Donald Kagan and Frederick Kagan, *While America Sleeps* (New York, 2000), p. 325.

[136] "Do Moderate Islamists Exist?" in *Militant Islam Reaches America* (New York, 2002) pp. 44–45.

[137] Kagan and Kagan, p. 425.

[138] In Sale, p. 235.

[139] Scheuer, *Marching Toward Hell* (New York, 2008), p. 77.

[140] Ibid.

[141] Wright, *Looming Tower,* pp. 323–24.

[142] In *The 9/11 Commission Report*, p. 114.

[143] Tyler, p. 487.

[144] In *The 9/11 Commission Report*, p. 136.

[145] *The 9/11 Commission Report*, p. 133. Executive Order 12333 requires a presidential Memorandum of Notification for "special activities" such as assassination.

[146] *The 9/11 Commission Report*, p. 187.

[147] *Marching Toward Hell*, pp. 104–05.

[148] Wright, *Looming Tower*, p. 330.

[149] *The 9/11 Commission Report*, p. 138.

[150] Ibid., 140.

[151] In Richard Clarke, *Against All Enemies* (New York, 2004), p. 224.

[152] See *The 9/11 Commission Report*, pp. 193–96.

[153] Scheuer, *Marching Toward Hell*, p. 33.

[154] See *The 9/11 Commission Report*, pp. 121–26, for a summary of these efforts.

[155] In Michael Rubin, "Taking Tea with the Taliban," *Commentary* (Feb. 2010), p. 11.

[156] In ibid., p. 13.

[157] Ibid., p. 14.

[158] Text available at http://archives.cnn.com/2001/US/09/20/gen.bush.transcript.

[159] See "Steering Committee for 'Peace,'" Ryan O'Donnell, available at www.discoverthenetworks.org/Articles/Peace percent20Movement.pdf.

[160] In Jamie Glazov, *United in Hate* (Los Angeles, 2009), p. 164.

[161] In D'Souza, p. 233.

[162] *New York Times*, 31 Oct. 2001.

[163] See *The 9/11 Commission Report*, pp. 273–76. For other examples of opportunities to uncover and prevent the 9/11 attack lost because of the "wall," see Wright, *Looming Tower*, pp. 382–89; *The 9/11 Commission Report*, pp. 266–77; George Tenet, *At the Center of the Storm* (New York, 2007), pp. 200–05.

[164] At http://www.aclu.org/national-security/surveillance-under-usa-patriot-act.

[165] "Osama bin Laden's Oath to America," in Ibrahim, *The al Qaeda Reader*, p. 193.

[166] Text available at news.findlaw.com/hdocs/docs/iraq/libact103198.pdf.

[167] For a detailed survey of the factors that led to the invasion of Iraq, see Douglas J. Feith, *War and Decision* (New York, 2008), pp. 179–212.

[168] Speech available at http://www.cnn.com/ALLPOLITICS/1998/02/17/transcripts/clinton.iraq.

[169] Text available at http://www.un.org/Docs/scres/2002/sc2002.htm.

[170] *Unholy Alliance* (Washington, D.C., 2004), p. 32.

[171] Text available at http://www.crocuta.net/Dean/Transcript_of_Dean_Sacramento_Speech_15March2003.htm.

[172] See Matthew Continetti, "Professor Mogadishu," *National Review* (31 Mar. 2003).

[173] Speeches available at www.crocuta.net/Dean/Dean_Speeches.htm.

[174] "Dean the Dream," *Wall Street Journal,* 19 Feb. 2004.

[175] In *Unholy Alliance,* p. 222.

[176] Adam Nagourney, "Democrats Attack Credibility of Bush, *New York Times,* 14 July 2003.

[177] Horowitz, p. 223.

[178] In D'Souza, p. 245.

[179] At www.michaelmoore.com/words/mikes-letter/heads-up-from-michael-moore.

[180] In Horowitz, *Unholy Alliance,* p. 237. Kerry's "nuisance" remark in Matt Bai, "Kerry's Undeclared War," *New York Times Magazine,* 10 Oct. 2004.

[181] In *Intellectuals and Society* (New York, 2009), p. 267.

[182] Text available at www.c-span.org/Content/PDF/hjres114.pdf.

[183] In Sowell, *Intellectuals and Society,* pp. 267–68.

[184] At www.cbsnews.com/stories/2007/04/20/politics/main2709229.shtml.

[185] In Sowell, pp. 269–71.

[186] At www.sfgate.com/cgi-bin/blogs/chroncast/detail?blogid=5&entry_id=26858 percent22.

[187] See Yoo, *War by Other Means,* pp. 168–87, for a discussion of the legal issues surrounding torture and enhanced interrogation techniques.

[188] Marc A. Thiessen, *Courting Disaster* (Washington, D.C., 2010), p. 163. Waterboarding is still part of SERE training for Air Force personnel.

189 *Courting Disaster,* p. 165. Emphases in original.

190 See Thiessen, pp. 7–9 for a catalogue.

191 *At the Center of the Storm,* p. 255.

192 *Courting Disaster,* p. 1.

193 See Thiessen, pp. 130, 157.

194 When President Bush left office, 242 detainees were left. President Obama has released 54.

195 Thiessen, p. 34.

196 "The Real Gitmo," *The Weekly Standard* (28 Dec. 2009).

197 In Thiessen, p. 279.

198 "Just Shut It Down," *New York Times* (27 May 2005); Schlesinger in D'Souza, p. 54.

199 "Un-American by Any Name" (5 June 2005)

200 Peter Finn, "Detainees Shown CIA Officers' Photo," *Washington Post* (21 Aug. 2009).

201 Thiessen, p. 290. For conditions in the detention centers, see Willy Stern, "Inside Our 'Secret' Afghan Prisons," *The Weekly Standard* (4 and 11 Jan. 2010).

202 Thiessen, pp. 287, 89; see also p. 309.

203 "Obama on Foreign Affairs," *Los Angeles Times* (17 Jan. 2009).

204 "Renewing American Leadership," *Foreign Affairs* (July/Aug. 2007).

205 Though compared to Carter, he is reticent on the issue of human rights. See Elliot Abrams, "People Not Placards," *Weekly Standard* (7 Dec. 2009).

206 "The Return of Carterism?" *Commentary* (Jan. 2009).

207 John R. Bolton, "Obama's Next Three Years," *Commentary* (Jan. 2010), p. 25. Obama's comment of 4 Apr. 2009 available at http://transcripts.cnn.com/TRANSCRIPTS/0904/04/cnr.01.html.

208 Text available at www.nytimes.com/2009/09/24/us/politics/24prexy.text.html.

209 Smith, *The Strong Horse,* p. 196. See also pp.188–91.

210 Helene Cooper, "U.S. Engagement with Iran Shifts to Worldview," *New York Times* (16 Feb. 2010).

211 Executive orders available at http://edocket.access.gpo.gov/2009/pdf/E9–1893.pdf.

212 "Obama Issues Directives to Shut Down Guantánamo," *New York Times* (22 Jan. 2009).

213 Thiessen, p. 12.

214 Ibid., p. 348.

[215] "Security Before Politics," *Washington Post* (25 Apr. 2009).

[216] "The American Promise," 28 Aug. 2008, available at obamaspeeches.com.

[217] 20 Jan. 2009. Available at www.whitehouse.gov/blog/inaugural-address.

[218] Ray Takeyh, "The Essence of Diplomatic Engagement," *Boston Globe,* 7 Oct. 2009.

[219] Text available at www.whitehouse.gov/the_press_office/Remarks-by-the-President-at-Cairo-University-6-04-09/.

[220] "Obama and the Malleability of History," *National Review Online,* 19 Dec. 2009. Available at www.victorhanson.com/articles/hanson121909.html.

[221] See Andrew Bostom and Bat Ye'or, "Andalusian Myth, Eurabian Reality," available at www.jihadwatch.org/2004/04/andalusian-myth-eurabian-reality.html.

[222] See Michael Ledeen, "We Have Met the Enemy . . . ," *Weekly Standard* (26 Oct. 2009); Geraghty, *Peacekeepers at War,* pp.196–97.

[223] "NASA Chief: Next Frontier Better Relations with Muslim World" (5 July 2010), www.foxnews.com/politics/2010/07/05/nasa-chief-frontier-better-relations-muslims/.

[224] Text available at www.religlaw.org/interdocs/docs/cairohrislam1990.htm.

[225] *Milestones,* p.141.

[226] See Michael Ledeen, "We've Been Talking to Iran for 30 Years," *Wall Street Journal* (30 Sept. 2009).

[227] In Scheuer, *Through Our Enemies' Eyes,* p. 72. For the consequences of Iran's acquisition of nuclear weapons, see Kori N. Schake and Judith S. Yaphe, *The Strategic Implications of a Nuclear-Armed Iran* (Washington, D.C., 2004).

[228] See the Aug. 2010 Brookings Report, at www.brookings.edu/reports/2010/0805_arab_opinion_poll_telhami.aspx.

[229] Borzou Daragahi, "Obama's New Year Greeting Met with Suspicion in Iran," *The Sidney Morning Herald* (23 Mar. 2009).

[230] Barbara Slavin, "U.S. Contacted Iran's Ayatollah Before Election," *Washington Times* (24 June 2009).

[231] In Stephen F. Hayes, "Obama's Iran Formula," *Weekly Standard* (5 Oct. 2009).

232 Bill Gertz, "Tehran Aiding al Qaeda Links," *Washington Times* (17 Mar. 2010).

233 David E. Sanger and Thom Shanker, "Gates Says U.S. Lacks Policy to Thwart Iran," (17 Apr. 2010).

234 See Ledeen, *Accomplice to Evil*, pp. 155–59, for a catalogue of the Bush administration's extensive efforts at outreach to Iran.

235 See Joe Becker and Ron Nixon, "U.S. Enriches Companies Defying Its Policy on Iran," *New York Times* (7 Mar. 2010).

236 See "Exclusive: China's Top Oil Firms Sell Gasoline to Iran," at http://www.reuters.com/article/idUSTRE63D1CY20100414.

237 Michael Slackman, "Some See Iran as Ready for Nuclear Deal," *New York Times* (14 Oct. 2009).

238 "Iran Outlook: Grim," *National Review* (19 Oct. 2009).

239 Jay Solomon, "Panetta Warns of Iran Threat," *Wall Street Journal* (27 June 2010).

240 "Osama bin Laden's Oath to America," 7 Oct. 2001, in Ibrahim, *The Al Qaeda Reader*, 194.

241 "Bin Laden's Truce Offer to the Americans," Jan. 2006, in Ibrahim, p. 225.

242 See Bowden, pp. 210–11.

243 In Bruce Bawer, *Surrender* (New York, 2009), p. 5.

244 In ibid., p. 8.

245 In Daniel Pipes, *The Rushdie Affair*, 2nd ed. (New Brunswick, 2003), pp. 156, 158, 179.

246 In Cohen, *What's Left?*, p. 335.

247 See www.religionnewsblog.com/9440.

248 "Those Danish Cartoons," *New York Times* (7 Feb. 2006); Bawer, p. 46.

249 At www.theparliament.com/no_cache/latestnews/news-article/newsarticle/eu-moves-to-new-media-rules-on-religion/. In 1937, after Goebbels complained to Lord Halifax about famed caricaturist David Low's cartoons critical of the Germans, Low was pressured by Halifax to stop drawing cartoons of individual Nazi leaders. See Faber, *Munich, 1938*, p. 191.

250 See http://yalepress.yale.edu/yupbooks/KlausenStatement.asp.; sandbox.blog-city.com/some_day_yales_prince_will_come.htm.

251 "The Pope's Words," *New York Times* (16 Sept. 2006).

252 Daniel Pipes, *Militant Islam Reaches America*, pp. 166–67.

253 "The Return of the Paranoid Style," *Atlantic Magazine* (Apr. 2008).

254 In Bawer, pp. 164–65.

255 Speech available at http://escholarship.org/uc/item/7n5515mx.

256 *Surrender,* pp. 72–73.

257 In Bawer, p. 85.

258 In Pipes, p. 97.

259 Shakir translation, at www.usc.edu/schools/college/crcc/engage-ment/resources/texts/muslim/quran/005.qmt.html.

260 In Pipes, p. 98.

261 Text available at www.presidentialrhetoric.com/speeches/09.20.01.html.

262 Stephen J. Hadley and Frances Fragos Townsend, "What We Saw in London," *New York Times* (23 July 2005).

263 See Daniel Pipes and Sharon Chada, "CAIR Founded by 'Islamic Terrorists'?" *FrontPageMagazine* (28 July 2005). Available at www.danielpipes.org/2811/cair-founded-by-islamic-ter-rorists. Also Daniel Pipes and Sharon Chada, "CAIR: Islamists Fooling the Establishment," *Middle East Quarterly* (Spring 2006), available at www.danielpipes.org/3437/cair-islamists-fooling-the-establishment.

264 *Militant Islam Reaches America,* p. 102.

265 *Surrender,* p. 156. Emphases in original.

266 *Why Terrorism Works* (New Haven, CT, 2002), p. 49.

267 Texts available at http://unispal.un.org/UNISPAL.NSF/vGARes?

268 Dershowitz, p. 54. In 1999 the Security Council condemned terrorist acts regardless of motive.

269 In Bawer, pp. 244–45.

270 See *Why Terrorism Works,* pp. 57–78.

271 In Bawer, p. 244.

272 See http://tundratabloid.blogspot.com/2010/03/david-littman-addresses-un-human-rights.html.

273 See www.jihadwatch.org/2009/05/un-bans-human-rights-activist-who-spoke-out-against-islamic-antisemitism.html.

274 See data at www.unwatch.org/site/c.bdKKISNqEmG/b.3820041/.

275 In Bret Stephens, "Iran Cannot Be Contained," *Commentary* (July/Aug. 2010), p. 66.

276 Text of Protocol I available at http://www.icrc.org/ihl.nsf/7c4d08d9b287a42141256739003e636b/f6c8b9fee14a77fdc125641e0052b079.

277 For the Geneva Conventions see Thiessen, pp. 29–33; Reagan quoted on p. 208.

278 *Courting Disaster,* p. 208.

279 *Reflections on a Ravaged Century* (New York, 2000), pp. 180, 182.

280 *Leviathan,* 17.

281 For a more detailed analysis of these affinities see McCarthy, *The Grand Jihad* (New York, 2010), pp.171–85.

282 *Milestones,* in John Esposito, *Unholy War* (New York, 2002), p. 57.

283 From *In the Shade of the Quran,* in Berman, pp. 69–70.

284 See Buruma and Margalit, pp. 110–16.

285 In Horowitz, *Unholy Alliance,* pp. 144–45.

286 In Ibrahim, *The Al Qaeda Reader,* pp. 244, 204, 212, 217.

287 In Rubin and Rubin, p. 148.

288 For the left and the Palestinians, see Horowitz, pp. 127–31.

289 These statements and over a hundred more have been collected and documented by the American Council of Trustees and Alumni in their report "Defending Civilization: How Our Universities Are Failing America and What Can Be Done About It," available at www.goacta.org/publications/reports.html. See too Horowitz, *Unholy Alliance,* pp. 31–37.

290 In David Horowitz and Peter Collier, *The Anti-Chomsky Reader* (New York, 2004), pp.169, 180.

291 In *The Wretched of the Earth,* trans. Richard Philcox (1963; New York, 2004), p. xiv.

292 *Tears of the White Man,* trans. William R. Beer (1983; New York, 1986), p. 4.

293 *Reflections on a Ravaged Century,* p. 252. See Ferguson, *Colossus,* pp. 173–83, for the real reasons for the economic and political failures of Europe's former colonies.

294 In D'Souza, p. 53.

295 *For Lust of Knowing* (London, 2007), p. 4.

296 *Ivory Towers on Sand* (Washington, D.C., 2002), p. 22.

297 See Justus Weiner, "'My Beautiful Old House' and Other Fabrications by Edward Said," *Commentary* (Sept. 1999).

298 *Culture and Imperialism* (New York, 1993), p. 22.

299 Edward Said, *Orientalism* (1978; New York, 1994), p. 3.

300 *Orientalism,* p. 204.

301 In Kramer, p. 35.

[302] In Lee Smith, *The Strong Horse,* p. 36.

[303] For Said's many blunders and contradictions see Ibn Warraq, *Defending the West* (Amherst, 2007), pp. 18–54; Irwin, pp. 277–309; Bernard Lewis, "The Question of Orientalism," in *Islam and the West,* pp. 99–118.

[304] Smith, p. 37.

[305] *Ivory Towers on Sand,* pp. 56–57.

[306] In Lee Harris, *The Suicide of Reason* (New York, 2007), p. 217.

[307] "Want to Understand Islam? Start Here," *Washington Post* (22 July 2007).

[308] Document available at www.investigativeproject.org/documents/misc/127.pdf.

[309] P. W. Singer and Elina Noor, "What Do You Cal a Terror(Jihad)ist?" *New York Times* (2 June 2008).

[310] Text available at www.whitehouse.gov/the_press_office/Remarks-by-John-Brennan-at-the-Center-for-Strategic-and-International-Studies/.

[311] See www.npr.org/templates/story/story.php?storyId=124494788.

[312] In D'Souza, p. 56.

[313] *Unholy War,* p. 65.

[314] Raymond Ibrahim, "Islam's Inherent Violence," *Middle East Quarterly* (Summer 2009), p. 5.

[315] In D'Souza, p. 178.

[316] Koran 9.5, 9.29, 9.123, 2.191, 8.12; Shakir translation available at www.usc.edu/schools/college/crcc/engagement/resources/texts/muslim/quran/.

[317] In Andrew Bostom, "All Islamic Things Not Considered at NPR," at www.andrewbostom.org/blog/.

[318] See Andrew Bostom, *The Legacy of Jihad* (Amherst, NY, 2005), pp. 24–124, for an overview of this tradition. For jihad in the Hadith, see pp. 136–40.

[319] In Rubin and Rubin, p. 29.

[320] In Robert P. Mitchell, *The Society of Muslim Brothers* in Andrew C. McCarthy, *The Great Jihad,* p. 56.

[321] See www.thereligionofpeace.com/ for a catalogue of attacks. On the propensity for violence among Muslim states, see Samuel P. Huntington, *The Clash of Civilizations* (New York, 1996), pp. 254–65.

[322] In "Balancing the Prophet," *Financial Times* (27 Apr. 2007).

323 In Michael Oren, *Power, Faith, and Fantasy* (New York, 2007), p. 27.

324 "Moderate Islam Is a Prostration to the West," in Ibrahim, p. 53.

325 In Karsh, *Islamic Imperialism*, p. 1; Khomeini statement in Farber, p. 184; Hassan in McCarthy, *The Great Jihad*, p. 361.

326 *Religion of Peace?* (Washington, D.C., 2007), p. 25.

327 *The Strong Horse*, p. 11.

328 *The Crisis of Islam*, pp.16–17.

329 In Pipes, *Militant Islam Reaches America*, pp, 52, 53.

330 "The Empire Strikes Back," *Village Voice* (9 Oct. 2001).

331 *Islamic Imperialism*, p. 23.

332 See medievalnews.blogspot.com/2009/08/medieval-churches-being-destroyed-and.html.

333 "Why We Are Fighting You," in Ibrahim, p. 198.

334 Testimony available at armed-services.senate.gov/statemnt/2010/03 percent20March/Petraeus percent2003–16 10.pdf.

335 Mark Landler and Helene Cooper, "Obama Phrase Highlights Shift on Middle East," *New York Times* (15 Apr. 2010).

336 Ethan Bronner, "Rift Exposes Splits in Views on Mideast," *New York Times* (28 Mar. 2010).

337 See Barry Rubin, *The Rubin Report* (9 Apr. 2010), available at rubinreports.blogspotcom/.

338 *The Strong Horse*, p. 205.

339 In D'Souza, p. 260.

340 *Intellectuals and Society*, p. 280.

341 *The Lion and the Unicorn. Socialism and the English Genius* (London, 1941), rpt. in *My Country Right or Left*, p. 74.

342 *Eurabia* (Madison and Teaneck, NJ, 2005), p. 9.

343 Interview of Dec. 1998, in *Messages to the World*, p. 93.

344 See Steven Stalinksy, "Dealing in Death," *National Review Online* (24 May 2004), available at old.nationalreview.com/comment/stalinsky200405240846.asp.

Conclusion

1 *The Muqaddimah*, trans. Franz Rosenthal, abr. and ed. N. J. Dawood (Princeton, 1967), p. 109.

[2] In *Turmoil and Triumph* (New York, 1993), p. 648.

[3] *Democracy in America*, 1.13. trans. Henry Reeve and Francis Bowen.

[4] *Reflections on a Ravaged Century*, pp. 12–13.

[5] Demosthenes 18.67, trans. Yunis.

[6] *Guide to the New World* (London, 1941), in George Orwell, *My Country Right or Left*, p. 140.

[7] David E. Sanger, "Obama Vows Fresh Proliferation Push as Summit Ends," *New York Times* (13 Apr. 2010).

[8] In Kenneth N. Waltz, *Man, the State, and War* (New York, 1954), p. 97.

[9] *The Lion and the Unicorn*, in *My Country Right or Left*, p. 56.

[10] Thucydides 2.43.1, trans. Benjamin Jowett.

[11] *Earthly Powers* (New York, 2006), pp. 14–15.

[12] *The Lion and the Unicorn*, in *My Country Right or Left*, p. 104.

[13] From *Tristes Tropiques*, in Pascal Bruckner, *The Tyranny of Guilt*, trans. Steven Rendall (2006; Princeton, 2010), p. 7.

[14] *The Lion and the Unicorn*, in *My Country Right or Left*, pp. 103–04.

[15] In the Preface to Helen Sikorska, *The Dark Side of the Moon* (New York, 1947), p. ix.

[16] *Faith, Reason, and the War against Jihadism* (New York, 2007), pp. 111, 116.

[17] *Colossus*, p. 301.

[18] *Of Paradise and Power* (New York, 2004), pp. 35–36.

[19] *Colossus*, p. 294.

Index